1 & 2 PETER

Brazos Theological Commentary on the Bible

Series Editors

R. R. Reno, General Editor
Creighton University
Omaha, Nebraska

Robert W. Jenson
Center of Theological Inquiry
Princeton, New Jersey

Robert Louis Wilken
University of Virginia
Charlottesville, Virginia

Ephraim Radner
Wycliffe College
Toronto, Ontario

Michael Root
Lutheran Theological Southern Seminary
Columbia, South Carolina

George Sumner
Wycliffe College
Toronto, Ontario

1 & 2 PETER

DOUGLAS HARINK

BrazosPress
a division of Baker Publishing Group
Grand Rapids, Michigan

© 2009 by Douglas Harink

Published by Brazos Press
a division of Baker Publishing Group
P.O. Box 6287, Grand Rapids, MI 49516-6287
www.brazospress.com

Printed in the United States of America

Library of Congress Cataloging-in-Publication Data
Harink, Douglas Karel, 1953–
    1 & 2 Peter / Doug Harink.
        p.   cm. — (Brazos theological commentary on the Bible)
    Includes bibliographical references and indexes.
    ISBN 978-1-58743-097-8 (cloth)
    1. Bible. N.T. Peter—Commentaries. I. Title. II. Title: First and Second Peter. III. Series.
BS2795.53.H36 2009
227'.9207—dc22   2009023400

09   10   11   12   13   14   15   7   6   5   4   3   2   1

For
Elmer[†] and Alida Harink
David E. Demson
J. Louis Martyn

CONTENTS

SERIES PREFACE

Near the beginning of his treatise against gnostic interpretations of the Bible, *Against the Heresies*, Irenaeus observes that Scripture is like a great mosaic depicting a handsome king. It is as if we were owners of a villa in Gaul who had ordered a mosaic from Rome. It arrives, and the beautifully colored tiles need to be taken out of their packaging and put into proper order according to the plan of the artist. The difficulty, of course, is that Scripture provides us with the individual pieces, but the order and sequence of various elements are not obvious. The Bible does not come with instructions that would allow interpreters to simply place verses, episodes, images, and parables in order as a worker might follow a schematic drawing in assembling the pieces to depict the handsome king. The mosaic must be puzzled out. This is precisely the work of scriptural interpretation.

Origen has his own image to express the difficulty of working out the proper approach to reading the Bible. When preparing to offer a commentary on the Psalms he tells of a tradition handed down to him by his Hebrew teacher:

> The Hebrew said that the whole divinely inspired Scripture may be likened, because of its obscurity, to many locked rooms in our house. By each room is placed a key, but not the one that corresponds to it, so that the keys are scattered about beside the rooms, none of them matching the room by which it is placed. It is a difficult task to find the keys and match them to the rooms that they can open. We therefore know the Scriptures that are obscure only by taking the points of departure for understanding them from another place because they have their interpretive principle scattered among them.[1]

---

1. Fragment from the preface to *Commentary on Psalms 1–25*, preserved in the *Philokalia*, trans. Joseph W. Trigg (London: Routledge, 1998), 70–71.

As is the case for Irenaeus, scriptural interpretation is not purely local. The key in Genesis may best fit the door of Isaiah, which in turn opens up the meaning of Matthew. The mosaic must be put together with an eye toward the overall plan.

Irenaeus, Origen, and the great cloud of premodern biblical interpreters assumed that puzzling out the mosaic of scripture must be a communal project. The Bible is vast, heterogeneous, full of confusing passages and obscure words, and difficult to understand. Only a fool would imagine that he or she could work out solutions alone. The way forward must rely upon a tradition of reading that Irenaeus reports has been passed on as the rule or canon of truth that functions as a confession of faith. "Anyone," he says, "who keeps unchangeable in himself the rule of truth received through baptism will recognize the names and sayings and parables of the scriptures."[2] Modern scholars debate the content of the rule on which Irenaeus relies and commends, not the least because the terms and formulations Irenaeus himself uses shift and slide. Nonetheless, Irenaeus assumes that there is a body of apostolic doctrine sustained by a tradition of teaching in the church. This doctrine provides the clarifying principles that guide exegetical judgment toward a coherent overall reading of scripture as a unified witness. Doctrine, then, is the schematic drawing that will allow the reader to organize the vast heterogeneity of the words, images, and stories of the Bible into a readable, coherent whole. It is the rule that guides us toward the proper matching of keys to doors.

If self-consciousness about the role of history in shaping human consciousness makes modern historical-critical study critical, then what makes modern study of the Bible modern is the consensus that classical Christian doctrine distorts interpretive understanding. Benjamin Jowett, the influential nineteenth-century English classical scholar, is representative. In his programmatic essay "On the Interpretation of Scripture," he exhorts the biblical reader to disengage from doctrine and break its hold over the interpretive imagination. "The simple words of that book," writes Jowett of the modern reader, "he tries to preserve absolutely pure from the refinements or distinctions of later times." The modern interpreter wishes to "clear away the remains of dogmas, systems, controversies, which are encrusted upon" the words of scripture. The disciplines of close philological analysis "would enable us to separate the elements of doctrine and tradition with which the meaning of Scripture is encumbered in our own day."[3] The lens of understanding must be wiped clear of the hazy and distorting film of doctrine.

Postmodernity, in turn, has encouraged us to criticize the critics. Jowett imagined that when he wiped away doctrine he would encounter the biblical text in its purity and uncover what he called "the original spirit and intention of the authors."[4] We are not now so sanguine, and the postmodern mind thinks

---

2. *Against the Heresies* 9.4.

3. Benjamin Jowett, "On the Interpretation of Scripture," in *Essays and Reviews* (London: Parker, 1860), 338–39.

4. Ibid., 340.

interpretive frameworks inevitable. Nonetheless, we tend to remain modern in at least one sense. We read Athanasius and think him stage-managing the diversity of Scripture to support his positions against the Arians. We read Bernard of Clairvaux and assume that his monastic ideals structure his reading of the Song of Songs. In the wake of the Reformation, we can see how the doctrinal divisions of the time shaped biblical interpretation. Luther famously described the Epistle of James as a "strawy letter," for, as he said, "it has nothing of the nature of the Gospel about it."[5] In these and many other instances, often written in the heat of ecclesiastical controversy or out of the passion of ascetic commitment, we tend to think Jowett correct: doctrine is a distorting film on the lens of understanding.

However, is what we commonly think actually the case? Are readers naturally perceptive? Do we have an unblemished, reliable aptitude for the divine? Have we no need for disciplines of vision? Do our attention and judgment need to be trained, especially as we seek to read scripture as the living word of God? According to Augustine, we all struggle to journey toward God, who is our rest and peace. Yet our vision is darkened and the fetters of worldly habit corrupt our judgment. We need training and instruction in order to cleanse our minds so that we might find our way toward God.[6] To this end, "the whole temporal dispensation was made by divine Providence for our salvation."[7] The covenant with Israel, the coming of Christ, the gathering of the nations into the church—all these things are gathered up into the rule of faith, and they guide the vision and form of the soul toward the end of fellowship with God. In Augustine's view, the reading of scripture both contributes to and benefits from this divine pedagogy. With countless variations in both exegetical conclusions and theological frameworks, the same pedagogy of a doctrinally ruled reading of scripture characterizes the broad sweep of the Christian tradition from Gregory the Great through Bernard and Bonaventure, continuing across Reformation differences in both John Calvin and Cornelius Lapide, Patrick Henry and Bishop Bossuet, and on to more recent figures such as Karl Barth and Hans Urs von Balthasar.

Is doctrine, then, not a moldering scrim of antique prejudice obscuring the Bible, but instead a clarifying agent, an enduring tradition of theological judgments that amplifies the living voice of scripture? And what of the scholarly dispassion advocated by Jowett? Is a noncommitted reading, an interpretation unprejudiced, the way toward objectivity, or does it simply invite the languid intellectual apathy that stands aside to make room for the false truism and easy answers of the age?

This series of biblical commentaries was born out of the conviction that dogma clarifies rather than obscures. The Brazos Theological Commentary on the Bible advances upon the assumption that the Nicene tradition, in all its diversity and controversy, provides the proper basis for the interpretation of the Bible as Christian

5. *Luther's Works*, vol. 35, ed. E. Theodore Bachmann (Philadelphia: Fortress, 1959), 362.
6. *On Christian Doctrine* 1.10.
7. *On Christian Doctrine* 1.35.

scripture. God the Father Almighty, who sends his only begotten Son to die for us and for our salvation and who raises the crucified Son in the power of the Holy Spirit so that the baptized may be joined in one body—faith in *this* God with *this* vocation of love for the world is the lens through which to view the heterogeneity and particularity of the biblical texts. Doctrine, then, is not a moldering scrim of antique prejudice obscuring the meaning of the Bible. It is a crucial aspect of the divine pedagogy, a clarifying agent for our minds fogged by self-deceptions, a challenge to our languid intellectual apathy that will too often rest in false truisms and the easy spiritual nostrums of the present age rather than search more deeply and widely for the dispersed keys to the many doors of scripture.

For this reason, the commentators in this series have not been chosen because of their historical or philological expertise. In the main, they are not biblical scholars in the conventional, modern sense of the term. Instead, the commentators were chosen because of their knowledge of and expertise in using the Christian doctrinal tradition. They are qualified by virtue of the doctrinal formation of their mental habits, for it is the conceit of this series of biblical commentaries that theological training in the Nicene tradition prepares one for biblical interpretation, and thus it is to theologians and not biblical scholars that we have turned. "War is too important," it has been said, "to leave to the generals."

We do hope, however, that readers do not draw the wrong impression. The Nicene tradition does not provide a set formula for the solution of exegetical problems. The great tradition of Christian doctrine was not transcribed, bound in folio, and issued in an official, critical edition. We have the Niceno-Constantinopolitan Creed, used for centuries in many traditions of Christian worship. We have ancient baptismal affirmations of faith. The Chalcedonian definition and the creeds and canons of other church councils have their places in official church documents. Yet the rule of faith cannot be limited to a specific set of words, sentences, and creeds. It is instead a pervasive habit of thought, the animating culture of the church in its intellectual aspect. As Augustine observed, commenting on Jeremiah 31:33, "The creed is learned by listening; it is written, not on stone tablets nor on any material, but on the heart."[8] This is why Irenaeus is able to appeal to the rule of faith more than a century before the first ecumenical council, and this is why we need not itemize the contents of the Nicene tradition in order to appeal to its potency and role in the work of interpretation.

Because doctrine is intrinsically fluid on the margins and most powerful as a habit of mind rather than a list of propositions, this commentary series cannot settle difficult questions of method and content at the outset. The editors of the series impose no particular method of doctrinal interpretation. We cannot say in advance how doctrine helps the Christian reader assemble the mosaic of scripture. We have no clear answer to the question of whether exegesis guided by doctrine is antithetical to or compatible with the now-old modern methods of

8. *Sermon* 212.2.

historical-critical inquiry. Truth—historical, mathematical, or doctrinal—knows no contradiction. But method is a discipline of vision and judgment, and we cannot know in advance what aspects of historical-critical inquiry are functions of modernism that shape the soul to be at odds with Christian discipline. Still further, the editors do not hold the commentators to any particular hermeneutical theory that specifies how to define the plain sense of scripture—or the role this plain sense should play in interpretation. Here the commentary series is tentative and exploratory.

Can we proceed in any other way? European and North American intellectual culture has been de-Christianized. The effect has not been a cessation of Christian activity. Theological work continues. Sermons are preached. Biblical scholars turn out monographs. Church leaders have meetings. But each dimension of a formerly unified Christian practice now tends to function independently. It is as if a weakened army had been fragmented, and various corps had retreated to isolated fortresses in order to survive. Theology has lost its competence in exegesis. Scripture scholars function with minimal theological training. Each decade finds new theories of preaching to cover the nakedness of seminary training that provides theology without exegesis and exegesis without theology.

Not the least of the causes of the fragmentation of Christian intellectual practice has been the divisions of the church. Since the Reformation, the role of the rule of faith in interpretation has been obscured by polemics and counterpolemics about *sola scriptura* and the necessity of a magisterial teaching authority. The Brazos Theological Commentary on the Bible series is deliberately ecumenical in scope, because the editors are convinced that early church fathers were correct: church doctrine does not compete with scripture in a limited economy of epistemic authority. We wish to encourage unashamedly dogmatic interpretation of scripture, confident that the concrete consequences of such a reading will cast far more light on the great divisive questions of the Reformation than either reengaging in old theological polemics or chasing the fantasy of a pure exegesis that will somehow adjudicate between competing theological positions. You shall know the truth of doctrine by its interpretive fruits, and therefore in hopes of contributing to the unity of the church, we have deliberately chosen a wide range of theologians whose commitment to doctrine will allow readers to see real interpretive consequences rather than the shadow boxing of theological concepts.

Brazos Theological Commentary on the Bible has no dog in the current translation fights, and we endorse a textual ecumenism that parallels our diversity of ecclesial backgrounds. We do not impose the thankfully modest inclusive-language agenda of the New Revised Standard Version, nor do we insist upon the glories of the Authorized Version, nor do we require our commentators to create a new translation. In our communal worship, in our private devotions, in our theological scholarship, we use a range of scriptural translations. Precisely as scripture—a living, functioning text in the present life of faith—the Bible is not semantically fixed. Only a modernist, literalist hermeneutic could imagine that this modest fluidity is a liability. Philological precision and stability is a consequence of, not a basis for, exegesis. Judgments about the meaning of a text fix its literal sense, not the other way around. As a result, readers should expect an eclectic use of biblical translations, both across the different volumes of the series and within individual commentaries.

We cannot speak for contemporary biblical scholars, but as theologians we know that we have long been trained to defend our fortresses of theological concepts and formulations. And we have forgotten the skills of interpretation. Like stroke victims, we must rehabilitate our exegetical imaginations, and there are likely to be different strategies of recovery. Readers should expect this reconstructive—not reactionary—series to provide them with experiments in postcritical doctrinal interpretation, not commentaries written according to the settled principles of a well-functioning tradition. Some commentators will follow classical typological and allegorical readings from the premodern tradition; others will draw on contemporary historical study. Some will comment verse by verse; others will highlight passages, even single words that trigger theological analysis of scripture. No reading strategies are proscribed, no interpretive methods foresworn. The central premise in this commentary series is that doctrine provides structure and cogency to scriptural interpretation. We trust in this premise with the hope that the Nicene tradition can guide us, however imperfectly, diversely, and haltingly, toward a reading of scripture in which the right keys open the right doors.

R. R. Reno

AUTHOR'S PREFACE

Too long ago now (and I am grateful for their patience) Rusty Reno and Rodney Clapp invited me to contribute this volume to the Brazos Theological Commentary on the Bible. I agreed on the basis of a desire to explore the message of 1 Peter more deeply, though (I'll confess) I was largely unaware of the treasures that awaited in the much neglected second epistle. The opportunity to write a commentary on these two very different letters has proven to be a rich and satisfying theological adventure, for which I am very grateful.

The adventure began in the 2005 Senior Seminar in Theology at the King's University College and continued in the 2007 Senior Seminar. I am grateful to the students in those seminars for their dedication to reading 1–2 Peter with me, asking the most important questions, and producing valuable research projects. Jonathan de Koning, Rachel Stolte, Jamie Ostercamp, and Lindsay Vanderhoek deserve special mention for their challenging and outstanding work.

In the summer and fall of 2005 I was granted a sabbatical leave by the King's University College and a residential membership at the Center of Theological Inquiry in Princeton. I am grateful to both of those institutions for their great generosity, which enabled me to do most of the work on the commentary on 2 Peter during my stay at CTI. I am especially thankful to the CTI staff, and its director William Storrar, for providing such a wonderful context in which to do theological research and writing—truly a theologian's sabbatical dream come true. Of course, what makes the dream is the characters in it, and here I must give thanks to the other scholars in residence at CTI while I was there, in particular Markus Bockmuehl, Chris Mostert, Anne Marie Reijnen, Robert Pope, and Steve Walton, each of whom contributed, through critical readings, conversations, research tips, and friendship to my understanding of theology, commentary writing, and 2 Peter.

Opportunities to present some of this material were generously provided by the Canadian Theological Society, the Canadian Evangelical Theological Association, and the amazing theological community of the parish of St. Margaret's Anglican Church in Winnipeg. I am grateful to Rev. Dr. David Widdicombe for the invitation to participate in and contribute to the St. Margaret's theological consultations in 2007 and 2008 and for making me an honorary member of the parish.

A number of people read smaller or larger portions of this commentary and provided very necessary critical perspectives and comments: the above-named CTI colleagues and Jane Barter-Moulaison, Tim Fretheim, and Debby Harink. Thanks to each of them for their good judgment and patience. Rusty Reno and George Sumner, series editors, each read the entire manuscript and provided significant critical suggestions for improvement. Though they graciously required nothing of me, nevertheless on many points in the commentary I learned from their engagements, on most I thought through the issues again, and on some I made substantial changes. In the end, alas, each of them would no doubt have written a very different commentary from mine (especially on 1 Peter), and no doubt a better one too. If this commentary is finally less or other than it should be, it is not for lack of trying on the part of Rusty or George or any of my other faithful early readers. All gratitude to them; all final responsibility to me.

The editorial staff at Brazos Press are a delight to work with. Lisa Cockrel makes sure that actual progress is made on a manuscript and that it gets done. David Aiken provides outstanding service as a manuscript editor; I am very fortunate to benefit from his careful and insightful work for the second time. Thanks to Brazos, its people, and its vision.

My work is always accompanied and made possible by colleagues, family, and friends. Arlette Zinck, dean of the faculty of arts at the King's University College, not only always encourages my work with words and friendship, but also honors and often protects the time I need to do it—time that might otherwise be spent on many pressing administrative tasks. My colleague in theology, Steve Martin, constantly graces me with good conversation, good theology, and friendship. My dear friend and fellow traveler in theology and the good life, Roy Berkenbosch, always lifts my spirits, and often drinks them—a dram fine Dutchman he is. Debby—companion of my heart, of my thoughts, of my love for Christ and the church, for more than thirty-five years—always bears with me, believes in me, encourages me, blesses me. God bless her, and our two wonderful daughters, Elizabeth and Allison.

I dedicate this book to four of my elders in life and in faith. My father and mother, Elmer and Alida Harink, instructed me in the scriptures and the Christian life from the very beginning. I thank God for their constancy, love, and witness. David Demson is my *Doktorvater*, from whom I learned Calvin, Barth, Frei, and all of the most important theological moves I know. I hope this work does him honor, though he may not agree with it all. Finally, Lou Martyn has blessed me not only with his work on the apocalyptic Paul, without which I can no longer imagine theology, but also with his friendship and encouragement. At one critical juncture in my journey with Paul, when Lou saw me taking a wrong turn, he spoke up: "O foolish Canadian, who hath bewitched thee?" I needed that. Thank you.

ABBREVIATIONS

General

→	indicates a cross-reference to commentary on a Petrine passage
DH	translation by the author
LXX	Septuagint
NIV	New International Version
NRSV	New Revised Standard Version

Biblical

Acts	Acts	Gal.	Galatians
Amos	Amos	Gen.	Genesis
1 Chr.	1 Chronicles	Hab.	Habakkuk
2 Chr.	2 Chronicles	Hag.	Haggai
Col.	Colossians	Heb.	Hebrews
1 Cor.	1 Corinthians	Hos.	Hosea
2 Cor.	2 Corinthians	Isa.	Isaiah
Dan.	Daniel	Jas.	James
Deut.	Deuteronomy	Jer.	Jeremiah
Eccl.	Ecclesiastes	Job	Job
Eph.	Ephesians	Joel	Joel
Esth.	Esther	John	John
Exod.	Exodus	1 John	1 John
Ezek.	Ezekiel	2 John	2 John
Ezra	Ezra	3 John	3 John

Jonah	Jonah		2 Pet.	2 Peter
Josh.	Joshua		Phil.	Philippians
Jude	Jude		Phlm.	Philemon
Judg.	Judges		Prov.	Proverbs
1 Kgs.	1 Kings		Ps.	Psalms
2 Kgs.	2 Kings		Rev.	Revelation
Lam.	Lamentations		Rom.	Romans
Lev.	Leviticus		Ruth	Ruth
Luke	Luke		1 Sam.	1 Samuel
Mal.	Malachi		2 Sam.	2 Samuel
Mark	Mark		Song	Song of Songs
Matt.	Matthew		1 Thess.	1 Thessalonians
Mic.	Micah		2 Thess.	2 Thessalonians
Nah.	Nahum		1 Tim.	1 Timothy
Neh.	Nehemiah		2 Tim.	2 Timothy
Num.	Numbers		Titus	Titus
Obad.	Obadiah		Zech.	Zechariah
1 Pet.	1 Peter		Zeph.	Zephaniah

INTRODUCTION

Two epistles more different from one another it would be difficult to find in the entire New Testament.

In the one, 1 Peter, we have an extended exhortation for the church to take up, dwell in, and live out of its identity as "the elect, the exiles of the Diaspora" (1:1 DH), a chosen people called out from the wider social and political orders to embody and display God's transforming holiness and love as its peculiar mission among the nations. In this messianic calling, the church, like the Messiah, will often encounter disdain, opposition, and even persecution from those who continue to live under the reign and by the rules of other gods and lords. In carrying out their mission, the people of the Messiah must therefore prepare themselves for suffering. At the very heart of this first epistle stands the figure of Jesus Christ as the one who suffers. As the suffering Messiah he defines the very character of messianic life. The people that has been called by God and redeemed through the Messiah's suffering and death, that shares in his resurrection and fullness of life, does not shrink from the wider world or go into hiding among the nations. It shares in the suffering and destiny of its Lord joyfully and full of confidence and lives without fear in the societies in which it finds itself. For the followers of Jesus know that God's justice is being done through them, and will be done for them, exactly because God demonstrated his justice for them and for the world in the crucifixion and resurrection of the Messiah. Their sharing in the Messiah's suffering, redemption, and resurrection life is their participation in, their enactment of, the hidden revolution in which God is bringing about a new creation. The greatest revolutionary power of this letter comes at that point where its words are likely to strike us as the most objectionable—in the "household code" (2:13–3:8) in which Peter's instruction is summed up in the repeated phrase "be subordinate." As we shall discover, difficult though that instruction is to swallow in our time, the revolutionary history of the world in its messianic sense begins with that phrase.

The term "messianic," appearing frequently in the commentary, needs some explanation. Why not simply "Christian"? What is signaled with the term "messianic"? First and most obviously the term links the people and way of life designated *messianic* with the *Messiah* Jesus. The "messianic" in the New Testament is not a free-floating concept awaiting our bestowal of attributes. On the contrary, it is fully enacted, summed up, and defined by the life, death, and resurrection of Jesus of Nazareth. As the Messiah, he *is* "the messianic." The messianic is originally, truly, and definitively revealed—"apocalypsed"—in him. Nevertheless, the concept also points to the varied but concrete theological, political, and economic messianic expectations that were current among Jews in the time of Jesus: in the gospel accounts the devil tempts Jesus to enact a messiahship in accordance with those very expectations. But Jesus fundamentally interrupts, suspends, and reconfigures them. Jesus trusts the word, will, and way of the Father as he discerns the godly shape of his messiahship on his journey from Bethlehem to Golgotha. In fact, radical trust in the Father is itself the very enactment and definition of the messianic. At the same time, Jesus does not substitute a "spiritual" or "religious" messiahship in the place of social, economic, and political ones. Rather, trusting in the Father, he enacts in his concrete historical life and death, within the concrete historical conditions of his time, an *alternative sociopolitical messianic life* and calls his followers to participate in and imitate that messianic life as their baptismal share in his own being and act as the incarnate Word, crucified, risen, exalted, coming again in glory. Of course, we turn most naturally and immediately to the canonical Gospels to discern just what that alternative sociopolitical vision looks like in Jesus's life and in the life of his followers. Nevertheless, we can also get a clear picture of it through a careful reading of 1 Peter.

Some readers of this commentary may worry that my presentation of the relationship between the messianic people of God and the wider world is insufficiently dialectical, that is, that it presents that relationship in too antithetical a manner. There is some truth to that judgment, but I think it is misplaced. Were I developing a general treatise on the church-world relationship I would indeed have to show greater sensitivity to the complexities intrinsic to shaping, say, a theology of culture or a political theology. In a commentary on 1 Peter, however, I am in the first place obliged to follow the text of this particular epistle. Peter's letter is not very dialectical. The believers to whom he writes are being scorned, abused, and made to suffer in various ways at the hands of their unbelieving neighbors and rulers. Peter instructs them how to live in that situation. If we are to be true to the letter then, we will more likely find ourselves exploring the themes of messianic martyrdom than those of how Christians transform societies in which Christian influence is taken for granted or perhaps even welcomed. Indeed, I will show how Peter's messianic/apocalyptic vision might lead us to reconsider some of our dearest beliefs about how Christians go about influencing and transforming the world.

The messianic interpretation of 1 Peter that I offer here is informed in large measure by those strands of theological tradition that resonate most deeply with the messianic sociopolitical vision of the epistle. Prominent in this regard is the Radical Reformation tradition, represented for me primarily by the work of John Howard Yoder. The reader familiar with Yoder's work will detect the presence of his messianic/apocalyptic theology throughout my exposition of the letter, even in those places where Yoder is not directly quoted or identified. But not only Yoder: also Karl Barth, whose apocalyptic/messianic theology, whether in the *Römerbrief* or in the *Church Dogmatics*, equips us to plumb the theological, christological, and ethical deeps of 1 Peter like no other. Again, while Barth is only infrequently quoted or referenced in the commentary, his influence is pervasive and will be obvious to those familiar with him. While working on this commentary, I discovered (but in relation to Paul rather than Peter) the work of (secular?) Jewish philosopher Walter Benjamin (1892–1940), in particular his revolutionary "Theses on the Philosophy of History," in which he develops a concept of the messianic, messianic time, and messianic agency. In his own way Benjamin grasps profoundly the kind of messianic existence that Peter calls forth from the people of the Messiah. Benjamin's theses have come to haunt this work in ways I could not have anticipated, and I commend them to the reader's consideration.[1]

Among the number of modern commentaries on 1 Peter that I use, I rely especially on two superb comprehensive works to guide me through the issues of text, language, history, and culture: Achtemeier 1996 and Elliott 2000. Boring 1999 is also invariably useful, and Calvin 1963 never fails to illuminate, instruct, and kindle a passion for God and his reign. Luther 1967 reveals his love both for the epistle and for the one to whom it testifies.

When we come to 2 Peter we find ourselves in an atmosphere very different from the first epistle, one not frequently breathed by Western (Protestant) Christian readers and that therefore requires a kind of acclimatization. What shall we think, for example, when the language of *gnōsis* ("knowledge") rather than *pistis* ("faith") predominates; when salvation is thought of as rescue from the corruption that comes from desire; when eschatological fulfillment is rendered as participation in the divine nature; when the Christian life is described most fully in terms of knowledge and virtue (*aretē*); when the transfiguration (rather than, say, the cross and resurrection) is put forward as the decisive christological event; when heretics are unremittingly (and ungraciously?) condemned; when the final parousia comes as a great cosmic conflagration? In view of all these things, shall we join Ernst Käsemann in his unrelenting theological attack (a "critical cross-examination," as he called it) on the epistle, concluding with him that 2 Peter is irredeemably

---

1. Walter Benjamin, "Theses on the Philosophy of History," in *Illuminations*, ed. Hannah Arendt, trans. Harry Zohn (New York: Schocken, 1968), 253–64. Michael Löwy's *Fire Alarm: Reading Walter Benjamin's "On the Concept of History"* (London/New York: Verso, 2005) provides a helpful translation and guide to Benjamin's "Theses."

"Hellenistic," "from beginning to end a document expressing an early Catholic viewpoint . . . perhaps the most dubious writing in the canon"?[2] That is one option. But it is not the one I pursue in this commentary. How shall we breathe the air of 2 Peter? How shall we become acclimatized to its quite obvious Hellenism? One way is to learn from those who are already used to it. And so I turn to Eastern Orthodoxy. For, which tradition has plumbed to greater depths (sometimes to the point of danger) the mystery of participation in the divine life? And which has meditated with more concentration and profundity—in both word and icon—on the transfiguration of our Lord? And where shall we find the intellectual and spiritual riches of Hellenism so thoroughly redeemed through subsuming and taking them up into the greater and more powerful riches of New Testament apocalypticism? Where, but in Orthodoxy? Maximus the Confessor and Gregory Palamas on deification, the Fathers (McGuckin 1986) and icons[3] on the transfiguration, Sergius Bulgakov and David Bentley Hart on apocalyptic eschatology[4]—these became my primary commentary on 2 Peter. By taking in some of the air of this tradition I was able to develop the lungs I needed to climb the mountain of 2 Peter; and climbing 2 Peter in turn opened up for me a vista on Orthodoxy.

In the first instance, however, I was delivered from Käsemann's hyper-Protestant judgment against 2 Peter not by reading in Orthodoxy, but by reading the outstanding 1983 commentary on the epistle by Richard Bauckham. Bauckham provides a definitive rejoinder to Käsemann. Bauckham's own reading of 2 Peter may be characterized as a kind of cautious hellenization thesis—but certainly not hellenization pure and simple. Bauckham demonstrates persuasively that what we find in 2 Peter is a "surprising combination of Hellenism and [Jewish cosmic] apocalyptic" (1983: 154).[5] That is the lead I followed, and the one that led me to explore some of the treasures of Orthodoxy as a means of discerning and understanding the theological treasures of 2 Peter. At the same time, both Calvin and Luther were again constant and illuminating companions in my journey through the epistle.

At the heart of 2 Peter is a profound and passionate declaration of the divine justice, authority, and glory of Jesus Christ revealed in the transfiguration, of

2. Ernst Käsemann, "An Apologia for Primitive Christian Eschatology," in his *Essays on New Testament Themes*, trans. W. J. Montague (Philadelphia: Fortress, 1982), 169.

3. See Andreas Andreopoulos, *Metamorphosis: The Transfiguration in Byzantine Theology and Iconography* (Crestwood, NY: St. Vladimir's Seminary Press, 2005); and Solrunn Nes, *The Uncreated Light: An Iconographical Study of the Transfiguration in the Eastern Church* (Grand Rapids: Eerdmans, 2007).

4. Sergius Bulgakov, *The Bride of the Lamb*, trans. Boris Jakim (Grand Rapids: Eerdmans, 2002); and David Bentley Hart, *The Beauty of the Infinite: The Aesthetics of Christian Truth* (Grand Rapids: Eerdmans, 2003).

5. Cf. Richard Bauckham, "2 Peter," in *Dictionary of the Later New Testament and Its Developments*, ed. Ralph P. Martin and Peter H. Davids (Downers Grove, IL: InterVarsity, 1997), 923–27. I also found Kraftchick 2002 and Harrington 2003 especially helpful.

his imminent glorious coming that will purify and transform all of creation and make it the home of righteousness, and of the absurdity and indeed great danger of the heresies that deny these truths. In view of these things it is regrettable that 2 Peter often hardly registers on the radar of theologians and ordinary Christian readers of scripture. I hope this commentary encourages another and deeper look at this important text.

Some readers may be troubled that I straightforwardly refer to the author of each of the epistles as Peter. On that, I simply follow the canonical text, and then also follow the connections from the Peter of the epistles to the other canonical accounts of Peter in the Gospels and Acts.[6] I assume the theological legitimacy of both of those moves without making a historical-critical judgment one way or another about the authorship of the epistles. Arguments about authorship are legion in the commentaries.

In the end, the reader of this book may well sense certain theological tensions between the commentaries on the two epistles, as between the epistles themselves. If so, then she or he will be sharing in my own experience. I have not tried to resolve those tensions completely—though perhaps something of a clue to the resolution might be found in the transfiguration as the apocalypse of Christ reigning in full divine glory. But such a resolution will have to be explored on another day. In the meantime I pray that God will use this commentary to guide the reader, in some small measure, into the fullness of truth in Christ Jesus, to whom each epistle is an indispensable witness.

6. See Brevard Childs, *The New Testament as Canon: An Introduction* (Philadelphia: Fortress, 1985), 462–76.

1 PETER

1 PETER 1

Apostle (1 Peter 1:1a)

Petros apostolos Iēsou Christou ("Peter, apostle of Jesus Christ" [DH]). With this self-identification Peter claims no other identity for himself and no other authority for sending his letter than his apostolicity; for in fact Peter's apostolic identity and authority are not his own to claim, but consist in his *having been chosen, called, and commissioned* and *thus* constituted as an apostle by the Lord Jesus Christ. "An Apostle can never come to himself in such a way that he becomes conscious of his apostolic calling as a factor in the development of his life. Apostolic calling is a paradoxical factor, which from first to last in his life stands paradoxically outside his personal identity with himself as the definite person he is."[1] This letter by Peter issues out of Jesus Christ's identity and authority, into which Peter's witness in writing is caught up by the Spirit's own witness, who speaks through the apostles only what he hears from Jesus Christ and who thereby guides us into all truth (John 15:26–27; 16:12–15). "St. Peter wants to say: I am an apostle of Jesus Christ; that is, Jesus Christ has commanded me to preach about Christ. Take note that all who preach human doctrines are immediately excluded.... If [Peter] preaches what Christ has commanded, this is no different from hearing Christ Himself in person" (Luther 1967: 5). Achtemeier notes: "Customarily, the second word [*apostolos*] is translated 'an apostle,' since there is no definite article, yet that tends to lessen the implied force of this claim. To be sure, Peter is one among at least twelve, but the force of the title is not that he is one of a group, but that what is being written carries apostolic authority" (1996: 79). Peter is not *an* apostle, as if in writing and sending the letter he is first himself and then also a member of a class; rather, in writing and sending this letter he fully and solely

1. Søren Kierkegaard, *The Present Age* and *Of the Difference between a Genius and an Apostle*, trans. Alexander Dru (London: Collins, 1962), 107.

is apostle, and nothing else. Martyn's comments on Paul's apostleship also apply to Peter's: "Bearing the ultimate message *from God* to human beings, he is a man whose identity is determined by the God who sent him and by the message God gave him to preach. To other human beings . . . , he is himself a stranger, a person who, in a profound sense, 'comes from somewhere else.'"[2] As *apostle* of Jesus Christ, Peter is an exile, homeless in relation to every other factor (genetic, ethnic, sociopolitical, etc.) that might constitute him as the personality that he is. Factors of Peter's personality become apostolic insofar as Jesus Christ appropriates them and renders them serviceable to Peter's calling and commission.

As the Gospels testify, Peter's name itself (*Petros*) is a sign of his exilic existence. In terms of his paternal origin and home, he is *Simōn Bariōna* ("Simon son of Jonah"; Matt. 16:17). But when Jesus calls Simon to be his follower, he gives him the Aramaic name *Kēphas* ("rock"; John 1:42). And when Simon utters the confession that Jesus is the Messiah, Jesus declares that Simon is *Petros*, the "rock" upon which Christ will build his church (Matt. 16:17–18). Jesus conscripts Simon son of Jonah into the messianic revolution; he becomes *Petros* and is thereby rendered a stranger among his own people. At the same time he is made a binding sign of the existence of the church that is, not first by social or political circumstance, but by God's election, calling, and sending, perpetually in exile, perpetually in Diaspora among the nations. Peter testifies to this when he writes in 1 Pet. 5:13 that both he and the church in Rome from which he writes—"chosen together with you"—are "in Babylon."

The People of God among the Nations (1 Peter 1:1b)

Peter thus also immediately addresses his readers in these terms: *eklektois parepidēmois diasporas* ("to the elect, to the exiles of the Diaspora"; DH). In these three Greek words we have what we might call Peter's dogmatic ecclesiology, his normative description of the church. With them Peter introduces, brings into sharp focus, and sums up a great deal of what he goes on to write in the letter about God's calling and purpose for the church, which is prefigured in the story of Israel's election, sanctification, and mission. While the themes introduced by these important words come up again throughout the letter, each of them is worthy of some extended reflection at this point.

With *eklektois* ("to the chosen/elect") Peter leads us to pay attention to the divine origin and constitution of the church: God's people is brought into being and constituted in the first place by God's gracious choosing or election. That is why Peter gives this word first place among the designations (recognized in NIV, but not NRSV). We see throughout 1 Peter that aspects of political and

2. J. Louis Martyn, *Galatians: A New Translation with Introduction and Commentary*, Anchor Bible 33A (New York: Doubleday, 1997), 95 (emphasis original).

social existence are always immediately intrinsic to the being and character of the people of God,[3] which the terms *parepidēmos* ("exile") and *diaspora* already clearly indicate; those aspects are rooted theologically in God's election of his people. God chooses and calls Abram, "a wandering Aramean" (Deut. 26:5), to be the ancestor of God's people, one whom God blesses with his particular promise and revelation and through whom God brings blessing to all the peoples of the earth (Gen. 12:1–3). "And because he loved your [Israel's] ancestors, he chose their descendants after them" (Deut. 4:37). Israel's very being is founded in God's particular love and choosing:

> For you are a people holy to the LORD your God; the LORD your God has chosen you out of all the peoples on earth to be his people, his treasured possession.
>
> It was not because you were more numerous than any other people that the LORD set his heart on you and chose you—for you were the fewest of all peoples. It was because the LORD loved you and kept the oath that he swore to your ancestors, that the LORD has brought you out with a mighty hand, and redeemed you from the house of slavery. (Deut. 7:6–8)

So also, through the reconciling death of Jesus Christ, God graciously reaches out from Israel to the not-chosen nations, that is, the Gentiles, those who "once . . . were not a people" but have now been made God's people (1 Pet. 2:10, quoting Hos. 2:23; cf. Rom. 9:24–26). "Blessed be the God and Father of our Lord Jesus Christ, who has blessed us in Christ with every spiritual blessing in the heavenly places, just as he chose us in Christ . . . to be holy and blameless before him" (Eph. 1:3–4). These passages indicate that to *be* God's people can never be an achievement of human will. It is possible only by God's election. "The language of election draws attention to the way in which the Church has its being in the ever-fresh work of divine grace. The Church is what it is in the ceaseless gift of its

3. While this matter will be taken up later (→2:4–10), it is important here to explain briefly my frequent use of the phrase "the people of God." In explanation I offer the words of Paul Minear, writing on the word *laos* ("people") in the New Testament: "People in general do not exist [e.g., How many people are in this room?]; there are only particular peoples. Every person belongs to a particular people, just as he belongs to a particular tongue or nation or tribe; and this people is not reducible to the mathematical aggregate of its members." This aspect of peoplehood is especially evident in Gen. 10, where the descendents of each of Noah's sons are described in terms of pluralities of particular peoples distinguished from one another "by their families, their languages, their lands, and their nations" (10:20; cf. also 10:5, 31). "Humanity is not visualized as a world-wide census of individuals [e.g., People are like that!], but as the separate peoples that, taken together, comprise mankind as a whole. Each people retains its own discrete unity. Therefore, to identify a particular society as the people of God is immediately to set it over against all other peoples. This people and it alone has been constituted in a special way by this God's action, by his taking it 'for his own possession.' Henceforth it can be spoken of as his people. To avoid . . . misconceptions, then, it is well to take the phrase as a whole and to accent the article and the prepositional phrase: *the* people *of God*." See Paul Minear, *Images of the Church in the New Testament* (Louisville: Westminster John Knox, 2004), 68.

being through the risen Christ and the Holy Spirit who accomplish the will of the Father in gathering a holy people to himself."[4]

Throughout history peoples have regularly constituted themselves by self-assertion, territorial control, military might, conquest, and expansion and sustained themselves by walls, weapons, and warfare; but such peoplehood is at best an approximation, at worst a simulacrum or parody of true peoplehood (see Gen. 11:1-9). God's sovereign election of Israel and church—and his appointment of the nations (see Gen. 10; Acts 17:26-27)—founds and sustains peoples in "grace and peace" (1 Pet. 1:2) rather than in self-assertion and violent struggle against neighbors.[5] Ancient conquering empires and modern military nation-states alike stand in contradiction of and resistance to God's will (but not beyond God's sovereignty: God continues to employ, ad hoc, "pagan" peoples [e.g., the Assyrians] and rulers [e.g., Cyrus of Persia] to accomplish his purpose [cf. Rom. 13:1-7]).

God's election of a people founds the biblical politics of peace. God elects Abram and Sarai so that their people might be a blessing to the nations, though they were not always so. When God in Christ elects from among the Gentile nations "a people for his name" (Acts 15:14), he breaks down the ancient wall of hostility between "the commonwealth of Israel" and the nations. Through the cross God reconciles the chosen Gentiles and chosen Israel (without eradicating the difference between them) into "one new humanity"; together they are made "citizens" and "members of the household of God" (Eph. 2:11-22). The people of God is able to put its full confidence in God and thus refuse self-assertion, hostility, violence, and war vis-à-vis its neighbors (a significant emphasis in 1 Peter), because its very being and ongoing life rests originally, perpetually, and finally, not in its self-constitution and self-preservation, but in the Father's sovereign love and election constituted in the life, death, resurrection, ascension, and intercession of the Son: "Who will bring any charge against God's elect?" Nothing in all creation can separate God's people from the love of God that is in Christ Jesus (Rom. 8:33-34). Just so, that people, of all peoples, should be able to dwell nonviolently among the nations, as a visible sign of God's grace and peace. With the word *eklektos* Peter thus acknowledges the whole economy of God's election in the constitution, preservation, and consummation of the people of God. Every-

4. John Webster, *Holiness* (Grand Rapids: Eerdmans, 2003), 56.

5. In Gen. 10, the genealogy of the sons of Noah, we see the peaceable founding of numerous peoples ("in their lands, with their own languages, by their families, in their nations"; 10:5; cf. 10:20, 31) according to God's command, appointment, and blessing: "be fruitful and multiply, and fill the earth" (9:1). In the tongues of Pentecost and in Paul's speech on the Areopagus (Acts 17:26) the legitimacy of the cultural-linguistic and even political plurality of peoples is again affirmed as God's good arrangement. By contrast, in the story of Babel in Gen. 11:1-9, God judges the imperial and totalitarian will of those who resist cultural-linguistic pluralizing and geographical and political spreading. Against their resistance, God makes it happen.

thing Peter writes in this epistle requires that we understand that economy and the church's identity and mission within it.[6]

With *parepidēmois* ("to the exiles/foreigners/strangers"; see also *paroikos* ["resident alien"] in 2:11) Peter acknowledges that God's choosing of a people for himself is at the same time God's setting that people apart from the other peoples of the earth, rendering it strange and foreign among peoples, making it a "holy" people that witnesses with the whole of its life to the being and character of God: "For you are a people holy to the LORD your God; the LORD your God has chosen you out of all the peoples on earth to be his people, his treasured possession" (Deut. 7:6). "You shall be holy to me, for I the LORD am holy, and I have separated you from the other peoples to be mine" (Lev. 20:26).[7] Through this kind of "exile" among the nations God establishes the holiness of the people of God in the holiness of God. Israel and the church are the people of this God and no other. "You shall have no other gods before me" (Exod. 20:3). The whole existence of the people of God—praise, politics, social and economic order, personal responsibility—begins with the distinction marked by the first commandment.

When God chooses Abraham, he also separates—exiles—him from his father's house and homeland and sends him to a land that is Abraham's only by promise, not by possession. "By faith Abraham obeyed when he was called to set out for a place that he was to receive as an inheritance. . . . By faith he stayed for a time in the land he had been promised, as in a foreign land, living in tents. . . . He looked forward to the city that has foundations, whose architect and builder is God" (Heb. 11:8–10). Israel is called to be God's people while still in Egypt, a land in which they are foreigners and slaves (but that had become like a homeland to them), and they are led out from that place to the land of promise. Before they enter the land of promise, they are given a law that, by being obeyed, renders them a nation permanently foreign among the nations, insofar as the nations follow other gods and other ways: "I am the LORD your God. You shall not do as they do in the land of Egypt, where you lived, and you shall not do as they do in the land of Canaan, to which I am bringing you. You shall not follow their statutes. My ordinances you shall observe and my statutes you shall keep, following them: I am the LORD your God" (Lev. 18:2–4). Even as they dwell faithfully in their own lands, therefore, Israel and the church are legal and political strangers among the nations, indicating by their very existence that their true citizenship is held "in

6. Peter develops neither a doctrine of the election of individual persons to salvation (cf. Calvin 1963: 229: "God knew before the world was created those whom He had elected for salvation") nor a doctrine of the relation of divine and human will (cf. Luther 1967: 6: "Our will is unimportant; God's will and choosing are decisive"). Nonetheless, Peter is clearly asserting and emphasizing God's priority and sovereignty in bringing the people of God into being.

7. "Electedness and holiness were traditionally correlated qualities of the people of God . . . that marked it as a covenant community selected and set apart by God from other peoples" (Elliott 2000: 319). On the theme of the holiness of God's people, Webster, *Holiness*, 53–76, is indispensable reading.

heaven," that is, rooted in God's own triune being and action (Phil. 3:20). They eagerly await the advent of their sovereign from heaven and their citizenship in the new Jerusalem that this sovereign will establish in the midst of nations. While they await that advent, exile for the people of God—its being the one holy people of the one holy God—is its normal state until God makes all things new.

The exilic character of the life of the people of God does not make it otherworldly, in the sense that Christians seek their souls' escape or deliverance from bodily and earthly existence or long for their departure to their heavenly home. That understanding has been and is a common error among Christians. A comment on 1 Pet. 1:1 from Didymus the Blind (ca. 313–98) exhibits the tendency: "The souls of all are like strangers who are joined to bodies for as long as they dwell in time. If these souls were thought to be the substance of the body, they would be natives on earth. But these souls are concealed in a covering of flesh and are in fact like strangers on earth" (quoted in Bray 2000: 65–66). Such understandings, many of them hardly avoiding gnostic heresy, are legion throughout the history of Christian theology. But scripture points in another direction altogether. What makes the life of the people of God foreign or exilic in character is that God's reign "as it is in heaven" is already (in some measure) being actualized and made visible, transforming the political, social, economic, and cultural life of God's people on earth according to the divine pattern revealed in the gospel. "Gospel discipline will require us to say both that the church's holiness is real and actual, a perceptible form of common human being and action, and also that the being and action of the church are holy only in so far as they have within themselves a primary reference to the work and the word of the holy God."[8] The church's divine election and holy calling become visible here and now by the power of the Holy Spirit among God's people, setting it apart from and often at odds with those peoples who worship false gods and practice unholy ways of life.

In the story of Israel, exile is largely the result of God's disciplining of an unfaithful, unjust, and rebellious people. But the disciplinary aspect of exile plays little role in Peter's letter. Rather, for Peter, *to be exiled means to be vulnerable with the vulnerability of Christ*, to live "out of control," to suffer under a foreign power, to long for the homeland, as we see profoundly expressed in Ps. 137:

> By the rivers of Babylon—
> there we sat down and there we wept
> when we remembered Zion.
> On the willows there
> we hung up our harps.
> For there our captors
> asked us for songs,
> And our tormentors asked for mirth, saying,
> "Sing us one of the songs of Zion!"

8. Webster, *Holiness*, 57.

How could we sing the LORD's song
   in a foreign land?
If I forget you, O Jerusalem,
   let my right hand wither! (Ps. 137:1–5)[9]

The life of exile therefore requires that the people of God put their whole trust in God, since they are at the mercy of those among whom they live: "You received without payment; give without payment. Take no gold, or silver, or copper in your belts, no bag for your journey, or two tunics, or sandals, or a staff; for laborers deserve their food. . . . See, I am sending you out like sheep into the midst of wolves; so be wise as serpents and innocent as doves" (Matt. 10:8–10, 16). When Israel is taken captive into Babylon it must remember once again to put its confidence in God's electing love, forgiving goodness, and redeeming power:

Remember these things, O Jacob,
   and Israel, for you are my servant;
I formed you, you are my servant;
   O Israel, you will not be forgotten by me.
I have swept away your transgressions like a cloud,
   and your sins like a mist;
return to me, for I have redeemed you.
Sing, O heavens, for the LORD has done it;
   shout, O depths of the earth;
break forth into singing, O mountains,
   O forest, and every tree in it!
For the LORD has redeemed Jacob,
   and will be glorified in Israel. (Isa. 44:21–23)

Peter's readers also know suffering and grief, born of their alienation from the wider society because of their trust in God's electing grace and their loyalty to Jesus Christ. Their being formed as God's people in Christ brings about a loss of social and political standing in their cities and villages because they have separated themselves from practices that honor the false "gods and lords" that ruled those cities, villages, lands, and the empire itself. "You shall have no other gods before me." They have been made strangers in their own cultural, social, and political contexts and are unable to control the events under which they suffer.[10] By inscribing their experience of suffering into the story of Israel's exile, Peter not only tells them that

9. Daniel L. Smith-Christopher's *A Biblical Theology of Exile* (Minneapolis: Fortress, 2002) provides an important comprehensive study of Israel's exile and its varied significance for the people. He also includes studies of exiled peoples in recent history to deepen and substantiate his understanding of Israel's exilic experience.

10. Recent commentators are generally agreed that Peter's original readers were not facing official, Rome-sponsored persecution; rather they were suffering a variety of forms of local social ostracism. "The persecution in view is the kind carried out not with fire and sword but with words—words of ridicule, slander and sometimes formal accusations of crimes against society (see 1 Pet. 2:12; 3:13–17;

they are not unique and that suffering must be expected; he also reminds them that their precarious existence in the world is their opportunity to know God's gracious care. In its vulnerability the church, like Israel, may joyfully put its hope in God and his power, rather than pine for a time when it will be able to assert its own control over events and nations. Not being in charge (i.e., being "slaves of God"; 1 Pet. 2:16 DH) is our true freedom and participation in Christ. Not being in charge is the normative condition of the people created by the gospel of the crucified Christ—who himself was exiled and cut off from his own people (Isa. 53:8–9), crucified "outside the gate" of Jerusalem (Heb. 13:12).[11] As Peter says later in the letter: "Dear friends, do not be surprised at the painful trial you are suffering, as though something strange were happening to you. But rejoice that you participate in the sufferings of Christ, so that you may be overjoyed when his glory is revealed" (1 Pet. 4:12–13 NIV).

Exile always also implies a homeland, a place of citizenship. The apostle Paul writes in Philippians that our "citizenship" (*politeuma*) is "in heaven"; but he goes on: "And it is from there [*ex hou*] that we are expecting a Savior, the Lord Jesus Christ. He will transform [*metaschēmatisei*] the body of our humiliation that it may be conformed to the body of his glory, by the power that also enables him to make all things subject to himself" (Phil. 3:20–21). The end of exile comes for the church not when Christ takes it away *to heaven*, but when he comes *from heaven* in sovereign glory and power and radically transfigures the church, the body of Christ, from its current humiliation, conforms it to his own glory, and grants it its rightful place *within the transfigured creation and among the healed nations*. The homeland from which the church for the time being is separated is not heaven, but creation itself, still suffering under bondage to powers opposed to the reign of God. In the fullness of his messianic reign, Jesus the Messiah subdues all rulers and authorities in heaven and on earth that would set themselves against God and his chosen people. According to 2 Pet. 3:13, God will reign finally over the newly purified and transfigured creation, where his justice will be "at home." God's glory will fill the whole earth. The exile of God's people ends when God makes the earth *his own home and kingdom* and, only thus, also the true home for God's people. At that time the members of Israel and the church receive their citizenship in the city of God: "See, the home of God is among mortals. He will dwell with them as their God; they will be his people, and God himself will be with them" (Rev. 21:3). Then the peoples of the earth

---

4:14–16)"; J. R. Michaels, "1 Peter," in *Dictionary of the Later New Testament and Its Developments*, ed. Ralph P. Martin and Peter H. Davids (Downers Grove, IL: InterVarsity, 1997), 919.

11. This important point is emphasized consistently in the writings of John Howard Yoder, especially *The Jewish-Christian Schism Revisited*, ed. Michael G. Cartwright and Peter Ochs (Grand Rapids: Eerdmans, 2003), 168–79 (an essay entitled "On Not Being in Charge"). Peter Ochs, a postliberal Jew responding to Yoder, appreciates Yoder's argument for exile as normative, but nonetheless qualifies this point with respect to the Jewish people, for whom landedness is intrinsic to the Jewish people's being and identity (179–80).

will be drawn to the light of God's glory and bring their glory into the new city of God, the gates of which are eternally open (21:24–26). The new creation is the hope and home of God's people. Until then, however, the people of God is a foreign people among the nations.

While "exile" describes the relationship between God's people and the wider society in terms of the alienation, homelessness, and vulnerability that results from election and obedience to the gospel, "Diaspora" (*diaspora*), in Pontus, Galatia, Cappadocia, Asia, and Bithynia, introduces another register and completes Peter's preliminary sketch of the existence of God's people. "Diaspora" means literally to be "sown abroad," as in the scattering of seeds in a field. According to Jesus's parable, the purpose of the scattering is that the seeds might land upon good soil, take root, grow, and produce an abundant crop—"some a hundredfold, some sixty, some thirty" (Matt. 13:8). Jesus Christ is the sower, and the people of God scattered among the nations, provinces, and cities of the world are the seeds. "'Though I scattered them among the nations, yet in far countries they shall remember me' (Zech. 10:9). According to God's will, the Christian church is a scattered people, scattered like seed 'to all the kingdoms of the earth' (Deut. 28:25). That is the curse and its promise. God's people must live in distant lands among the unbelievers, but they will be the seed of the kingdom of God in all the world."[12] If exile is the church's *separation-from*, then Diaspora is its *sending-into, taking-root-in, flourishing-among* the pagan nations. These two movements, separation (or sanctification) and sending, are always intrinsic to one another since they are each rooted in God's election of a people through the gospel, a people that is chosen and set apart *to be a witness* of God's grace to the world.

The exile of Israel into Babylon was certainly, from one point of view, a devastation and loss of all that might otherwise (i.e., apart from God's election) constitute Israel as God's people—homeland, monarchy, temple. As we saw above, the lament of Ps. 137 brings that devastation and loss poignantly and powerfully to expression. The exiles who sing this psalm deal with their present distress by refusing to participate in, or perhaps to be forcibly assimilated into, the cultural life of an alien nation. And in certain circumstances that is surely one important and crucial mode of response for the people of God among the nations. But it is not the only one.

Jeremiah sends a letter to the Israelites who have recently been taken into exile in Babylon. In that context the exile is God's discipline of a disobedient people and thus a condition that they must survive. But it is much more than that. It is also a condition in which God calls them to thrive. The exiles are sent away from Judah and Jerusalem with a mission:

12. Dietrich Bonhoeffer, *Life Together* and *Prayerbook of the Bible*, trans. Daniel W. Bloesch and James H. Burtness, Dietrich Bonhoeffer Works 5 (Minneapolis: Fortress, 1996), 28.

Thus says the LORD of hosts, the God of Israel, to all the exiles whom I have sent into exile from Jerusalem to Babylon: Build houses and live in them; plant gardens and eat what they produce. Take wives and have sons and daughters; take wives for your sons, and give your daughters in marriage, that they may bear sons and daughters; multiply there, and do not decrease. But seek the welfare [*shalom*] of the city where I have sent you into exile, and pray to the LORD on its behalf, for in its welfare you will find your welfare. (Jer. 29:4–7)

God turns exile into dispersion—Diaspora—and the unique kind of cultural, social, and political existence that that came to mean for Jews from that time forward: settling down and making home away from the homeland; flourishing, growing, and sustaining life as a distinct people among the nations; faithfully observing Torah yet participating in many ways in the cultural, social, and political life of the foreign city, working toward its flourishing, and praying to God on its behalf; remembering the homeland and hoping for a return to it. A Diaspora people is a people that is at the same time both separated from its home, which it nonetheless holds in memory, and settled in its present location, toward which it nonetheless sustains a measure of critical distance through specific liturgies, polities, and practices that form and sustain its identity. The social, cultural, and political strangeness of God's Diaspora people often makes it an irritant among the host people, a critical (perhaps even subversive) question to that people about its taken-for-granted way of life and supposed stable identity. Consider how Hasidic and Orthodox Jews and Amish, Hutterite, and Mennonite Christians are often regarded by the wider society. At the same time the residency and participation of God's faithful people in a particular place might also become, in their life together and with their unbelieving neighbors, a witness of cultural, social, and political order obedient to the Lord of the universe, an icon through which the wider society, by God's grace, might behold its own true form and destiny. A Diaspora people among the nations is not simply vulnerable (though it is often that, and thus subject to persecution and expulsion); it is also in the power of the Holy Spirit a site of unique, transformative potentials and powers *for the nations*, precisely because of its diasporic mode of existence.[13]

13. A helpful and important account of the Jewish Diaspora in the period during which 1 Peter is written may be found in Erich S. Gruen, *Diaspora: Jews amidst Greeks and Romans* (Cambridge: Harvard University Press, 2002). An account of the enduring powers of the Jewish Diaspora both to sustain itself and to unsettle and effect real change in modern societies is given in Jonathan Boyarin and Daniel Boyarin, *Powers of Diaspora: Two Essays on the Relevance of Jewish Culture* (Minneapolis: University of Minnesota Press, 2002). John Howard Yoder reflects extensively on the significance of the Jewish Diaspora for ecclesiology and Christian witness in his *For the Nations: Essays Public and Evangelical* (Grand Rapids: Eerdmans, 1997) and *Jewish-Christian Schism Revisited*. Each of these volumes contributes significantly to our understanding of 1 Peter. See also George A. Lindbeck, *The Church in a Postliberal Age*, ed. James J. Buckley (Grand Rapids: Eerdmans, 2002), 223–52; and Arne Rasmussen, "The Politics of Diaspora: The Post-Christendom Theologies of Karl Barth

Yoder invites us to consider whether Jesus himself, in his messianic commission, teaching, and pattern of life and death, was calling first-century Judean Jews to live as if they too were in Diaspora, *even though they were dwelling in "their own" land*. The reign of God comes upon Israel, Jesus taught, not when the people of God control their own territory, temple, and throne, but when "two or three" gather in the "name" of Jesus, that is, when they gather to reenact Jesus's practice, mission, and identity in their life together. Jesus Messiah called Israel to refuse the option of being or seeking to be politically and militarily in charge—that option of garnering a measure of state power that motivated the strategic alliances with Rome by the Herodians and Sadducees, as well as the revolutionary hopes of the Zealots—and instead to enact social and economic justice in the land and entrust their destiny as a people to God while living peaceably, albeit vulnerably, among their enemies. Exactly in that way they would participate in the strange, alternative politics of messianic life, God's right-making justice, otherwise known as mercy, *which is the divine power of history*. "Jesus' impact on the first century added more and deeper authentically Jewish reasons, and reinforced and further validated the already expressed Jewish reasons, for the already well established ethos [in the Diaspora] of not being in charge and not considering any local state structure to be the primary bearer of the movement of history."[14] As it turned out, only a few of the Judean Jews of Jesus's time paid heed to his call. The Romans crushed the subsequent destabilizing attempts of Jewish revolution in 70 and 135.

Remarkably, however, the sociopolitical existence of the Jews that developed in Diaspora following the failed revolts of 70 and 135 in fact bears, according to Yoder, a striking resemblance to the way of life that Jesus had called for:

> Occasionally privileged after the model of Joseph, more often emigrating, frequently suffering martyrdom non-violently, they were able to maintain identity without turf or sword, community without sovereignty. They thereby demonstrated pragmatically the viability of the ethic of Jeremiah and Jesus.
>
> In sum: the Jews of the Diaspora were for over a millennium the closest thing to the ethic of Jesus existing on any significant scale anywhere in Christendom.[15]

When Peter writes of the church in terms of the Jewish Diaspora, he requires the church to learn something of the shape of its own life among the nations from the sociopolitical pattern of Jewish Diaspora, because in that pattern there is a concrete and visible witness to the messianic politics of Jesus.[16]

---

and John Howard Yoder," in *God, Truth, and Witness: Engaging Stanley Hauerwas*, ed. L. Gregory Jones et al. (Grand Rapids: Brazos, 2005), 88–111.

14. Yoder, *For the Nations*, 69.

15. Yoder, *Jewish-Christian Schism Revisited*, 81–82. Peter Ochs provides a Jewish response to Yoder's suggestive interpretation of Jesus and Diaspora on pp. 89–92.

16. This is, of course, a Christian assessment and, to some extent, appropriation of Jewish Diaspora existence—without, I hope, being an expropriation; see George A. Lindbeck, "What of

Peter's description of the church under the phrase *eklektois parepidēmois diasporas* is a *normative description* or, as I have suggested, a terse dogmatic ecclesiology, guiding all that Peter writes in his letter. Peter does not address the church in the language of simile, as those who are *like* chosen exiles in Diaspora. Rather, the church is addressed *directly* as those who *are* such. Each word reveals primarily an aspect of *God's own act* in making the church what it is. The church is not created out of its own action; it does not choose itself, does not separate itself, does not send itself, and yet it is truly a chosen, holy, and sent people. When the church takes seriously the normativity of its being "elect exiles of the Diaspora" it must on the one hand be wary of all forms of Constantinianism, Christendom, and other ecclesial subordinations to or identifications with the social, economic, political, and national powers of this age. Under such forms the church has all too readily and frequently confused or substituted its divine messianic identity and mission with an identity and mission defined by the worldly powers under which it lives. The German Christians in the 1930s and '40s are of course the notorious example. American Christians after September 11, 2001, have also been strongly tempted in this direction, and many American churches and Christians have capitulated to a spirit of patriotic nationalism and militarism under which the gospel is subsumed and of which it becomes a servant—thereby ceasing to be the gospel.[17] On the other hand, being defined as "elect exiles of the Diaspora" is not a call for the church to be otherworldly or escapist, but rather to be a called-out people whose political, social, economic, and cultural life is continually being conformed to its divine messianic origin, constitution, and end. As a people thus formed, it enters confidently into critical, creative, and flexible relationships with its wider cultural, social, and political environments, sharing in the life of the nations, seeking the peace and well-being of earthly cities, engaging them hopefully in the confidence that God also works in earthly cities (even through the church) to bring about a measure of justice, good order, and peace. But the people of God does not look to the earthly city's pride, power, progress, or protection to sustain or provide direction for its own life. The power and grace of God given in the Word and Spirit are sufficient for the life of God's people.[18]

---

the Future? A Christian Response," in *Christianity in Jewish Terms*, ed. Tikvah Frymer-Kensky et al. (Boulder, CO: Westview, 2000), 357–66. Whether Jews see the correspondence between the Diaspora way of life and the life to which Jesus called his disciples is for Jews themselves to decide. The Boyarins (*Powers of Diaspora*, 1–33), who argue for Diaspora as normative Judaism, nonetheless worry about Christians (like 1 Peter) and others co-opting or generalizing the language of Diaspora in such a way that it loses its unique power as a Jewish phenomenon.

17. I show how the apostle Paul (together with the witness of Stanley Hauerwas) equips the church to resist being co-opted by worldly powers in my *Paul among the Postliberals: Pauline Theology beyond Christendom and Modernity* (Grand Rapids: Brazos, 2003), 67–103.

18. I show how the apostle Paul critically and creatively engages the wider culture in my *Paul among the Postliberals*, 209–54.

The Holy Trinity Creates the People of God (1 Peter 1:2)

Peter first describes the being of the church in terms of Israel's election, exile, and Diaspora. But he immediately goes on to say that those terms are themselves grounded more fundamentally in the being and work of the Trinity.[19] Translations of 1:2 generally link God the Father's foreknowledge directly to the election of God's people (cf. NIV, NRSV, New King James Version, Revised English Bible), but then they tend to leave the last two phrases of 1:2 dangling on their own and theologically separated from 1:1. However, the Greek text may well be read as drawing all of 1:1 into the theological reality described in the three phrases of 1:2: "To the elect exiles of the Diaspora . . . according to [*kata*] the foreknowledge of God the Father, in [*en*] the sanctification of the Spirit, because of [*eis*] the obedience and blood-sprinkling of Jesus Christ" (DH).[20] In other words, the church just is what it is, "elect exiles of the Diaspora," because of the foreknowing, sanctifying, and justifying action of God the Father, Spirit, and Son.

By "according to the foreknowledge of God the Father" we see that the election, exile, and dispersion of God's people is no afterthought in God's purpose to bring all creation into communion with the Trinity, but the very outworking of that purpose for all creation. The election of Abram and Sarai from among the nations in Gen. 12 is a new creative act of God, an additional act of differentiating, separating, and fructifying within the created order, in keeping with the other such acts described in Gen. 1. The election of Israel creates *another difference*, constituting a distinct people, in all of its ethnic, social, cultural, and political particularity, among the divinely intended plurality of distinct peoples that spread across the face of the earth according to Gen. 10. The election of Abram and Sarai prefigures and prepares for the incarnation, while the incarnation is the eternal basis of the election of Abram and Sarai. We might say, then, that theologically prior to being a *soteriological* act in response to human sin and the fall (which it also is), the election of Abraham as the father of God's "family" among the families of the earth

19. "The referent of the divine activity described in these three phrases [1:2] is to be construed as ἐκλεκτοῖς rather than ἀπόστολος, since the apostolicity of Peter is not at issue in this letter, while the reality of divine election for estranged and persecuted Christians goes to the heart of the problem this epistle is addressing" (Achtemeier 1996: 86). On the theme of the foundation of the church in the work of the Holy Trinity, see Webster, *Holiness*, chaps. 2–3.

20. My translation follows Elliott in rendering *eis* as causative (see *A Greek-English Lexicon of the New Testament and Other Early Christian Literature*, by W. Bauer, F. W. Danker, W. F. Arndt, and F. W. Gingrich, 3rd ed. [Chicago: University of Chicago Press, 2000], 291 #10a) and *Iēsou Christou* as a subjective genitive: "With *Jesus Christ* as subjective genitive, the three phrases of v 2a–c assume a balance in which God, Spirit, and Jesus Christ each is assigned an active role in Christian election, its origin, mediation, and cause. Taking *eis* to indicate purpose and assuming the elect believers to be the subject of *obedience* but Jesus Christ as the subject of *sprinkling*, on the other hand, results in an awkward syntactical construction . . . that obscures the balance of these three phrases [in 1:2], which appear to focus exclusively on the action of God, Spirit, and Jesus Christ" (Elliott 2000: 319). On this understanding, Peter's thought in this phrase is close to Paul's in Rom. 5:12–19.

is another *creational* act by which God separates one people, Israel, from the rest and promises not only to bless this people, but also to bless all peoples in their God-ordained linguistic, cultural, social, and political diversity and particularity through this one people, which from the beginning bears the flesh of the Messiah. The election, sanctification, and witness of Israel furthers God's original creational intent that the Son of God should become incarnate in Israel's flesh and that through him the Spirit of God should be poured out on all flesh—an intent established in God's foreknowledge of the consummation for which he created all things in the first place.[21] As Maximus the Confessor writes:

> He who, by the sheer inclination of his will, established the beginning of all creation, seen and unseen, before all the ages and before that beginning of created beings, had an ineffably good plan for those creatures. The plan [even before the sin and fall] was for him to mingle, without change on his part, with the human nature by true hypostatic union, to unite human nature to himself while remaining immutable, so that he might become a man, as he alone knew how, and so that he might deify humanity in union with himself. Also, according to this plan, it is clear that God wisely divided "the ages" [*aiōnes*] between those intended for God to become human, and those intended for humanity to become divine.[22]

Israel belongs to that age that is fulfilled in the incarnation of the Son as Israel's Messiah,[23] while the church belongs to that age that is fulfilled in the "deification" of humankind and the healing of the nations. These ages meet and are held together forever in Jesus Christ. In God's creational and soteriological purpose the church is thus eternally joined to Israel in Christ, which is precisely the point of Peter's description of the church in Israel's terms: the elect, the exiles of the Diaspora. Paul also makes this clear when he speaks of the "grace given to [him] to bring to the Gentiles [the nations = *tois ethnesin*] the news of the boundless riches of Christ, and to make everyone see what is the plan of the mystery hidden for ages in God who created all things; so that through the church the wisdom of God in its rich variety might now be made known to the rulers and authorities in the heavenly places. This was in accordance with the eternal purpose that he has carried out in

21. The constitutive and enduring (that is, nonsuperseded) place of Israel among the nations in God's economy of creation, blessing, and consummation is crucially argued in R. Kendall Soulen, *The God of Israel and Christian Theology* (Minneapolis: Fortress, 1996), 109–77. At the same time (going beyond Soulen), Israel itself is created by, in, and for Jesus Christ, who is himself the redemption and consummation of creation. (George Sumner reminded me of this necessary correction of Soulen.)

22. *Ad Thalassium* 22, in Maximus the Confessor, *On the Cosmic Mystery of Jesus Christ*, trans. Paul M. Blowers and Robert Louis Wilkins (Crestwood, NY: St. Vladimir's Seminary Press, 2003), 115.

23. We should also note that in Jesus Christ we have the redemption and glorification not only of human nature (in the generic sense) but also specifically of Israel, inasmuch as the incarnate, crucified, risen, and glorified Messiah is not only "son of Adam, son of God" (Luke 3:38), but also "the son of David, the son of Abraham" (Matt. 1:1).

Christ Jesus our Lord" (Eph. 3:8–11). The list of specifically named provinces in
1 Pet. 1:1—"Pontus, Galatia, Cappadocia, Asia, and Bithynia"—reveals that God's
eternal purpose, to bless the particular and diverse peoples of the earth with his
riches and wisdom in Jesus Christ through Israel and the church, is already coming
to fruition in the particular churches of those provinces to which Peter writes. In
those churches, sharing in the particular languages and cultures of those places in
that time, the triune God is beginning to redeem the nations. That is the eternal
divine purpose of God's people in all particular times and places.

While the origin and purpose of the people of God lies in its election according
to the foreknowledge and purpose of the Father, its holiness, that is, its distinct
exilic existence as a people "set apart" (*hagios*) among the nations, is the work of
the Holy Spirit: "in the sanctification of the Spirit" (*en hagiasmō pneumatos*). The
Holy Spirit creates and sustains the bond between the election and the holiness
of the people of God by distinguishing the people of God from other peoples.
Circumcision in Israel is a sign of the Spirit, who is the bond of the covenant
between the holy God and his chosen holy people, named and set apart for God's
purpose. The Spirit is also the pillar of cloud by day and the pillar of fire by night
that both guides the exilic journey of God's people among the nations and guards
it from the attack of the enslaving enemy (Exod. 13:21–22; 14:19–20). The Holy
Spirit is the power of God's covenant with the church as well as with Israel. The
sign of the Spirit's power in the church is baptism, in which we are named and
set apart as God's covenant people. "For all who are led by the Spirit of God are
children of God. For you did not receive a spirit of slavery to fall back into fear,
but you have received a spirit of adoption" (Rom. 8:14–15). Thus the sanctifying
Spirit of God not only creates and sustains God's covenant with his people, but
also brings about the visible signs of God's messianic reign among them: "For the
kingdom of God is . . . righteousness and peace and joy in the Holy Spirit" (14:17).
The Holy Spirit creates "the fruit of the Spirit" among the people of God (Gal.
5:22–25) and pours out "gifts" for building up the body politic of Christ (1 Cor.
12). The Spirit is "the bond of peace" that unites the body politic of Christ as one
people (Eph. 4:3–6). It is the very presence and powerful working of the Holy
Spirit, rather than their own decision to "be different," that distinguishes God's
people from the wider world. "Nothing is holy but the holiness that God works
in us" (Luther 1967: 6).

With the words "because of the obedience and blood-sprinkling of Jesus Christ"
we are reminded that we are made participants of God's triune life through the
vicarious obedient life and sacrificial death of Jesus Christ. The Father's election
and foreknowledge rests first and directly upon his Son, Jesus Christ, as Peter says
later: "He was destined [*proegnōsmenou*, i.e., having been foreknown] before the
foundation of the world, but was revealed at the end of the ages for your sake"
(1 Pet. 1:20; cf. Eph. 1:4–5). He is the one "chosen and precious in God's sight"
(1 Pet. 2:4). It is *through* this same Christ that we ourselves are chosen and made
able to put our "trust in God" (1:21). As Paul writes in Rom. 5:19: "By the one

man's [Christ's] obedience the many will be made righteous." We are made righteous "by his [Christ's] blood" (5:9). This is what Paul means when he writes of the *pistis Iēsou Christou* ("the faithfulness of Jesus Christ") in Rom. 3:22, 26; Gal. 2:16; 3:22; Phil. 1:27; 3:9; Eph. 3:12. "*Pistis Christou* is an expression by which Paul speaks of Christ's atoning faithfulness, as, on the cross, he died faithfully for human beings while looking faithfully to God."[24] So too, Peter writes that we were "ransomed . . . with the precious blood of Christ, like that of a lamb without defect or blemish" (1 Pet. 1:18–19). With the clause "because of the obedience and blood-sprinkling of Jesus Christ" the apostle is pointing us to the costly work of the crucified Son, rather than to the believers' obedience, as the creating, confirming, and sustaining power at work in the church. In so doing, Peter completes his description of how the being, life, and mission of the messianic people of God is constituted through the work of the Holy Trinity, and thereby as participation in the life of God.

Peter concludes his greeting (1:2) with words of benediction: "May grace and peace be yours in abundance." These words are not mere formalities or throwaways, because in fact the whole being of the people of God is a testimony to God who, out of sheer grace, elects, justifies, and sanctifies it; and the whole purpose of that people is to witness among the nations to the triune peace in which it is established. "For we who have been captured from among the nations have been overcome and conquered by the grace of his word" (Origen, *First Principles* 4.1.5). The entire message of Peter's letter might well be summed up in the two words "grace and peace," for throughout the letter the apostle exhorts the church to be a people of peace as the quality both of its inner life and of its relationship to the wider world. It is able to be that kind of people because it does not constitute and sustain itself as a people through its own powers or in dependence on any worldly powers: rather the eternal triune God is the one who graciously creates, upholds, works in, and completes it.

Blessing God and Living Hope (1 Peter 1:3-5)

"In this foreword [1:3–9] you see a truly apostolic speech and an introduction to the theme. . . . For here St. Peter begins without further ado to tell us what Christ is and what we have acquired through Him. . . . These are genuinely evangelical words. They must be proclaimed" (Luther 1967: 9–10). Peter begins his "evangelical" introduction to the themes of his letter by *blessing* God. The first and constitutive act of God's people is to praise God (cf. 2 Cor. 1:3; Eph. 1:3; and the many psalms of blessing and praise). Praise is our grateful acknowledgement of God's

---

24. Martyn, *Galatians*, 271. For interpreting Paul's phrase *pistis Iēsou Christou* as "faith(fulness) of Jesus Christ" rather than "faith in Jesus Christ," see Richard B. Hays, *The Faith of Jesus Christ: The Narrative Substructure of Galatians 3:1–4:11*, 2nd ed. (Grand Rapids: Eerdmans, 2002); and Harink, *Paul among the Postliberals*, 26–45.

being, works, and ways, our joyous and thankful declaration of the truth about God and the world created, reconciled, and redeemed by God. Thus our praise is always specific: we specifically bless or praise the *revealed* God of the gospel: "Blessed be the God and Father of our Lord Jesus Christ." As Peter has already made clear in 1 Pet. 1:2, this God is not a vague and numinous "transcendence," an empty sublime awaiting "naming" by our imaginative theological "constructions."[25] The post-Kantian agnostic strain in modern and postmodern theology is often defended as a way to guard the transcendence of God and ward off idolatry; and yet, it is not the way of scripture.[26] According to scripture, God actively establishes and demonstrates his own transcendence—or rather, his freedom—both by naming himself: "I AM WHO I AM" (Exod. 3:14); and by keeping covenant with his chosen people: "The LORD, the God of your ancestors, the God of Abraham, the God of Isaac, and the God of Jacob" (3:15). We know that God is God and not a human construct because he declares and reveals that he is *this God and not another*. We are saved from idolatry not by positing a finally empty and indefinite transcendence, but because God reveals himself to us in his own freedom and truth. Calvin writes:

> As formerly [God] marked the difference between Him and all fictitious gods by calling Himself the God of Abraham, so now after He has manifested Himself in His own Son, He wills to be known only in Him. Hence those who conceive of God in His naked majesty apart from Christ have an idol instead of the true God. ... Whoever then seeks really to know the true God must regard Him as the Father of Christ, for, whenever our mind seeks God, unless it meets Christ it will wander and be confused, until it is wholly lost." (Calvin 1963: 231–32)[27]

In view of this, we see that Peter draws us directly to that event and proclamation in which the words "Father" and "Lord" are given specific content and meaning—the gospel of Jesus Christ. The God whom Jesus of Nazareth calls "Father" is the God of Abraham, Sarah, Isaac, Jacob, Moses, Miriam, David, and the prophets. This God speaks to Jesus at his baptism in the Jordan River and at his transfiguration

25. Understanding theology as a primarily constructive task is endemic to a great deal of modern and postmodern theology, for which Immanuel Kant's *Critique of Pure Reason* (1781) always stands in the background. Essential reading in this regard is William C. Placher's *The Domestication of Transcendence: How Modern Thinking about God Went Wrong* (Louisville: Westminster John Knox, 1996); and David Bentley Hart's *The Beauty of the Infinite: The Aesthetics of Christian Truth* (Grand Rapids: Eerdmans, 2003), 43–93, who provides a rigorous critique of such theology.

26. While the provenance of the modern version of theological agnosticism is predominantly Kant, R. Kendall Soulen notes that there have been other versions throughout history, including in ancient Egypt and Greece, against which the biblical writers had to contend; see "'Go Tell Pharaoh'; or, Why Empires Prefer a Nameless God," Society for Scriptural Reasoning (2005–2006), online at http://etext.lib.virginia.edu/journals/jsrforum/writings/SouPhar.html (accessed 1/22/2008).

27. Karl Barth's entire theology may be seen as an extensive application of Calvin's rule here— indeed, in his doctrines of election and predestination Barth applied it more consistently than Calvin did.

on Mount Tabor and calls Jesus his beloved "Son." God speaks as Jesus when Jesus instructs his disciples to baptize "in the name of the Father and of the Son and of the Holy Spirit" (Matt. 28:19). We simply get it wrong if we attempt to fill out the theological content or significance of words like "Father," "Son," and "Lord" from our own human concepts and experiences (positive or negative) of parents, children, and rulers. Instead we must be consistently oriented to and by the gospel narratives in which the identity of the triune God is given to us in the specific acts and relations of the Father, Son, and Holy Spirit depicted in those narratives.

Further, we praise "the God and Father of our Lord Jesus Christ" because of the *specific benefits* that he bestows upon his people. In the first instance we have been "begotten anew" (*anagennēsas*) by God "through the resurrection of Jesus Christ from the dead," and this because of the "great mercy" of God (1:3). Once again Peter draws our attention to the gracious priority and power of God's act.[28] No one becomes a daughter or son of God, no one has God truly as Father, no one can "see the kingdom of God," by virtue of natural birth (see John 3:1–10), for that birth and subsequent life have been laid hold of by the powers of sin, death, and "bondage to decay." As Paul makes clear in Rom. 8, the womb of creation has become a tomb of corruption; all creation groans in labor pains but is not able to give birth to living children of God or to its own freedom. We are prisoners and slaves. We become children of God by God's own act of redemption and new creation, of delivering us from bondage and begetting us anew by the power of the Holy Spirit. The crucifixion and resurrection of Jesus are that act. In the cross the powers that enslave are defeated. Through the bodily resurrection of Jesus Christ, God's unconquerable power of life is unleashed upon the creature delivered from bondage to decay. Sin and death cannot corrupt the risen body of Jesus Christ; he is delivered, transfigured, taken up into the inexhaustible livingness of God. "So if anyone is in Christ, there is a new creation" (2 Cor. 5:17). Those who are joined to Christ's risen body by the Holy Spirit through faith, baptism, and participation in the messianic community are already begotten anew to a "living hope," even as they still await, beyond death, the final redemption and resurrection of their own natural bodies. "When one wants to preach the Gospel, one must treat only of the resurrection of Christian. . . . For this is the chief article of our faith. . . . For if there were no resurrection, we would have no consolation or hope, and everything else Christ did and suffered would be futile (1 Cor. 15:17)" (Luther 1967: 12–13). Peter states this crucial truth at this point in the letter, because a good deal of what he goes on to write has to do with God's exilic people suffering persecution as the form of their sharing in Christ's sufferings. The living hope of resurrection sustains the

28. "The nuance of this active aorist participle 'begotten anew' (*anagennēsas*) is to emphasize the action of God in begetting the Christian anew—thus the translation '(God) has begotten us anew' rather than 'being born again'"; Senior 2003: 31.

people of God in its faithfulness to the cruciform way of life, the politics of suffering to which it is called.

The end toward which Christian hope is directed is called an "inheritance . . . kept in heaven for you" (1 Pet. 1:4). The persistent popular habit of construing this inheritance as something that we receive when we "go to heaven" is perhaps rooted partly in Jesus always using in the Gospel of Matthew the Jewish circumlocution "the kingdom of heaven." According to popular interpretation, that kingdom is contrasted in turn with an earthly, political kingdom, such as the land and nation of Israel that the Jews have always viewed as their inheritance, to be restored to them in the messianic age. The kingdom of heaven, so it is thought, is more spiritual than that. But in Mark and Luke the words that Jesus uses are rendered as "the kingdom/reign of God," and Jesus teaches his disciples to pray, "Your kingdom come; your will be done, on earth as it is in heaven." Jesus declares that "the kingdom of God is in the midst of you." It is clear that Jesus is not speaking of an inner or other place or dimension to which his disciples must go, but rather proclaiming the actuality and quality of God's reign *on earth among his people Israel* and teaching his disciples to pray for God to enact that reign even here and now. The inheritance kept (literally) "in the heavens" is given to God's people when God himself comes in power to deliver and purify his people, to establish the new Jerusalem in the midst of the nations, and to make creation the home of his own righteousness (2 Pet. 3:11–13). The inheritance of the people of God is the new creation in which "the home of God is among mortals" (Rev. 21:3). Precisely because God graciously reigns in the new creation with his own presence, holiness, and glory, the inheritance of God's people in turn participates in the eternal qualities of God's own life; it is "imperishable, undefiled, and unfading" (1 Pet. 1:4). We no longer suffer the corrosions of sin, bondage, and death. That is what is meant by the inheritance "having been kept [*tetērēmenēn*] in the heavens for you" (DH). This is not a statement about where the inheritance is located; it is a statement about its divine origin and quality—God's eternal life, glory, and reign is itself our inheritance. "And this is eternal life, that they may know you, the only true God, and Jesus Christ whom you have sent" (John 17:3).

While God preserves or himself is and gives our inheritance in its incorruptibility, the people of God are also "being guarded [*phrouroumenous*] by the power of God through faith" (1 Pet. 1:5 DH).[29] The protection envisaged here is not that God will save his people from all suffering and adversity. The next few verses and the whole of Peter's letter assume that God's people are being persecuted in some manner and that they should continue to expect danger from the surrounding society, just because they are "elect exiles of the Diaspora" called to a cruciform,

---

29. "The picturesque participle *phrouroumenous* ('guarded') is related linguistically to the term *phrouria* denoting the numerous 'forts' or 'fortifications' dotting the rural areas of Pontus, Cappadocia, and Galatia . . . and used by local rulers and later Roman garrisons for securing the villages and countryside" (Elliott 2000: 337).

godly way of life. When Jesus calls, empowers, and sends out his disciples with
the good news and power of the kingdom, he makes clear to them not only that
there is no guarantee of their safety, but that their message and deeds will in fact
become the occasion of conflict (Matt. 10:16–42). Resistance to the reign of
God and the mission of God's people is often fierce and violent.[30] Jesus does not
assure us that no sparrow will fall, but that a sparrow, though it fall, does not fall
"apart from" (*aneu*; 10:29) the Father's knowledge and care; and disciples are
more valuable than sparrows.

How, then, are we protected by God's power? Luther draws attention to the
relationship between the power of God and faith in Peter's words:

> God's power must be present and work faith in us, as Paul says in Eph. 1:17–19:
> "That God . . . may give you a spirit of wisdom . . . that you may know . . . what is the
> immeasurable greatness of His power in us who believe, according to the working
> of His great might." It is not only God's will but also His power to spend a great
> deal. For when God creates faith in man, this is as great a work as if He were to
> create heaven and earth again. . . .
>
> But what does Peter mean when he says that you are guarded for salvation by
> the power of God? This is his meaning: The faith which works in us the power of
> God—which dwells in us and with which we are filled—is such a tender and precious
> thing that it gives us a true and clear understanding of everything that pertains to
> salvation, so that we are able to judge everything on earth and say: "This doctrine
> is right. That one is false. This life is right. That one is not. This work is good and
> well done. That one is evil." What such a person concludes is right and true; for
> he cannot be misled but is preserved and protected, and he remains a judge of all
> doctrine. (Luther 1967: 14–15)

Luther helps us to see that the graver danger for God's people living as exiles is
not from attacks directed toward their physical welfare, but from subtler attacks
that distort and destroy their spiritual ability to make judgments in accordance
with the truth of Christ. Those attacks may come as readily in the form of in-
traecclesial pressures and temptations as in the form of enmity and torture. A
people whose being is defined as "elect exiles of the Diaspora" is summoned to
faith in the God who has chosen them. Apart from that faith our judgments
are potentially pressured and tempted in two directions, each as a mode of *self-
preservation*: either toward uncritical assimilation to the wider culture's norms
and practices, or toward uncritical separation from them. *God's* salvation, on
the other hand, stands "ready to be revealed in the last time." It is by looking
toward that imminent salvation that we are directed away from our attempts at
self-preservation and called instead to trust in God in this time before the "last

30. Where that is not the case, the church may have to examine the faithfulness of its own witness. See Stanley Hauerwas's essay "No Enemy, No Christianity: Preaching between Worlds," in his
Sanctify Them in the Truth: Holiness Exemplified (Nashville: Abingdon, 1998), 191–201.

time."[31] Through trust in God's protection and deliverance, God enables his people to make good and faithful judgments about their responses to the beliefs, norms, actions, practices, and habits of the wider society.[32] As Peter writes later, God's judgment of the world begins with "the household of God" (4:17)—not least through the godly judgments that God's "household" makes about the character of its own life in the midst of the nations.

Joy in the Time of Trial (1 Peter 1:6–9)

With the phrase "ready to be revealed at the last time" (*hetoimēn apokalyphthēnai en kairō eschatō*; 1:5) Peter emphasizes not so much the futurity of God's salvation, as its *imminent nearness*—it stands "ready" (*hetoimēn*) to be revealed. "The end of all things is near" (4:7). The salvation of the "last time" is never simply separated from the present by a span of time, whether short or long. To be sure, we await the promised return of Christ and resurrection, which has not yet come. But, the "last time" is also already upon us: "When the fullness of time had come, God sent his Son" (Gal. 4:4). Christ is already risen, "the first fruits of those who have died" (1 Cor. 15:20); through Christ's resurrection, as Peter has said, Christians are already begotten anew into a *living* hope—a hope that is not inert, but that has real and present effects. The Holy Spirit is already poured out, as Peter declares at Pentecost: "In the last days it will be, God declares, that I will pour out my Spirit upon all flesh" (Acts 2:17, quoting Joel 2:28). The church is the messianic community upon whom, already, "the ends of the ages have come" (1 Cor. 10:11). God's "last time" salvation already invades the present and conditions the time in which we live: "the time has been shortened . . . ; the present form of this world is passing away" (1 Cor. 7:29, 31). As Boring writes: "The eschatological existence of the believer, the 'living hope' of which 1 Peter writes (1:3) is not an explanation that someday there will be a resurrection and things will be different, but a celebration that there has already been a resurrection, and things are already different" (1999: 65). For that reason Christians do not only *wait* for the day of God's salvation; they already "greatly rejoice" or "exult" (*agalliasthe*) in it (1 Pet. 1:6). They both wait for and *hasten* the day of God's coming (2 Pet. 3:12) because the power of "last time" salvation is already at work among the messianic people even now, even today, enabling it to face the present brief time

31. See Karl Barth's discussion of how God upholds the church against the pressures and temptations toward self-preservation in *Church Dogmatics*, vol. 4/2: *The Doctrine of Reconciliation*, trans. G. W. Bromiley (Edinburgh: Clark, 1958), 667–70.
32. The "divine guarding is now visibly appropriated by the Christians' trust διὰ πίστεως, which becomes the instrument whereby the divine protection becomes reality. Such Christian faith is therefore the visible evidence of the unseen reality evoking that trust" (Achtemeier 1996: 97).

of testing in a hostile context.[33] And yet, as Calvin notes, Peter does not mini-mize the "grieving" or "suffering" that also is part of the "trials" that come upon the Christian community: "The faithful are not logs of wood, nor have they so divested themselves of human feelings as to be unaffected by sorrow, unafraid of danger, unhurt by poverty, and untouched by hard and unbearable persecutions. Hence they experience sorrow because of evils, but it is so mitigated by faith that they never cease at the same time to rejoice. Thus sorrow does not prevent their joy, but rather gives place to it" (1963: 234).

The cross of Christ, which is itself the riches, wisdom, and power of God for those who believe and take up its way, is viewed by the world as poverty, foolish-ness, and weakness. The gospel's apocalyptic inversion of the usual standards of status, success, and security is often met with skepticism, revulsion, and hostility, rather than with faith and conversion. "For the gate is narrow and the road is hard that leads to life, and there are few who find it" (Matt. 7:14). When the church and its members keep faith with the gospel's inversion, testifying to it by their strange, exilic lives, they often encounter ridicule, persecution, and suffering at the hands of those still in the grip of the powers of the old eon. That suffering, as Peter puts it (1 Pet. 1:6), amounts to a purifying "trial" (*peirasmos*).

It is crucial at this point, and throughout Peter's letter, that we pay attention to the specificity of the suffering and testing in view here. It is neither natural calamity nor a generalized suffering of any and every sort, as the popular phrase "bearing my cross" has come to mean. Not all suffering is cross-bearing. "The cross of Calvary was not a difficult family situation, not a frustration of visions of personal fulfillment, a crushing debt, or a nagging in-law; it was *the political, legally-to-be-expected result of a moral clash with the powers ruling his society.*"[34] The suffering and trials of which Peter writes are those that come upon believers when our lives are being morally, socially, and politically conformed to the way of Jesus Christ, a conformity that may put us at odds with the prevailing moral, social, and political realities of the wider world.

Jesus teaches his disciples to pray, "Do not bring us to the time of trial [*peir-asmos*], but rescue us from the evil one" (Matt. 6:13), because he knows well that when our faithfulness to the way of Jesus Christ is tested against the seemingly self-evident and self-legitimating ways of the real world, we often fail the test, as did Peter himself in the time of Jesus's trial. Nevertheless, even as Jesus taught his disciples to pray that prayer, *he himself entered into the time of trial*—that is, he encountered the opposing and finally violent ways of the powers of this age—*and he called his disciples to follow him.* For disciples and the church, the time of trial and suffering should not catch us by surprise. Where the messianic community is not

---

33. Most commentators agree that "in which" (*en hō*) beginning the thought in 1:6 refers back to the "salvation ready to be revealed" in 1:5. Rejoicing now is produced by the present effective power of the *kairos eschatos*.

34. John Howard Yoder, *The Politics of Jesus: Vicit Agnus Noster*, 2nd ed. (Grand Rapids: Eerd-mans, 1994), 129 (emphasis added).

under trial in the world, it may as much be a sign that it is too closely conformed to the way of the worldly powers, as it is that those powers have conformed to the truth of the gospel and its judgment upon their ways. Jesus confronted the ruling powers of the day and conquered them not by their own violent means, but by allowing himself to suffer and be killed by them. In so doing, he gave himself into the hands of the Father. Trusting that the Father would deliver him, he revealed in that way that he was the divine Son of God. That was his time of trial, and it is the church's as well: "Since therefore Christ suffered in the flesh, arm yourselves also with the same intention" (1 Pet. 4:1). The "authenticity" (*dokimion*) of the church's faith is always "being authenticated" (*dokimazomenou*), to see whether it is faithful to Jesus Christ's merciful, nonviolent means of engaging and overcoming evil (1:6). That kind of faith participates in the very reality of Jesus Christ and so too shares in the "praise and glory and honor" that is due to him when he is "apocalypsed" (*apokalypsei*) to the world (1:7). Indeed, the church's witness to Jesus Christ by that kind of authentic faith is itself, in some measure, an apocalypse of Jesus Christ, an intrusion of the messianic era into the time of the world.

With "whom, not having seen, you love" (1:8 DH) Peter writes that love traverses the distance between our not seeing Jesus and our following him to the end. Jesus said to Thomas, "Have you believed because you have seen me? Blessed are those who have not seen and yet have come to believe" (John 20:29). The power of the "not-seeing" in which we yet come to believe ("in whom, now not seeing, but believing"; 1 Pet. 1:8 DH) is the proclamation of the gospel itself. "It was before your eyes that Jesus Christ was publicly exhibited as crucified" (Gal. 3:1), as Paul writes to the Galatians, who themselves had not seen Jesus Christ and yet had indeed seen him in Paul's proclamation. "Faith comes from what is heard, and what is heard comes through the word of Christ" (Rom. 10:17). Christ himself is present in the proclamation of the gospel—the telling in word and sacrament of the story of his life, crucifixion, resurrection, and ascension. His crucified and risen beauty draws us to himself; his gracious Spirit turns our hearts of stone into hearts of flesh, eliciting our love for him and our willingness to joyfully take up his difficult way and embrace the form of his suffering.

When we share in Christ through faith, love, and imitation, we also share in the joy and glory that is his: we "rejoice with joy unspeakable and full of glory" (1 Pet. 1:8 King James Version). It was for the sake of "the joy that was set before him" that Jesus "endured the cross, disregarding its shame," and entered into his glory, taking "his seat at the right hand of the throne of God." As such he is the "pioneer and perfecter of our faith" (Heb. 12:2). "The addition *full of glory* admits of two explanations. It means either what is magnificent and glorious, or what is contrary to that which is empty and fading, of which men will soon be ashamed. Thus 'glorified' has the same meaning as that which is solid and permanent, beyond the danger of being brought to nothing" (Calvin 1963: 236). The church must take note of this: its only hope of resisting the now pervasive nihilism in Western societies—governed by the enslaving regime of "empty and fading" consumer choice—is believing, living, and telling the "solid and permanent" truth of Jesus Christ in his crucified and risen glory. When through faith and love we share in Christ, we receive the substance and permanence of his joy and glory, and in our own joy we experience something of the "salvation of [our] souls" even here, even now (1 Pet. 1:9).

Messianic Interpretation (1 Peter 1:10–12)

Believing in and loving Jesus Messiah, and taking up his way, the church now shares in the divine power (the "grace" 1:10) of the messianic age, an age that nonetheless still awaits its completion and fullness. But to those to whom the Messiah has now been revealed, it becomes clear that the Messiah did not come lately upon the scene—unprecedented, unanticipated, and unheralded—as if only those who live after the birth and death of Jesus share in the grace of the Messiah. The Spirit of the Messiah (*pneuma Christou*) was already at work long ago, inciting in the prophets of Israel an intense inquiry into the *kairos* of the Messiah and bearing advance witness (*promartyromenon*) through them to his sufferings and subsequent glorification (1:11). The prophetic testimony of the Old Testament to the Messiah should not be understood as a prediction or multiple predictions that lead up to and come true when Jesus arrives. Rather, through Christ's death and resurrection it is revealed to the church that the prophets discerned *the pattern of messianic suffering and glorification* that is already *the divine secret of Israel's history* and sought out "what sort of person or propitious time" (*eraunōntes eis tina hē poion kairon*; 1:11, translation by Elliott 2000: 329) would bring that pattern to its full revelation.[35]

Christian interpretation of the Old Testament acknowledges that the messianic pattern "apocalypsed" in Christ also pervades Israel's memory. From the beginning God's work in Israel is characterized by this pattern: "God chose what is foolish in the world to shame the wise; God chose what is weak in the world to shame the strong; God chose what is low and despised in the world, things that are not [*ta mē onta*], to reduce to nothing things that are [*ta onta*]" (1 Cor. 1:27–28). The pattern is revealed in the weakness of Abraham, whose "body . . . was already as good as dead" (Rom. 4:19) and in the shame of Sarah who "was barren; she had no child" (Gen. 11:30); but God, the one "who gives life to the dead and calls into existence the things that do not exist [*ta mē onta hōs onta*]" (Rom. 4:17), chooses Abraham and Sarah and gives them the glorious inheritance that they were promised. The pattern is revealed in Joseph, who is cast into the

35. Peter may well have intentionally used the ambiguous word *tina* in 1:11, which can mean either "who" (i.e., the person of the Messiah) or "what" (i.e., the circumstances of the Messiah's coming), since the point is that the prophets were searching out matters that were not revealed clearly to them. Commentators differ in their readings of *tina*, but it seems better for the matter to remain unresolved.

pit, sold into slavery, put into prison, and forgotten, but who is chosen and raised up by God to share in the glory of Pharaoh and receive honor from his father and brothers. The messianic pattern is revealed in Moses, a fugitive in the wilderness, separated from his own people, whom God chooses to lead the people of Israel out of bondage in Egypt. The messianic pattern is there in David, the least of the sons of Jesse, whom God chooses and anoints as the great king of Israel. In each of these we see a figure of "the sufferings of Messiah and, after these, the glories" (1 Pet. 1:11 DH). The messianic figure receives its fullest prophetic depiction in the chosen servant of the Lord of Isa. 52–53, in whose suffering and vindication is the salvation of Israel and the nations. Finally, however, the "messianic secret"— God's way of making history, to which these figures all testify—is fully revealed in the suffering and glorification of Jesus of Nazareth, the servant of the Lord, the incarnate Son of God who "is before all things" and in whom "all things hold together" (Col. 1:17). He himself precedes all of the messianic patterns; he is their form and substance and goal. Peter's entire letter is written in the conviction that the chosen people of God, as sharers "in the Messiah," cannot but also be sharers in the pattern of his sufferings and glorification. As Paul also writes, "if [we are] children [of God], then heirs, heirs of God and joint heirs with Christ—if, in fact, we suffer with him so that we may also be glorified with him" (Rom. 8:17).

As the prophets diligently sought out the "propitious time" of the coming of Messiah, "it was revealed [*apekalyphthē*] to them that they were serving not themselves but you" (1 Pet. 1:12), that is, they were serving those to whom the good news of the Messiah's arrival would be announced.[36] What was revealed in anticipation to the prophets, however, had to be completed by the revelation (*apokalypsis*) of Jesus Christ (1:13), in order for the messianic community to discern that the prophetic writings of Israel were serving the gospel and the church. Origen discerns this point precisely: "Before the sojourn of Christ, the law and the prophets did not contain the proclamation that belongs to the definition of the gospel, since he who explained the mysteries in them had not yet come. But since the Savior has come and has caused the gospel to be embodied, he has by the gospel made all things as gospel."[37] This kind of *retrospective messianic hermeneutic* of the Old Testament is evident throughout Peter's letter, whose words here echo Paul in Rom. 4:23–24 ("now the words, 'it was reckoned to him,' were written not for his sake alone, but for ours also") and 1 Cor. 10:11 ("these things [events of the Israelites in the wilderness] happened to them to serve as an example [*typikōs*,

36. "The OT prophets had presentiments that the divine intervention they announced was not intended for their day [e.g., Num. 24:17; Deut. 18:15; Hab. 2:1–3], and the notion that prophets served not themselves but others became a commonplace in apocalyptic literature [*1 Enoch* 1.2] and at Qumran [1QpHab 7.1–8]" (Achtemeier 1996: 111; the references are from Achtemeier's footnotes).

37. Origen, *Commentary on John* 1.33, quoted in John Behr, *The Mystery of Christ: Life in Death* (Crestwood, NY: St. Vladimir's Seminary Press, 2006), 91.

literally 'types'], and they were written down to instruct us, on whom the ends of the ages have come").[38]

The apostolic announcement of the gospel "by the Holy Spirit sent from heaven" (1 Pet. 1:12) constitutes for the church the "time of legibility" of Israel's scriptures,[39] the decisive moment of reading the scriptures "in the Messiah" in which the prophetic writings speak their timely word to the church about the Messiah and thus find their messianic fulfillment. At that moment the messianic figures and patterns of the Old Testament become for the church "legible" or recognizable for what they are, anticipations or types of Christ, who is himself the "time of the now" in which all of the figures and types are "recapitulated." In messianic *typology* a relation is established "between every event from a past time and *ho nyn kairos* ['the now time'], messianic time.... What matters ... is not the fact that each event of the past—once it becomes a figure—announces a future event and is fulfilled in it, but is the transformation of time [and history] implied by this typological relation.... [A] tension [is created] that clasps together and transforms past and future, *typos* and *antitypos*, together in an inseparable constellation. The messianic is not just one of two terms in this typological relation, *it is the relation itself.*"[40] In messianic *recapitulation* "what is decisive is that the *plērōma* of *kairoi* [the fullness of times] is understood as the relation of each instant to the Messiah—each *kairos* is *unmittelbar zu Gott* ['immediate to God'], and is not just the final result of a process.... Each time is the messianic now ..., and the messianic is not the chronological end of time, but the present as the exigency of fulfillment, what gives itself 'as an end.'"[41] This drawing together of times past, present, and future "in an inseparable constellation" constitutes the time of the messianic community, the church (and Israel, in another sense), and the time of scriptural interpretation. Specifically, the risen Jesus Messiah freely gives *himself* "as an end" (or rather, as *the* end) to the church through the hearing and preaching of scripture, and scripture in turn finds its own true end in serving testimony to "the sufferings destined for Christ and the subsequent glory" (1 Pet. 1:11). Jesus says to the disciples on the road to Emmaus, "'Was it not necessary that the Messiah should suffer these things and then enter into his glory?' Then beginning with Moses and all the

38. I take the idea of a retrospective messianic hermeneutic of the Old Testament (in contrast to a prospective or predictive one) from a discussion of Paul by Douglas A. Campbell, *The Quest for Paul's Gospel: A Suggested Strategy* (London/New York: Clark, 2005), 142–44.

39. The phrase "time of legibility" is from Walter Benjamin, quoted in Giorgio Agamben, *The Time That Remains: A Commentary on the Letter to the Romans*, trans. Patricia Dailey (Stanford, CA: Stanford University Press, 2005), 145, who provides a helpful analysis of Benjamin's idea of *Jetztzeit* ("now-time") and *das Jetzt der Lesbarkeit* ("the now of legibility"). Benjamin's probing of the concept of messianic time is profound and germane to the discussion of messianic hermeneutics touched upon here; see his "Theses on the Philosophy of History," in *Illuminations*, ed. Hannah Arendt, trans. Harry Zohn (New York: Schocken, 1968), 253–64.

40. Agamben, *Time That Remains*, 74 (emphasis original).

41. Ibid., 76.

prophets, he interpreted to them the things about himself in all the scriptures" (Luke 24:26–27).

Christian interpretation of scripture, that is, Christian theology, is "messianic" or, we might say, "apocalyptic." "Theology begins . . . with the opening of the scriptures by the risen Lord."[42] Messianic hermeneutics as practiced and displayed by Peter and Paul and others is the gift and task of the church, since the messianic "time of legibility" of the scriptures is inaugurated wherever the risen and reigning Messiah is present and active, himself interpreting the scriptures "where two or three are gathered." When the scriptures are heard and preached in the congregation, and the same Holy Spirit who was "sent from heaven" upon the apostles comes again upon the church, we are enabled also to read our present time through the stories, patterns, and types of scripture. The scriptures, read according to the messianic pattern of crucifixion and resurrection, constitute for the church the true description and analysis of our present world under messianic judgment, the hermeneutical lens through which time, history, and personal, social, and political life are discerned in their truth.

Hope and Holiness (1 Peter 1:13–16)

The "elect exiles of the Diaspora" live in the time of the Messiah, that "propitious time" that the prophets sought and inquired about in the "Spirit of Christ," that the apostles proclaimed as "good news" by the Holy Spirit, and that the angels longed to glimpse before its arrival. Messianic time is the time of God's invasive and decisive reign. It is the time of God's impartial judgment and gracious patience. We await that time in its fullness. But that time is also now! "The Messiah has already arrived, the messianic event has already happened, but its presence contains within itself another time, which stretches its parousia, not in order to defer it, but, on the contrary, to make it graspable."[43] Messianic time is that definite yet open time defined by Jesus Christ, and thus the time within which the messianic people of God are exhorted to flourish in hope and holiness of life and in so doing to anticipate the fullness of the reign of the Messiah. "From the greatness and excellency of grace [Peter] draws an exhortation, that it was their duty to receive the grace of God more readily, as the more bountifully He bestows it upon them" (Calvin 1963: 242).

The first imperative verb in Peter's exhortation beginning in 1:13 is "hope."[44] Not just "hope," but "hope completely" (*teleiōs elpisate*). Boring notes: "*The first*

42. Behr, *Mystery of Christ*, 141. This crucial point is made powerfully in John Webster, *Holy Scripture: A Dogmatic Sketch* (Cambridge: Cambridge University Press, 2003); and idem, "Resurrection and Scripture," in *Christology and Scripture: Interdisciplinary Perspectives*, ed. A. Lincoln and A. Paddison (London: Clark, 2007), 138–55.

43. Agamben, *Time That Remains*, 71.

44. Achtemeier 1996: 117 issues a caution against reading the several participles in these verses as imperatives. The two true imperatives are "hope" and "become holy."

'true' imperative in the letter is the command to 'hope.' . . . 'Hope' is seen here not as one quality among others in the Christian life, but as the comprehensive term that summarizes Christian existence as such" (1999: 74–75, emphasis original). Messianic hope is rooted in the comprehensive alteration of reality already brought about through the crucifixion, resurrection, and ascension of Jesus Christ. By Christ's death, resurrection, and ascension God has both subjected the "angels, authorities, and powers" to Christ (3:22) and set Christ's own glorious inheritance as the destiny of the people of God (1:4). While their life as often-persecuted "exiles" might suggest to the messianic people that the powers of this age are still in charge and that the church's only "inheritance" is the shame and vulnerability of social and political marginalization, we must know that the *real* situation is otherwise. In the face of often seemingly powerful evidence that the powers are victorious ("Be realistic!" as they say), what is called for from the church is an act of hopeful resistance, an act of disciplined "counterintelligence" in which the already present and coming messianic age is grasped in thought and action as the all-determining truth of the church's life, and indeed of the life of the world.

The church comes to hope completely in the gospel, Peter says, by "girding up the loins of your intelligence [*dianoias*]" (1:13 DH). This strange-sounding description that, as Calvin points out, "doubles the metaphor by ascribing loins to the mind" (1963: 243) nonetheless makes its point powerfully.[45] In those parts of the ancient world in which long garments were normal for men and women, the robes needed to be tied up around the waist to clear the knees for doing hard work or walking quickly and running. A specific and self-conscious act of preparation was required before the activity was undertaken. Peter's double metaphor suggests that the mental activity required for hoping in Christ demands both preparation ("girding up") and exertion (working "the loins of the intelligence"). How can we hope completely in the reality of the messianic age without bringing its substance and contours clearly before our minds, and giving attentive and strenuous thought to it? Christian faith always evokes rigorous intellectual work, which asks, What does the messianic age, which in the crucifixion and resurrection of Jesus is already pressing in upon us, look like? Is it a vague ideal we wistfully hope to realize some day? Is it a mythical otherworld to which we hope to escape after death? No, the hope to which we are called is both more difficult and more glorious than that. The work of hope begins for us with an "intellectual vision" (*dianoia*) of actual messianic life, a vision constituted and formed by the specific narratives about the Messiah, canonically given to us in the four Gospels of the New Testament. "Let this pattern of thinking [*phroneite*] be in you that was also in Christ Jesus" (Phil. 2:5 DH), Paul writes, after which he sets out the way of Jesus Christ (which each of the Gospels also tells in its own way) from eternal glory, through incarnation, Spirit-empowered mission, confrontation of the powers, humiliation, and

---

45. Elliott 2000: 355 suggests "having rolled up the sleeves of your mind" as an idiomatic English equivalent. NRSV translates accurately, but blandly: "prepare your minds for action."

crucifixion, to exaltation and glorification (2:6–11). Since Christ himself is the true human being, we may not imagine that the path to our own true humanity (in other words, our hope) will be different from his; rather, the path to our own eternal inheritance, which is to share in Christ's life, reign, and glory, can only be a sharing in his mission, humiliation, and suffering. Jesus's destiny is our own human destiny. Christ himself is our *dianoia*, our intellectual vision. The messianic community must fix its mind upon him.

The author of Hebrews makes this same point. The abiding truth about humanity, he says, is that God has made humans to be rulers over all creation, "'subjecting all things under their feet.' Now in subjecting all things to them, God left nothing outside their control" (Heb. 2:8, quoting Ps. 8:6 LXX). However, the truth of ordinary human history is much different, as every Christian who has suffered persecution knows: "As it is, we do not yet see everything in subjection to them." How utterly true! But, like Peter and Paul, the author of Hebrews does not leave our minds floundering in a sea of ambiguity between the ideal and the real, between optimism and cynicism, left to wonder and guess at what human dominion might look like and how it might be attained. Rather, he directs our minds immediately to the one who himself constitutes the very substance and form of human dominion over all things and the manner in which it is to be attained: "*But we do see Jesus*, who for a little while was made lower than the angels, now crowned with glory and honor because of the suffering of death" (Heb. 2:9). The truly Christian intelligence is focused on, centered in, and governed by "seeing Jesus," even or especially in the midst of a human situation that by and large escapes human control. And what labor of spiritual insight and intellectual effort is required to form such a vision? Conversely, an intellectual vision *un*formed by the specific gospel narrative of Jesus (which is our means of "seeing Jesus") is simply inadequate to the task of Christian hope, for the content of that hope is itself the "grace" of receiving the "*apokalypsis* of Jesus Christ" (1 Pet. 1:13).[46]

The next imperative verb in this text is "become holy" (*hagioi ... genēthēte*; 1:15). Holiness is in the first place an attribute of God—"he who called you is holy"—and so Peter quotes Lev. 19:2: "You shall be holy, for I am holy." We see again (→1:2) that the holiness of God's people is rooted first of all in God's very own being, then in God's action of calling and setting apart a people for himself, and finally in God's people reflecting God's character and action in its life before God and among the nations. God's people must *become holy* because they are first *made holy* by God who himself *is holy*. Becoming holy is a matter of being transformed by, conformed to, and sharing in the prior action and character of God, and that in turn is a matter of obedience and the right orientation of desire.

46. While most commentators prefer a future meaning for *en apokalypsei Iēsou Christou* in 1:15, Elliott 2000: 357 argues that it refers to the good news of the gospel already announced to the readers. Luther 1967: 29 does the same, translating it "because Jesus Christ is revealed to you." But as Elliott notes, "In either case, the original manifestation of Jesus as Messiah and his final revelation in glory mark the boundaries of the endtime and of the period of lively hope."

Before we were, through Christ, "appropriated by God" (Achtemeier 1996: 121) and thereby made holy, we were ignorant of God's holiness, and our desires were subsumed, shaped, and directed (*syschēmatizō*, "conformed"; 1 Pet. 1:14) by that ignorance. We were "darkened in [our] understanding, alienated from the life of God because of [our] ignorance and hardness of heart" (Eph. 4:18). As Paul makes clear in Rom. 1:18–23, human ignorance of God is not the result of a natural or historical accident, but of our culpable turning away from God, failing to give God the honor and thanks due him, exchanging the glory of God for images of creatures, and exchanging the truth about God for a lie. In response, God "hands us over" (*paradidōmi*) as prisoners (1:24, 26, 28; cf. 11:32; Gal. 3:22) to our self-chosen ignorance and to powerful human desires no longer oriented to their proper ends. Paul goes on to show that the resulting profound disorientation of desire affects all of human life, from worship, to sexual relations, to every aspect of personal and social existence (Rom. 1:24–32). "Unholiness" is a moral failure, an act of willful disobedience by which we refuse to be the creature made in the image of God, whose very being is to worship God and to honor one another. Unholiness is subsequently an epistemological failure, an intellectual bondage in which we are no longer capable of the proper perception of God and our true end. Finally it is a failure of desire in which all human actions and relationships suffer various forms of distortion, disruption, and destruction. As Paul's Letter to the Romans demonstrates, we cannot deliver ourselves from unholiness by our own decisions and actions. It is only through God's grace, election, and powerful deliverance in Christ that we are freed once again to become holy, to be truly human as we were meant to be. God "chose us in Christ before the foundation of the world to be holy" (Eph. 1:4). "If we are elected to holiness, then we have been extracted from the sphere of human autonomy."[47]

Becoming holy requires that we are "children of obedience" (*tekna hypakoēs*; 1 Pet. 1:14), those who once again hear and recognize the voice of the Father and do what that voice commands. But the capacity to do so, as we have seen, was lost to us. We are enslaved to the dictates of our own ignorance and disordered desires and to the powers of sin and death. Being children of obedience must first mean, then, that we are delivered from that enslavement and joined to Jesus Christ by faith and baptism, for he himself is the original, only, and truly obedient Son, the one who listens to the Father's voice and obeys it: "By the one man's obedience the many will be made righteous" (Rom. 5:19). Because we have been assumed by the power of the Holy Spirit *into* the obedience of the Son, we too are now freed to be obedient children. Being joined to Christ, and together with him, we are once again able to pay careful attention, to hear, and to do the will of the Father, that is, to obey him.

Becoming holy requires further that our "desires" (*epithymiais*) are delivered from their bondage to ignorant disorientations (1 Pet. 1:14). Through Christ we come once again to know the truth of God in his power, glory, wisdom, and

47. Webster, *Holiness*, 80.

holiness. In Christ we see the true image of humanity in all of its dignity and beauty, a humanity "not conformed" (*mē syschēmatizomenoi*) to the desires that we formerly pursued in "ignorance" (*agnoia*), but one whose only desire is to do the will of the Father and to return to the Father with all of those whom the Father has chosen. When we are joined to Christ by faith and baptism, we are freed again to desire the Holy One who called us, and our lives are changed. We see God, ourselves, and all of creation, in truth. Origen writes:

> The soul is driven by a heavenly desire and lust when it has detected the beauty and comeliness of the Word of God, and has been captivated by him, and at his hand has received a certain dart and wound of desire. For this Word is "the image and shining brightness of the invisible God, the Firstborn of all creation, in whom all things are created, both things in heaven and things on earth, whether visible or invisible" (Col. 1:15ff.). If, then, one has the mental capacity to hold together in one's mind and to contemplate the loveliness and grace of all these things that have been created in him, then—struck by the elegant beauty and the magnificent splendor of the things themselves and, as the prophet says, pierced through by "a chosen arrow" (Isa. 49:2)—one will receive from him the wound that is saving and will burn with the blessed fire of the desire of him.[48]

Becoming holy requires being "captivated" by the word and receiving the saving "wound of desire" that comes from the word. In this we are granted a renewal of the mind: the culpable ignorance (*agnoia*) that resulted in disordered desire and unholiness of life is replaced by the holy intelligence (*dianoia*) of a desire reordered to "the elegant beauty and the magnificent splendor" of created things, kindling in us the "blessed fire" of desire for the true image of God in Christ.

Peter's exhortation to hope wholly and become holy in 1:13–16 weaves the threads of intelligence, obedience, and desire into a complex theological anthropology of human being transformed by the grace of Christ and the holiness of God. We are reminded of Paul's exhortation in Rom. 12:1–2: "By the mercies of God . . . present your bodies as a living sacrifice, holy and acceptable to God, which is your reasonable [*logikēn*] worship. Do not be conformed [*mē syschēmatizesthe*] to this world, but be transformed [*metamorphousthe*] by the renewing of your minds, so that you may discern what is the will of God" (NRSV margin).

Exilic Witness: Holy Reverence in Redeemed Time (1 Peter 1:17–21)

The people of God are those who "call upon" (*epikaleisthe*; 1:17) God as their Father, as the Holy Spirit enables them to do so: "When we cry, 'Abba! Father!'

48. Origen, *Commentary on Song of Songs*, quoted in Richard A. Norris, ed./trans., *The Song of Songs: Interpreted by Early Christian and Medieval Commentators*, The Church's Bible (Grand Rapids: Eerdmans, 2003), 5.

it is that very Spirit bearing witness with our spirit that we are children of God" (Rom. 8:15–16). "Our Father in heaven"—while those words bespeak an intimacy with God that comes through our participation in Christ's own sonship, that is not all they bespeak. Peter reminds us that the one we call upon as Father is at the same time "the one who judges each one's work impartially" (1 Pet. 1:17 DH). While the *dignity* of every human being is theologically founded in the royal calling and mandate of the *imago Dei*, the *equality* of every human being is established theologically in the doctrine of God's impartial judgment. As Qohelet says, "The sum of it all: fear God, and keep his commandments, for that is the sum total of humanity. For God will bring every deed into judgment, everything done in secret, whether good or evil" (Eccles. 12:13–14 DH).

Christian theology neither presupposes nor proposes the possession of a stable and identical universal human essence as the basis of human equality and the foundation of universal human rights. Such a modern account of the human is, in any case, increasingly under postmodern suspicion, criticism, and deconstruction, insofar as any supposed universal human essence is always being defined in a particular way, by a particular political, social, and cultural tradition. In a Christian vision, the human is constituted as such only by its *divine* origin, mandate, and end; in the gospel of Jesus Christ the truly human one is revealed. Therefore, without reference to Jesus Christ, the true image, the truth of human nature cannot be discerned. The justice of human "action" (*ergon*; 1:17) is established in and as the "justice" (*dikaiosynē*) of God revealed and enacted in Jesus Christ (Rom. 1:16–17); human justice is our participation in and correspondence to *that* justice, according to which the deeds of every human being will be judged. The single most important contribution that the exilic people of God can and must make to the establishment of justice in the world is to *witness* by its messianic life to *God's* justice and to the coming day when "God[, who] shows no partiality, . . . through Jesus Christ, will judge the secret thoughts of all" (2:11, 16). And this judgment is the *gospel—good news*!

Therefore Peter exhorts us to live by this gospel, that is, to "live in reverent fear [*en phobō . . . anastraphēte*] during the time [*chronon*] of your exile [*paroikias*]" (1 Pet. 1:17), because justice on earth, as well as judgment, begins with the household of God (cf. 4:17). The nearness of God's judgment evokes from the church the reverent acknowledgment (*phobō*) that God is the source and standard of all goodness and justice. The Christian community endures, even embraces, its precarious, vulnerable, and dispossessive messianic existence as a sojourner and exile in an ungodly society, because it is confident that its cause is ultimately secured by God's justice in the cross and resurrection and not by its ability either to secure and control its own place and safety in the wider world or to have its civil rights granted, acknowledged, and protected by the wider world—even though security, safety, and civil recognition may indeed be relative goods for which the church is grateful. When Christians and the church fear God, they do not fear their marginalization, nor even their "death" in the wider society. They are prepared for martyrdom. "Christians have no fantasy that we may get out of life alive."[49] Their purpose is not to be influential and powerful, to change the world, but to be witnesses. There is a stark contrast between Peter's vision of justice for the church and the world and that often represented by, for example, champions of a vision of "Christian America" and the claim of the church to a privileged place in the American empire. While historical and sociological factors seem to give hope that Christianity's privilege in America, and power in the world through that privilege, might continue (though there are reasons to be doubtful too), there is nothing intrinsic in the nature, calling, and mission of the church that warrants the idea of Christian America—and much that warns against it.[50] Most fundamentally, however, it betrays a failure to discern messianic time, as Peter goes on to show.

Holy fear in the "last time" (*ep' eschatou tōn chronōn*; 1:20) fills life with substance and seriousness, with "faith and hope" (1:21) in contrast to the "empty way of life" (*mataias . . . anastrophēs*) handed down from the time of our ancestors or presented to us by the wider society. We must grasp Peter's messianic chronology, which is hardly linear.[51] The time of the church's exile, the present time, is simultaneously the "last time," in which Jesus Christ is revealed. *The revelation of Jesus Christ creates the church's time of messianic exile.* This same Jesus Christ nonetheless is not a latecomer upon the scene; he precedes and contains all times: he is foreknown "before the foundation of the world" (*proegnōsmenou men pro katabolēs kosmou*; 1:20). He is "older" than any ancestor (Green 2007: 37), yet never "ancient." In comparison with him, silver and gold (which, like diamonds, seem to be "forever") are shown in fact to be merely "perishable things" (*phthartois*).

49. Stanley Hauerwas, "Why Did Jesus Have to Die? An Attempt to Cross the Barrier of Age," *Princeton Seminary Bulletin* n.s. 28 (2007): 190.

50. Despite its many gifts to the church catholic, the journal *First Things* often displays in its pages a hope and vision for Christian America. Such a vision is egregiously displayed in Stephen H. Webb's *American Providence: A Nation with a Mission* (New York: Continuum, 2004), in which virtually all of the scriptural attributes of the mission of Israel and the church in the world, and God's particular providence through them, are appropriated to the American nation. To be critical of that vision is not to be, as Webb suggests, "leftist" or "liberal"; it is simply to assert a catholic theological vision of the people of God that accords with the teaching of scripture about the purpose of Israel and the church. Indeed, the leftist, liberal agenda gets its own version and champion of Christian America in the journal *Sojourners* and in Jim Wallis's *God's Politics: A New Vision for Faith and Politics in America* (San Francisco: Harper, 2005). Wallis no less than Webb appropriates the attributes and mission of Israel and the church to the American nation and calls the church to serve it.

51. Here we must resist drawing an arrow of time, beginning with "primordial time" and ending with "resurrection," as, for example, in Green 2007: 36. Likewise Boring 1999: 183–201 engages in an effort to describe "The Narrative World of 1 Peter" by construing a time line from creation to eschaton (185) and concluding that "the orientation of the author [of 1 Peter], and the shape of the projected narrative world delineated by his letter, is horizontal, not vertical. The axis of the story is the moving line of history, not the vertical line to the heavenly world" (199–200). These are not the only two alternatives. Peter's theology of time is more complex, neither horizontal nor vertical, but time interrupted, dissolved, constituted, and fulfilled by God in the death and resurrection of Christ and the church's participation in that.

Christ is able to "ransom" (*elytrōthēte*) his people from mere "empty" time, whether that of "the ancestors" (1:18) or of our own late capitalist society, through his "precious blood," because his messianic suffering and sacrifice revealed in the "last time" bears the weight and power of his own eternity. Therefore the church, through its participation in Christ, is already in exile from *time as mere successive history*, from "one damn thing after another." Already in their worship of Christ, Christians know something of the *fullness* of time, the time of resurrection, which both conquers time as the power of death and gives time for Christian witness. The time of Jesus Christ cannot be represented by an arrow, a progressive movement "in time"; rather, the time of Jesus Christ interrupts the arrow of chronological time and redeems and reconstitutes time in relation to the "last time" that is already upon us in Christ's living presence. In the crucifixion, resurrection, and glorification of Jesus, God creates a rupture in the trajectory from past through present to future; those empty times are pulled into the ransoming power of that apocalyptic rupture and there given their true and enduring substance. The past is, in Christ, not dead and gone. It is retrieved, made alive, transfigured: Moses and Elijah speak with Jesus on the holy mountain. Past, present, and future are spun together, gathered up, ransomed from futility, in the "uncreated light" of God in Christ (→2 Pet. 1:16–18).

Therefore, as Peter makes clear in 1 Pet. 1:21, Christians do not trust in the future; rather, they set their faith and hope on God "who raised [Jesus Christ] from the dead and gave him glory." The church's time now is a time of exile, not because it is running out of time or because it lives beyond time—as if it were lifted out from the real stuff of worldly history—but because, in contrast to the present form of this world that is "passing away" (1 Cor. 7:31), it has all the time it needs, for its time is already being taken up and filled with the glory of eternity through its share in Jesus Christ. *The church's exile in worldly time comes from plenitude rather than lack.* The church's time of exile testifies to its anticipatory share in God's eternal plenitude, experienced in faith and hope. But because the world still enslaves itself to empty time, seeking to fill up time's lack by grasping after fame, wealth, power, or just stuff, the church's witness to the fullness of time takes shape now in its conformity to the sufferings of Christ. The church's time now is the time of its cruciform witness in an often hostile world. For that reason Peter emphasizes that our "faith and hope are set on God." "Faith is our victory against the world (I John 5:4), and what is it that makes it victorious, except that Christ, the Lord of heaven and earth, has us under His guardianship and protection?" (Calvin 1963: 251).

Conceived by the Word (1 Peter 1:22–25)

Peter writes: "Now that you have purified your souls by your obedience to the truth" (1:22). Purity is often thought of in terms of avoiding certain things or abstaining from certain actions that might bring contamination upon a person: "Do not handle, Do not taste, Do not touch" (Col. 2:21). Certainly many of the Jewish purity laws in Lev. 11–15 appear to have that character; it is common in contemporary Western societies, as well as the church, to think of purity in that way and therefore to scorn it as a fearful, prudish, and exclusivist concern of antique cultures. To say, in the contemporary North American context, that Christians might be concerned with purity is to sound strange and archaic, perhaps even offensive and dangerous.

To be sure, at the Council of Jerusalem (Acts 15) the apostles determined that the Jewish ritual purity laws were not to be imposed upon Gentile believers. But the concern for purity does not disappear in the New Testament. It acquires a new content and focus in the gospel: Jesus Christ is the fount of purity. Purity comes from Christ to those who confess him, put their trust in him, and devote themselves to his way with singularity of mind and heart (*katharas kardias*; 1 Pet. 1:22). Indeed, the purity of the Christian community is given in the singularity of its devotion to the truth of Christ: as Peter writes, we "have purified [*hēgnikotes*] [our] souls by [our] obedience to the truth."[52] The truth is the gospel, which is not only the message about Jesus Christ, but also the way of life conformed to the pattern of his life that the gospel evokes from God's people. On this understanding, the idea of purity assumes in the first place a positive content: it is the condition of the people that is gathered around Christ as its "common object of love" (Augustine, *City of God* 19.24). Singular devotion to Christ, as obedience to him and his way, creates purity; indeed, as Calvin writes: "Purity of soul *consists in* our obedience to God" (1963: 251, emphasis added).

Peter here does not present purity as an end in itself, an extrinsic goal toward which the Christian strives; *hēgnikotes* is not the imperative verb in 1:22.[53] Rather, purity—undivided love and obedience toward Jesus Christ—is the condition *in which* the end might be attained, in which believers might "love one another constantly" (*allēlous agapēsate ektenōs*).[54] "Love" is the imperative. That the members of the messianic community love one another with "unhypocritical [*anypokriton*] brotherly love" (DH) is both the result (*eis*) of purity and the imperative that is

52. Achtemeier 1996: 136 notes that *hēgnikotes* is "drawn from the same root as the ἅγιοι the Christians were commanded to become in v. 15."

53. *Hēgnikotes* is a perfect participle: "That the participle is perfect, and thus describes a present state growing out of a prior action, shows the author's assumption that that command has in fact been obeyed. It is the reality created by that obedience that now makes the next step in Christian life possible, namely, the wholehearted love of the other members of the Christian community" (Achtemeier 1996: 136). Luther's exegesis at this point implicitly takes the verb as an imperative. Oecumenius is surely wrong to make purity the goal and brotherly love the means to it: "And since there is a purification or preparation which must come before obedience, Peter wants to bring in as many helpers as possible. This is the role of brotherly love, which makes our neighbors also partakers of the good things which we have found" (*Commentary on 1 Peter*, quoted in Bray 2000: 80).

54. Achtemeier 1996: 137 and Elliott 2000: 387 both emphasize the *constancy* of love in the adverb *ektenōs*, rather than its depth or sincerity.

rendered doable by it.[55] From the perspective of the gospel, the offense and danger of the church's language of purity is not that it is strange and exclusionary, but that it names exclusive loyalty to the crucified one who renders the messianic community a revolutionary power in the world. Purity's dangerous power is the common life (*philadelphia*) of the Christian community in its cruciform "love" (*agapē*), which is always a threat to the powers of this age.

In 1:23 Peter returns to a theme already introduced in 1:3—being begotten anew—and here in its passive participial form, "having been begotten anew" (*anagegennēmenoi*), it speaks again of the prior act of God by which the constancy of love in the messianic community is made concretely possible. God begets us anew; therefore we love our brothers and sisters. Love is only truly love if it endures—indeed, endures eternally! But where shall such love be found among the ruins created by human greed, lust, pride, envy, anger, and violence, those characteristics of personal, social, and political life that are seemingly much more fundamental and enduring than love, even when we look not only at the world, but also at the church? It appears that the evidence is in: all human endeavor, "all flesh," including, it seems, our feeble attempts to love one another, "is like grass and all its glory [*doxa*] like the flower of grass. The grass withers, and the flower falls" (1:24, citing Isa. 40:6–8). "Perishable!"—that is the last word.

Nevertheless . . . we have received a word beyond that last word. We have received a revelation. God is love. God is eternal love in his being as Father, Son (Word), and Holy Spirit, and the source of all love. God is love in his giving himself to us in the life, crucifixion, and resurrection of Jesus Christ. God is love in his choosing and coming to his people in the Holy Spirit. Love in the messianic community is not self-generated—all such love is merely flesh. Rather, the enduring love necessary for this community to *be messianic* is generated of the "imperishable seed" (*sporas . . . aphthartou*) of God's word. That Word is Christ himself—or, as Peter says in 1:25, that "Word" (*rhēma*) is the gospel proclaimed. When we have heard and believed and received the Word of God, he bestows upon us his own eternal life and constancy, since he himself is "the living and enduring word [*logos*] of God" (1:23).[56] That is good news for the *dia-spora* people of God, born of the imperishable *spora*, living vulnerably among the nations:

> While the citation from Isaiah [40:6–8, in 1 Pet. 1:24–25] confirms the imperishable and abiding nature of the word of God, which is the seed by which Christians have been rebegotten . . . , the contrast between what is transitory and what is permanent embodied in the quotation would be highly appropriate for a beleaguered community of Christians facing what gave every appearance of being the permanent,

---

55. Not too much should be made (as often happens) of the distinction between love as *philia* (as in *philadelphia*) and love as *agapē* here. Boring 1999: 86 aptly notes: "The special quality of Christian love is not a matter of Greek vocabulary but of christological content."

56. Peter moves fluidly between the words *logos*, *spora*, and *rhēma*, each referring finally to the eternal Word or "speech" of God who takes our perishable flesh upon himself.

even eternal, power and glory of the Roman Empire. In such a situation, the announcement that the glitter, pomp, and power of the Roman culture was as grass when compared to God's eternal word spoken in Jesus Christ, available through the gospel preached to and accepted by the Christians of Asia Minor, would give them courage to hold fast to the latter while rejecting the former. Even the hostility of that overwhelming power becomes more bearable when its ultimately transitory nature is revealed. (Achtemeier 1996: 142)

Joined to the Word by the Spirit, God's people are delivered from perishability and made imperishable. "The grass withers, and the flower falls, but the word [*rhēma*] of the Lord endures forever" (1:24–25). Having thus been begotten anew by God, we are freed from all fearful and competitive efforts to establish and secure our own existence over against our brothers and sisters; we are freed to love one another with the constancy of God's love. "It is not sufficient for us to be once called by the Lord, unless we live as new creatures. This is the long and short of it" (Calvin 1963: 256). The word given and received in the gospel announced to us "begets" a new people whose life together might itself become, in turn, good news to the world.

1 PETER 2

Nourished by the Word (1 Peter 2:1–3)

A people begotten by the enduring word of God, who live in confidence of their imperishability in that word, may now begin to "put away" the perishable life of the flesh (2:1), that is, all those emotions, attitudes, and habits that would undermine and finally destroy the common life and love of the messianic community: "all malice [*kakia*, 'evil'], and all guile [*dolon*], insincerity [*hypokriseis*; cf. 1:22], envy, and all slander." It is fear that begets these, the fear of our own perishability—the vanity, fragility, and brevity of life itself—that drives us greedily to admire and desire and acquire for ourselves whatever belongs to God and our neighbor. "That's all there is to life; grab what you can!" Fear opens the door of death, and through fear of death we become slaves of our own desires. As Paul makes clear in Rom. 1:18–32, the vices that Peter lists are the destructive fruits of not abiding in the goodness of God revealed in creation and turning instead to seek from creatures what only the creator can give. When we turn creatures into gods we also seek to turn stones into bread, rather than living by *the* bread of life (John 6:25–59) that comes from God.

But, as Peter says, God gives us everything we need! He gives us, from his very own breast as it were, the abundantly flowing "guileless milk of the word [*logikon adolon gala*]" (1 Pet. 2:2 DH).[1] As those newly begotten by God through the

1. The phrase *logikon adolon gala* clearly registers the connection of *gala* ("milk") to the *logos* at the center of this passage. Just as the children of God are born of the word, they are also continually fed by the word. Elliott 2000: 400 also notes the connection between *adolon* ("guileless") here and *dolon* ("guile") in 2:1. Elliott's remarks (405) on Peter's use of language shed light on this text: "In this development of thought [1 Pet. 1:22–2:3] we find not only wordplays ('unhypocritical'— 'hypocrisy,' 'guile'—'guileless,' *logos/logikos*) but also merged metaphors ('word' as 'seed,' as speaking [*rhēma*], as 'good news,' and as 'milk'; 'milk of the word' and 'Lord' as objects of 'hunger'/'tasting'). These metaphors are consistent with imagery employed in early Christian tradition for proclaiming the good news and illustrating the nature of Christian baptism. Such blendings of images and

word, we now, like hungry infants, turn all of our desire toward that "milk of the word" with which our lives are fully nourished until the day of our salvation. We receive this nourishment through the church's preaching and sacraments. We receive it in the *sanctorum communio*, the concrete, gathered life together of the messianic community. We receive it through the practices of corporate and personal scripture reading and study under the rule of faith. We receive it through the testimony of the saints and the writings of the Christian tradition. In each of these ways, and more, *Christ gives himself to us as our food*.

Here we might pause briefly over the word *logikon*, which is often rendered in the translations as "spiritual" (so NRSV and NIV), no doubt intending to indicate the metaphorical rather than literal character of this "milk." But that translation is susceptible to misunderstanding: the milk of which Peter speaks is not only spiritual food for the soul. This milk also abundantly nourishes the *intellect*. The *Logos* of God is *logikos* ("rational"): it feeds thought. Rationality that is both founded and fed by the word of God is rationality in the true sense; it is understanding conformed to the truth of the gospel. As Calvin sees it, guilelessness and rationality belong together: "Thus [Peter] bids them to desire milk free from guile, but drawn from right understanding. We now see for what purpose he joins these two words λογικὸν and ἄδολον. Simplicity and quickness of understanding are two things apparently opposite, but they ought to be mixed together, in case simplicity becomes insipid, and malicious craftiness creeps in in the place of understanding. This well regulated mingling is in line with what Christ says, 'Be wise as serpents, and harmless as doves' (Matt. 10:16)" (1963: 257).

Finally, quoting Ps. 34:8 in 1 Pet. 2:3, "Taste and see that the Lord is good," Peter subtly and imaginatively makes an aural connection between milk or food and Christ himself. Muers writes: "The passage we are considering [1 Pet. 2:2–3] is not explicitly Christological, but the words of verse 3—in their materiality, in the sounds they make—contain an echo; *chrestos ho kurios*, 'the Lord is good,' *Christos ho kurios*, Christ is Lord. This echo in turn serves as a reminder that the addressees of 1 Peter are being asked to relearn their desire in relationship to Jesus Christ. The indispensable condition of their need being met, of their being able to 'grow up into salvation,' is a particular human body."[2] Peter appeals to our spiritual *sense*: the food that is Christ himself is not merely "good for us" because of its "nutritional value." It is also delectable: it *tastes good*! Our desire for this food is moved not only by hunger, but also by delight; not only by need, but also by

traditions are typical of this letter and are found elsewhere in 1:13–21; 2:4–10, 21–25; 3:18–22; and 4:12–19. Both wordplays and metaphors, moreover, serve to integrate these verses into a coherent line of thought."

2. Rachel Muers, "Demand Feeding and the Desire for God: A Brief Play at Exegesis," *Journal of Scriptural Reasoning* 7/1 (Jan. 2008), online at http://etext.lib.virginia.edu/journals/ssr/issues/volume7/number1/ssr07_01_e04.html (accessed 5/27/2008). Boring 1999: 94 notes: "The word for 'good' is *chrēstos*, which, though written differently, sounds exactly like 'Christ' (*christos*) in hellenistic Greek, thus facilitating a serious pun: 'The Lord is Christ/good.'"

attraction; not only from our lack, but also from the savory allure of that which will abundantly fill it—God's goodness. "He has filled the hungry with good things" (Luke 1:53). Having once experienced this gourmet offering, which is truly good beyond imagining, how could we wish to return to the flavorless fast foods offered in the markets, malls, and carnivals of our society? In the kingdom of God the glorious, life-giving banquet is the big attraction (cf. Isa. 25:6; Luke 14:12–24). The aroma and flavor of Christ's sheer goodness invite us: Come and dine!

Cornerstone, Temple, Priesthood, Nation (1 Peter 2:4–12)

Peter next focuses on Christ: "As you come to him" (2:4 NIV), that is, to Christ himself, the seed, the word, the good news, the milk, the Lord, and now the "living stone" (*lithon zōnta*). The church begins here, with Christ, and with those who have indeed come to him as the one who "draw[s] all men to [him]self" (John 12:32 NIV). With the words *eklektois parepidēmois diasporas* ("to the elect, the exiles of the Diaspora") in →1:1b, the apostle gave us a brief sketch of his ecclesiology. In 2:4–10 the ecclesiological sketch is extended onto a larger canvas in which we are able to discern a sharper and deeper picture of the founding, being, and purpose of the church. As Boring notes: "This passage presents one of the most dense constellations of ecclesiological imagery in the New Testament" (1999: 98).

Christ is the "living stone," the foundation on which the church is built. This phrase sets before us a remarkable juxtaposition; we do not readily associate livingness with a stone. But with the phrase "living stone" Peter speaks powerfully of the eternity ("living") and faithfulness ("stone") of Christ. Christ as the living stone is the eternal divine Son of God in his communion with the Father and the Spirit. In the Old Testament the God of Israel is "the Rock" (Deut. 32:4), "the Rock of Israel" (2 Sam. 23:3; Isa. 30:29), "the LORD GOD [in whom] you [Israel] have an everlasting rock" (Isa. 26:4). The psalmist calls out, "O LORD, my rock and my redeemer" (Ps. 19:14; cf. 62:2, 6–7).[3] That the "rock" in these and other Old Testament texts is none other than Yahweh, the God of Israel, and that Peter here identifies Christ as that rock, clearly testifies to the divine identity of Jesus Christ. In this way, then, Peter roots the church in the life of the Son in the Holy Trinity; his livingness is not derived and contingent, but original and eternal, and therefore utterly substantial, utterly sure, and trustworthy—he is the Rock of Ages. So Peter says, "Come to him" (if we take *proserchomenoi* as an imperative—so NRSV) or "as you come to him" (if indicative—so NIV); either

3. A number of theological problems surround the identification of the God of Israel with the Son alone, or the Father alone, or the Trinity. For clarification of those problems and a proposal for their resolution, see Bruce D. Marshall, "Israel: Do Christians Worship the God of Israel," in *Knowing the Triune God: The Work of the Spirit in the Practices of the Church*, ed. James J. Buckley and David S. Yeago (Grand Rapids: Eerdmans, 2001), 231–64.

way the result of our coming to the living stone is that our lives and the life of the church find in him their living origin, power, and end.

Our coming to him, however, is not a self-generated movement, a journey as it were to a monolith that immovably awaits our approach and ascent. In the very next phrase, "rejected by men" (*hypo anthrōpōn men apodedokimasmenon*; 1 Pet. 2:4 NIV), Peter makes it clear that this living stone *has already come to us* and has, in his earthly historical coming and actuality, confronted humanity with the decision to trust him or reject him.

> Then the owner of the vineyard said, "What shall I do? I will send my beloved son; perhaps they will respect him." But when the tenants saw him, they discussed it among themselves and said, "This is the heir; let us kill him so that the inheritance may be ours." So they threw him out of the vineyard and killed him. . . . [Jesus] looked at them and said, "What then does this text mean:
>
> > 'The stone that the builders rejected
> > Has become the cornerstone'?"
>
> Everyone who falls on that stone will be broken to pieces; and it will crush anyone on whom it falls. (Luke 20:13–15, 17–18)

Peter's words "rejected by men" echo these words of Jesus, as well as the prologue of the Gospel of John: "He was in the world, and the world came into being through him; yet the world did not know him. He came to what was his own [*eis ta idia*], and his own did not accept him.[4] But to all who received him, who believed in his name, he gave power to become children of God, who were born, not of blood or of the will of the flesh or of the will of man, but of God" (John 1:10–13). The stone, now revealed to us in its human reality, gives himself to human acceptance or rejection. His human flesh lacks the obvious solidity, durability, and impenetrability of rock. He is ordinary, weak, killable. He is pierced by thorn, nail, and spear. There is nothing statuesque to commend him to us. "He had no form or majesty that we should look at him, nothing in his appearance that we should desire him. He was despised and rejected by [men]; a man of suffering and acquainted with infirmity; and as one from whom [men] hide their faces he was despised, and we held him of no account" (Isa. 53:2–3). Because he gives himself to suffering and death, the living stone, come in the flesh, is not acknowledged by humankind as the utterly trustworthy foundation and orientation of life that he is. To trust this vulnerable one seems to us to be foolishness: by "men" he is not chosen, but rejected.[5]

---

4. This follows NRSV, but leaves out the word "people" (i.e., "his own people"), which does not appear in the Greek text.

5. Boring 1999: 97 rightly notes that at this point Peter is not making a distinction between those who accept Jesus and those who do not, but rather between human rejection of Jesus and God's vindication of him.

But, while "men" reject this stone, God does not. This one is "chosen" (*eklekton*) of God and "esteemed" (*entimon*; 1 Pet. 2:4, 6). "Here is my servant, whom I uphold, my chosen, in whom my soul delights" (Isa. 42:1). "This is my Son, the Beloved, with whom I am well pleased" (Matt. 3:17; 17:5). The weight of human rejection is not at all equal to the divine decision and delight by which the living stone is vindicated and exalted: the crucified one is raised from the dead. He lives! And he bestows his own life on all of those who "come to him"; they too become "living stones" (*lithoi zōntes*; 1 Pet. 2:5) through participating in his own living reality. Their life reflects his. Therefore the church that is constituted in Christ as the "elect exiles of the Diaspora" (1:1) must not be surprised when it also finds itself homeless and vulnerable among the nations and often subject to rejection and persecution. That is its normal way. The church is not above its Lord: "By a perversion of justice he was taken away" (Isa. 53:8). His way of vulnerability, suffering, and exile from the world is the normative pattern for the people of God. But that same pattern also offers a sure hope: "Therefore I will allot him a portion with the great, and he shall divide the spoil with the strong; because he poured out himself to death, and was numbered with the transgressors" (53:12). In Christ the people of God is assured of its own final vindication and exaltation among the nations. "We suffer with him so that we may also be glorified with him" (Rom. 8:17).

Christ in his divine-human unity is both the temple of God (John 2:19–21) and the high priest who offers himself as the acceptable sacrifice to the Father (Heb. 9:11–14). *In union with him*, therefore, the "living stones" are likewise being built up into the "house" or "temple of the Spirit" (*oikos pneumatikos*) in order that they too as a "holy priesthood" (*heirateuma hagion*) may offer "spiritual sacrifices" (*pneumatikas thysias*) acceptable to God (1 Pet. 2:5).[6] The living stones become through grace and participation "in Jesus Christ" (*dia Iēsou Christou*) what the living stone himself is by nature and resurrection from the dead. "For we do not bear Him, but He bears us" (Luther 1967: 57). Here Peter marks both the identification of the church with Christ, and its differentiation from him. The church is the temple of God only because Christ is originally the temple; the church is a priesthood because Christ is the original priest; the church offers acceptable sacrifices because Christ himself is the original sacrifice. Reflecting on the phrase "the body of Christ," but with no less pertinence to Peter's image of the temple, Jenson writes: "Though we rely on the church as on the presence of God, we do so just in that the church within herself directs us to a presence of God that is not

6. Achtemeier 1996: 155 sorts out the difficult grammar of 2:5: "Perhaps the best way to resolve the meaning is to take the verb [*oikodomeisthe*, 'being built up'] as a reverential passive, with God understood as the subject, 'you' as the object, modified by 'living stones,' and 'spiritual house' as object complement, thus deriving the sense: 'God is constituting you, who are like living stones, a spiritual house, to the end [εἰς] that a holy priesthood offer spiritual sacrifices.'" Elliott 2000: 414–18 argues against understanding *oikos* as "temple," taking it instead as "house(hold)," indicating primarily the family or community of God's people.

identical with herself. . . . The church *is* the body of Christ for the world and for her members, in that she is constituted a community by the verbal and 'visible' presence *to* her of that same body of Christ. The body of Christ is at once this sacramental presence within the church's assembly, to make that assembly a community, and is the church-community herself for the world and her members."[7] As Peter makes clear later (2:9, 12), Christ creates and indwells this corporate body as his own temple, priesthood, and sacrifice in order that the nations may *see* in the church, that is, in its lived correspondence to the crucifixion and resurrection of Jesus Christ, the very power, goodness, and glory of God himself (see also Eph. 2:19–22).

The Protestant doctrine of the priesthood of all (individual) believers has traditionally sought warrant in 1 Pet. 2:5. But neither here nor in 2:9 is Peter thinking in terms of individual believers.[8] His focus is consistently corporate and oriented toward the world (Achtemeier 1996: 156; Green 2007: 61). The emphasis is not on the believer's individual immediacy to God, or on priestly mediation among individual believers, or, of course, on the establishment of a priestly order in the church, but on the church itself as the mediation of the gospel to the world (cf. 2:9). The "spiritual sacrifice" that this corporate priesthood and temple offers is its holy, cruciform life as a godly people in the midst of the nations, and for their sake.

In 2:6–8 the apostle reflects further on Christ the stone, now identifying him as the "cornerstone" (*lithon akrogōniaion*) spoken of by the prophet Isaiah (Isa. 28:16) and the psalmist (Ps. 118:22). As the living stone, Christ comes to humankind in the scandal of the crucifixion. As the cornerstone, the crucified one confronts us with the decision about whether we will build our house upon him or seek another. We are confronted with the question of believing or not believing, of standing or

7. Robert W. Jenson, *Systematic Theology*, vol. 2: *The Works of God* (New York: Oxford University Press, 1999), 167–68 (emphasis original).

8. In my own Baptist tradition the doctrine of the priesthood of all believers has often and tragically been taken as the justification of extreme individualism in the Christian life. Consider one classic statement by Baptist theologian Francis Wayland (1796–1865): "Another truth which has always been inscribed on our [Baptist] banner is, the absolute right of private judgement in all matters of Religion. We have always believed that the New Testament was not given by God to a priesthood, to be by them diluted, compounded, and adulterated, and then retailed by the pennyworth to the people; but, on the contrary, that the whole revelation in its totality, in all its abundance of blessing, with all its solemn warnings, and its exceeding great and precious promises, is a communication from God to every individual of the human race. . . . With such a revelation, and such a spiritual aid [i.e., the Holy Spirit guiding the individual reading scripture], every man is required to determine for himself what is the will of God" (quoted from Curtis W. Freeman, James W. McClendon Jr., and C. Rosalee Velloso da Silva, eds., *Baptist Roots: A Reader in the Theology of a Christian People* [Valley Forge, PA: Judson, 1999], 222). In recent years strong protests against and correctives to such radical individualism are being issued by Baptist theologians; see Steven R. Harmon, *Towards Baptist Catholicity: Essays on Tradition and the Baptist Vision* (Waynesboro, GA: Paternoster, 2006); and Barry Harvey, *Can These Bones Live? A Catholic Baptist Engagement with Ecclesiology, Hermeneutics, and Social Theory* (Grand Rapids: Brazos, 2008).

stumbling, of being honored or shamed. Whether Christ is the cornerstone of the church according to God's reckoning is never the question: as we have seen, he is chosen and esteemed of God from eternity, and the church in him. The question is whether *we* will believe and esteem this one—who appears most obviously to be one rejected, shamed, fallen—as the stone upon which we must most surely build our lives, or will we cast him aside? Will the crucified cornerstone set the orientation and alignment of the whole house, that is, will he be "the very head of the corner," or will he be "the stone that the builders rejected" (1 Pet. 2:7), the "scandalous rock" (*petra skandalou*; 2:8) over which we stumble? That question stands at the heart of Peter's whole letter, indeed, at the heart of the gospel itself as it is believed and lived. Everything that we must say about the church in relation to earthly powers (2:13–17) and about Christians in relation to current social orders (2:18–3:7) depends on whether this crucified cornerstone is believed in, built upon, lived by. He is the one *logos* (2:8) of God whom we must hear and obey. Those who refuse to obey that word, that "scandalous rock," are "appointed" (*etethēsan*) to stumble and fall upon it.

By contrast, the people founded on the crucified and risen cornerstone, obedient to his word, is appointed to an incomparable place and purpose in the midst of the nations. That place and purpose is none other than that which God appointed to the people Israel as they stood at the foot of Mount Sinai, ready to hear his word: "And now if you will indeed hear my voice, and keep my covenant, you shall be to me a peculiar people above all nations [*laos periousios apo pantōn tōn ethnōn*]; for the whole earth is mine. And you shall be to me a royal priesthood [*basileion hierateuma*] and a holy nation [*ethnos hagion*]" (Exod. 19:5–6 LXX). Isaiah also writes of Israel as "my chosen race [*genos . . . eklekton*], even my people whom I have preserved [*laon mou hon periepoiēsamēn*] to tell forth my praises" (Isa. 43:20–21 LXX). Explicitly borrowing these phrases, Peter reiterates: "But you are a chosen race [*genos eklekton*], a royal priesthood [*basileion hierateuma*], a holy nation [*ethnos hagion*], God's own people [*laos eis peripoiēsin*]" (1 Pet. 2:9). With these phrases the community of the Messiah is thoroughly inscribed into the being, destiny, and mission of Israel; what is ascribed to Israel is now ascribed also to the people founded on the cornerstone.

"A chosen race [*genos*]," a phrase borrowed from Isa. 43:20, combines two thoughts already explored at length above, namely the election of God's people (→1:1b) and its being a people "born anew" and having common descent in Christ (*anagennaō* in 1:3, 23). This people is neither self-chosen nor self-generating; its being is not fundamentally explicable in terms of elective affinity or biological continuity. Rather, it is the "new thing" (Isa. 43:19) that God himself brings about and treasures. Peter's account of the constitution of the church is thoroughly theological: the church is a "clan" (*genos*) (Green 2007: 61) whose being is rooted solely in God's creative decision and power of new life. It is a "peculiar" (*peripoiēsin*) people because God himself is utterly peculiar; he alone brought this people into being, and it belongs to him alone. This people testifies by its very being to this God.

The phrase "a royal priesthood" is taken directly from Exod. 19:6. Here we see the indivisibility of the kingly and priestly calling of the people of God. There is no separation of religion and rule, no division into spheres of the spiritual and the political. As a *genos* and an *ethnos*, the church, like Israel, takes its place among the nations as a people among peoples, but with its own distinct political raison d'être, authority, calling, and practice. Its political character is decisively and critically embodied in and given to it by its own sovereign, the crucified and risen Jesus Christ. But, just because Christ's political sovereignty is so fundamentally different from the sovereignties of the rulers of this age ("my sovereignty is not of this world; if my sovereignty were of this world my followers would be fighting"; John 18:36 DH), we often think of it as something other than political—an invisible, inner, spiritual sovereignty "of the heart" perhaps, but not visible, material, bodily, political. In which case, we understand the community formed under Christ's sovereignty as a purely spiritual priesthood that deals with the religious issues of life and relates as such to worldly sovereignties as priest to king, faith to politics, church to state. But that is not how Peter thinks, for he tells us that the church is incorporated into the election, calling, and sending of *Israel* as a *basileion hierateuma*, a kingly, royal, *sovereign* priestly people. The priesthood of Israel as a people is itself political, its politics priestly. What might such an Israel-like existence mean for messianic Gentile communities scattered among the provinces of Asia Minor in the first century and the nations of the world in the twenty-first?

We have already in good measure anticipated one answer to that question in the exegesis of *eklektois parepidēmois diasporas* ("to the elect, the exiles of the Diaspora") in →1:1b. The messianic *ekklēsia* is theo-socio-politically Israel-like in living that same kind of exilic, diasporic existence that many Jews entered into during the exile to Babylon and continued among the nations for two and half millennia since. Indeed, even in Exod. 19:3–6 it is not entry into and possession of the land of Canaan that constitutes the people of Israel as a royal priesthood and holy nation. Occupying the promised land is not the sine qua non of that identity and calling. Rather, Israel is a royal priesthood and holy nation under no other terms than that this people will hear the voice of and keep loyal covenant with the sovereign who defeated the enslaving powers of Egypt, rescued his people, "bore [them] on eagles' wings and brought [them] to [him]self" (19:4–5). The terms under which the church is a royal priesthood are no different: it too is such only as it trusts and obeys the sovereign whose "mighty acts" have "called you out of darkness into his marvelous light" (1 Pet. 2:9).

A further and more decisive answer to the question of the character of royal priesthood is found in the being, authority, form, and mission of the king and priest whose people this is. From him alone, but determinatively, come the being, authority, form, and mission of the messianic political community. O'Donovan writes: "Describing the church as a political society means to say that it is brought into being and held in being, not by a special function it has to fulfil, but by a government that it obeys in everything. It is ruled and authorized by the ascended Christ alone and supremely; it therefore has its own authority; and it is not answerable to any other authority that may attempt to subsume it."[9] The royal priesthood of the messianic *ekklēsia* consists in its recapitulating the life of the kingly, priestly Messiah: "Through the Spirit the church recapitulates the whole saving event, Advent, Passion, Restoration and Exaltation. In Christ it is represented in that event; in the Spirit it participates in it. These two aspects of the one relation to the representative act confer the church's political identity upon it. Represented, it is authorized to represent Israel, the people of the Kingdom, possessed of the identity promised to the patriarchs. Participating, it is authorized to be the gathering nations, finding the new world order in the rule of Israel's God."[10] Through Christ, by the Spirit, in the church, Israel and the Gentile nations are now, in an anticipatory apocalyptic gesture, gathered together, reconciled, and raised up as a "new humanity" and, as such, the church *represents, mediates, and proclaims* the final messianic destiny of Israel and the nations to the whole world (Eph. 2:11–22). As Paul writes in Ephesians, the new political reality of the *ekklēsia* is itself the "messianic mystery" (*to mysterion tou Christou*; 3:4), "hidden for ages in God" (3:9), which has now been "apocalypsed" (3:5) to the apostles by the Spirit, "so that through the church the wisdom of God in its rich variety might now be made known to the rulers and authorities in the heavenly places" (3:10). Likewise the book of Revelation declares that through the blood of the slain Lamb a new priestly political reality comes into being: "saints from every tribe and language and people and nation" are "ransomed for God" and "made . . . to be a kingdom [*basileian*] and priests [*hiereis*] serving our God, and they will reign [*basileusousin*] on the earth" (5:9–10). This royal priesthood gathers around the throne of God and the Lamb and leads the whole angelic host and all of creation in praise of the Lamb of God. Royal priesthood is the politics of doxology, that is, the people of God making history and discerning its "progress" through the crucified, risen, and exalted Christ whom it worships.[11]

The last phrase from Rev. 5:10 ("and they will reign on the earth") leads to a final reflection on the character of "royal [*basileion*] priesthood." How does this priesthood *enact* its royalty, its "sovereignty" (*basileuō*), among the nations? To sum up simply, it reigns in the world when it worships the slaughtered Lamb in praise and in works. As we have already noted, the distinctive mode of sovereignty of the messianic *ekklēsia* is decisively and critically embodied in and given to it by its own royal sovereign, the crucified Messiah. Its sovereignty is a participation in and reflection of his. Therefore, the church enacts and makes visible its "lordly"

9. Oliver O'Donovan, *The Desire of the Nations: Rediscovering the Roots of Political Theology* (Cambridge: Cambridge University Press, 1996), 159.

10. Ibid., 161.

11. John Howard Yoder, *The Royal Priesthood: Essays Ecclesiological and Ecumenical*, ed. Michael Cartwright (Grand Rapids: Eerdmans, 1994), 127–40.

freedom in the patience, suffering, and "witness" (*martyrion*) it shows in the face of enmity and oppression.[12] Martyrdom is the church's crucial material witness to the Messiah's own political rule; martyrdom is the bodily, visible sacrament of the church's participation in Christ's sovereignty among the nations, for the nations—the manner in which it is a "royal priesthood."[13]

Peter goes on to describe the church as "a holy nation" (→1:1b; →1:13–16). Here we pause over the word "nation" (*ethnos*). If any word stands against the thoroughly individualistic understandings of Christian faith that are now prevalent, this one does. It signifies a singular, corporate, cultural, social, political entity—an entity corresponding to the people Israel in the Old Testament. According to Peter, that entity is what we are, and what we are called to be. He issues no general call to become a Christian and then, as a subsequent and perhaps optional move, for individual Christians to join together into a voluntary association that might serve and promote our projects of being individual Christians. Quite the contrary! In biblical logic the sovereign (YHWH, Jesus Christ) precedes the people and elects and creates the people; the people precedes the person; the person is constituted as such *by* the sovereign *through* incorporating the person into the people. That logic is no less true of the New Testament than of the Old. The mystery of the ages apocalyptically revealed in Jesus Christ the king is not the salvation of individual Jews and Gentiles. It is the reconciliation of Israel and the nations in Jesus Christ (cf. Rom. 15:7–13), the creation of a new humanity the reality of which is anticipated in the new theo-socio-political entity, the church (cf. Eph. 2:11–3:12). As James says in Acts 15:14, "God [has] looked favorably on the nations [*ethnōn*], to take from among them a people [*laon*, singular] for his name" (DH). Our (individual) share in the coming new creation is given to us in no other way than

---

12. At this point we might ponder again, but this time critically, some further words of O'Donovan: "In the second place, however, we assert that the political character of the church, its essential nature as a governed society, is hidden, to be discerned by faith as the ascended Christ who governs it is to be discerned by faith. Experienced from within, the church is a community of obedience and freedom, a society under the law of Christ, heedful of his commands and direction and enjoying the freedom from all other lordships that he has won for it. Looked at from the outside, it presents the appearance of a functional religious organism rather than a political one, having no visible source of government and right save that which is from time to time borrowed or imposed by other rulers" (*Desire of the Nations*, 166). Here O'Donovan fails to note that in the Gospels and Epistles the crucifixion is itself the revelation (visibility) of Christ's government and that the place to *look for* the corresponding true government in and of the church is among those who wash feet, give themselves for the building up of the body, and suffer at the hands of enemies. Given that our mode of perception is so often simply identical with that of the forms of government that "crucified the Lord of glory" (1 Cor. 2:8), it is no wonder that we conclude that "the political character of the church, its essential nature as a governed society, is hidden." But as Paul makes clear in 1 Cor. 1–2, our very *perception* must be changed by the cross, in order that the cruciform political character of the church might not be hidden from us.

13. See Tripp York, *The Purple Crown: The Politics of Martyrdom* (Scottdale, PA: Herald, 2007); and Craig Hovey, *To Share in the Body: A Theology of Martyrdom for Today's Church* (Grand Rapids: Brazos, 2008).

through sharing in the reality and life of this "people" (*laos*), this "nation" (*ethnos*). Further, no such nation is created and sustained apart from a common founding, a common constitution, a common governance, a common history, a common *telos*—all of which shape and guide the life of the nation through shared stories, symbols, anthems, liturgies, leaders, beliefs, and practices. What makes this nation holy is, in the first place, that it has its common origin, history, and end in the life of its holy sovereign, the triune God—it is "God's own people" (1 Pet. 2:9). Second, its stories, symbols, liturgies, practices, and so on conform to the way, truth, and life of Jesus Christ the king as given in the testimony of the apostles and prophets. In both of these ways it will itself be marked as other, holy, in the midst of the nations.

God's people exists, Peter sums up, through the "mighty acts" (*aretas*; 2:9) of God, acts that correspond to the creation of the world from nothing. In the beginning God spoke, and the light shone in the darkness. Likewise, God's people have been "called... out of darkness into his marvelous light" (2:9). In the beginning God said, "Let there be," and there was. Once there was not a people, now there is; once they were not recipients of God's mercy, now they are (2:10). "We now learn the result of God's call from darkness to light: it is the creation of a people that before did not exist" (Achtemeier 1996: 167). God's people is God's creation, pure and simple. It can never try or claim to be the product of *autopoiēsis* ("self-making"). It is a people of *peripoiēsis* (2:9), having been made and claimed by another: it lives eternally only as the creature of God's mercy.

Peter reiterates at this point the fact with which he began his letter: that the people of God is a body of "aliens and exiles" (*paroikous kai parepidēmous*; 2:11) among the nations. In St. Augustine's terms, it is the "city of God" dwelling amid the "earthly city." As a creature of God's mercy, the church is not a natural and normal political entity, having its origin in the will-to-power of human rulers and the survival motive of human collectives. Those are "the desires of the flesh" (*tōn sarkikōn epithymiōn*) that normally create and sustain—and often destroy— persons, communities, and the nations of the earth. We know them well, even from firsthand experience (4:2–3). It is those same desires that "wage war" against the "soul" (*psychē*, singular) of the people of God (2:11) founded as the creature of God's mercy. And so Peter urges his "beloved" to "abstain" from such desires of the flesh. Being a people that lives "by the mercies of God" (Rom. 12:1) and not by the will to power and survival, this holy nation can only continually look to God's mercy to sustain it. And while the desires of the flesh wage war even against this holy nation, its own warfare is only ever against those temptations and dark powers that attack and destroy its confidence in God's people-making mercy in Jesus Christ. It can never wage war against flesh and blood itself, that is, against other humans and nations (Eph. 6:12). In the midst of nations created and sustained by ungodly desires, powers, and violence, the people of God's own merciful making can appear only as a body of "aliens and exiles"—those who do not fit the normal order of things; those who are therefore themselves "malign[ed]

. . . as evildoers [*kakopoiōn*]" (1 Pet. 2:12) among the nations, ruled "out of order," and banished.

The people of God are called to abstain from the desires of the flesh that found the politics of violence. They are also called to resist *their own* temptation to vengeance when they are mistreated, scorned, and persecuted. Despite their being wrongly maligned as evildoers, they are nonetheless called not to mount a revolt in kind against the enemy, not to repay evil for evil, but rather to enact a wholly other politics, the politics of the good (a "good way of life" [*anastrophēn . . . kalēn*] and "good works" [*kalōn ergōn*]; 2:13) rooted in and generated by the merciful goodness and power of God. This is how they "make history." Corresponding to and sharing in God's mercy, the people of God enacts the messianic politics of mercy that it has learned from its Lord and Savior Jesus Christ. That is how it overcomes evil. This is the politics that, from the perspective of "the Gentiles," looks like it is not one (cf. Matt. 20:24–28). As Barth writes on Rom. 12:21: "*Overcome evil with good*. What can this mean but the end of the triumph of men, whether their triumph is celebrated in the existing order or by revolution? And how can this end be represented, if it be not by some strange 'not-doing' precisely at the point where men feel themselves most powerfully called to action?"[14] That "strange 'not-doing'" takes the shape of service, mercy, and forgiveness, which is the true form of personal, social, and political justice revealed in Jesus the Messiah and is therefore also the messianic political revolution to be enacted by the church. That is the church's "belligerent" response to the destructive desires of the flesh. That is how the sovereignty, justice, and goodness of God become *visible* among the nations, for the sake of the nations. That is how the nations themselves might catch a glimpse of God's advent and in the day of his coming enter with the church into the politics of the doxology of the Lamb: as Peter says, "Live the way of goodness among the nations, so that . . . they may see your good deeds and glorify [*doxasōsin*] God when he comes in the day of visitation"; 2:12 DH).

Messianic Revolution (1 Peter 2:13–17)

Having called us to "the way of goodness," Peter now goes on to specify what this way, the messianic revolution, looks like in the concreteness of daily political and social life amid the orders of this world that are "passing away" (1 Cor. 7:31). The first, determinative, and abiding word for this revolution is this: "be subordinate" (*hypotagēte*: "submit" in King James Version, "submit yourselves" in NIV; forms of *hypotassō* are found in 1 Pet. 2:13, 18; 3:1, 5, 22; 5:5).[15] We now know immediately

14. Karl Barth, *The Epistle to the Romans*, trans. Edwyn C. Hoskyns (Oxford: Oxford University Press, 1933), 481.

15. The NRSV rendering, "accept the authority of," here and elsewhere reads a note of acquiescence into the word *hypotagēte*. Achtemeier 1996: 182 suggests that the "meaning is closer to 'subordinate' than to 'submit' or 'obey,' and advocates finding one's proper place and acting

that this messianic revolution is a strange one indeed, one that both creates and befits a people that is itself alien and exiled in its native cities and provinces. "Be subordinate"—this is the shocking, invasive, liberating word of the gospel, creating another history amid the oppressive structures and powers of society, whether in Peter's time or ours. This is the revolution that looks like it is not one. Barth writes on Rom. 13:1:

> **Let every man be in subjection** [*hypotassesthō*] **to the existing ruling powers.** Though subjection may assume from time to time many various concrete forms, as an ethical conception it is here purely negative. It means to withdraw and make way; it means to have no resentment [cf. Nietzsche], and not to overthrow [cf. Marx and Lenin]. . . . Even the most radical revolution can do no more than set what *exists* against what *exists.* Even the most radical revolution—and this is so even when it is called a "spiritual" or "peaceful" revolution—can be no more than a revolt; that is to say, it is in itself simply a justification and confirmation of what already exists. . . .
>
> It is evident that there can be no more devastating undermining of the existing order than the recognition of it which is here recommended, a recognition rid of all illusion and devoid of all the joy of triumph. . . . No-revolution is the best preparation for the true Revolution, but even no-revolution is no safe recipe. To *be in subjection* is, when it is rightly understood, an action void of purpose, an action, that is to say, which can spring only from obedience to God. Its meaning is that men have encountered God, and are thereby compelled to leave the judgement to Him. The actual occurrence of this judgement cannot be identified with the purpose or with the secret reckoning of the man of this world.[16]

The "true revolution" begins in "an action void of purpose." Our subordination, as participation in Christ, is to "every human creature" (*pasē anthrōpinē ktisei*; 1 Pet. 2:13).[17] Such subordination is its own end, an end given over to the redeeming

---

accordingly, rather than calling upon one to give unquestioning obedience to whatever anyone, including governing authorities, may command." While that improves on "accept the authority of," the notion of "finding one's proper place" loses the dynamism of subordination, which, if it is to "every human creature," is an action that is never completed. Both Achtemeier 1996: 179 and Elliott 2000: 484 render the first clause of 2:13 as "be subordinate to every human creature because of the Lord." How can such a radical downward movement be a finished action? I follow their translation here, but "finding one's place in" or "obeying" existing social and political institutions is not what is being called for. And we certainly cannot follow Achtemeier when he slips into the language of "loyalty" to civil powers (1996: 180, twice) and "political loyalty" (185). Peter calls for no such thing and makes no argument that Christians owe their loyalty (*pistis*) to any other than Jesus Christ.

16. Barth, *Epistle to the Romans*, 481–84 (emphasis original).

17. As already indicated in a previous note, I render this phrase, following Achtemeier and Elliott, as "every human creature." The temptation to think in terms of "human institution" (NRSV; Jobes 2005: 174) or "created structures" (Senior 2003: 68) should be avoided. With this phrase Peter is precisely seeking to think of even highly exalted persons in terms of their human creatureliness, rather than thinking of hypostasized social and political institutions. Subordination and honor are

power of God. The one who is Lord of all became the servant of all not for the sake of an end other than that. He did not take "the form of a slave" *so that* he might accomplish *another* revolutionary end (say, the abolition of slavery) or *so that* he might be exalted. Becoming a slave *is* the Messiah's revolution. It *is* his revelation of the goal of history: "*Therefore* [that is, because he took the form of a slave and was crucified] God also highly exalted him" (Phil. 2:6–11). Therefore too we bow our knee to him, confess him, obey him, imitate him. *Serving "every human creature" is the messianic revolution to which we are called.* It is our sharing in God's life. It is the gospel's liberating power in history. "Owe no one anything, except to love one another; for the one who loves another has fulfilled the law" (Rom. 13:8). There is no other or higher revolutionary purpose than that. As Peter says, we "subordinate" ourselves "because of the Lord" (*dia ton kyrion*; 1 Pet. 2:13); it is the authority, example, command, and grace of Jesus Christ that calls us to this self-subordination to others.

Some human creatures (the *basileus*, "emperor") claim the "superauthority" (*hyperechonti*) for whatever reason (Peter does not say: he does not attribute their authority to God's ordination or commission) to rule empires; while others (the *hēgemosi*, "governors") under the command of the emperor punish those who do evil and praise those who do good (2:14). No matter! Peter offers no argument for or validation of the proper authority or legitimate role of emperors and governors, presidents and prime ministers. They are there, and they do what they do. On occasion God sovereignly uses them as *servants* to accomplish his purpose (Rom. 13:1–7), though their service as such is indeed a matter of God's free sovereign action and not a mandate inherent in their rule and authority, as if their very being and action were the outworking of God's sovereignty. For insofar as such rulers ignore, despise, or persecute God's people, they are shown up by the gospel to be "foolish" (*aphronōn*) and "ignorant" (*agnōsias*) of the real political authority that is being enacted among them in the messianic revolution. For what the "authorities" seem to be authorized to do (i.e., to punish and praise) is finally a matter of indifference to messianic revolutionaries, who are always authorized, "free" (*eleutheroi*), "as God's slaves" (*hōs theou douloi*; 1 Pet. 2:16), to do the will of God, to do the good, to be the servants of all: "All their works are performed without compulsion and for nothing" (Luther 1967: 77). The good is this: "Honor everyone. Love the family of believers. Fear God. Honor the emperor" (2:17). Without ignoring that the rulers are there doing what they do as rulers (even with respect to the people of God, whether for good or ill), Peter calls us to a way of life and a political practice that operate completely beneath and simultaneously completely beyond their rule. It is our godly freedom and calling in the Messiah ("because of the Lord") to give rulers the honor that they are due *as human creatures along with everyone else,* thereby rendering them both less and more than they are

---

owed to persons, whatever their station, not to institutions as such. That in itself, of course, does not make Peter anti-institutional.

according to their own or others' vaunted estimation of their superiority.[18] In this way even the rulers are brought into the sphere of redemption.

It is true that the church itself is always in some sense both a society and a political institution in the ordinary worldly sense: any actual local congregation or global ecclesial communion is empirical proof of that in the most obvious way. It is an entity that *exists* among other such entities, sometimes jostling for position and rights in the same sociopolitical space. If in no other way than in the physical bodies of its members (not to mention its leaders, buildings, and economies), the church occupies a place in the world. It might thus also become (as it often has become) a conservative or progressive or reactionary or revolutionary institution in the ordinary sense, making a contribution (whether for good or ill) to the social and political course of history. We cannot deny that God may also sovereignly work his purposes in the world through the church in those ways, insofar as the church sometimes makes itself more or less at one with the world that God also loves and continues patiently to preserve and bless, even in its rebellion against him. Moreover, God continues to preserve, judge, bless, and use the church (like Israel) as his "chosen" (*eklektos*) body in history, even if at times the church (like Israel), in its social and political formation and practice, seems almost indistinguishable from the enslaved world.

But the true revolutionary power of the church does not consist in its ability to be an effective power in the world, to bring about changes in history, whether in collusion with or in opposition to the existing powers. Its revolutionary sociopolitical power lies rather in its union with, imitation of, and testimony to the crucified sovereign (*dia ton kyrion*; 2:13) who has already invaded the world and wrought the decisive revolution (see 2:21–25; 3:21–22), the reconciliation of the world. Bonhoeffer writes:

> It is intrinsic to God's revelation in Jesus Christ that it occupied space in the world. It would, however, be fundamentally wrong simply to explain this space empirically. When God in Jesus Christ claims space in the world—even space in a stable because "there was no other place in the inn"—God embraces the whole reality of the world in this narrow space and reveals its ultimate foundation. So also the church of Jesus Christ is the place [*Ort*]—that is, the space [*Raum*]—in the world where the reign of Jesus Christ over the whole world is to be demonstrated and proclaimed. This space of the church does not, therefore, exist just for itself, but its existence is already always something that reaches far beyond it. . . . The space of the church is not there in order to fight with the world for a piece of its territory, but precisely to testify to the world that it is still the world, namely, the world that is loved and reconciled by God. It is not true that the church intends to or must spread its space out over the space of the world. It desires no more

---

18. "The motivation 'for the Lord's sake' removes from the βασιλεύς, the 'king,' the sacral and ideological splendor with which both the continuation of the ancient oriental cult of the ruler and political philosophy and poetry had surrounded him"; Leonhard Goppelt, *A Commentary on 1 Peter*, ed. Ferdinand Hahn, trans. John E. Alsup (Grand Rapids: Eerdmans, 1993), 184–85.

space than it needs to serve the world with its witness to Jesus Christ and to the world's reconciliation to God through Jesus Christ. . . . When one therefore wants to speak of the space of the church, one must be aware that this space has already been *broken through, abolished and overcome* in every moment by the witness of the church to Jesus Christ.[19]

Messianic revolutionary power does not perpetuate, oppose, or destroy what *exists*: as Barth writes, God's revolution does not "set what *exists* against what *exists*."[20] Rather, messianic revolutionary power *seeks only the good of what exists* and does so by *doing the good* as revealed and defined by its Lord, that is, by subordinating itself, giving itself, in the bodies of its members, even to suffering and death, *for the sake of what exists*.[21] That is its witness to Jesus Christ. Paul writes, "Bless those who persecute you; bless and do not curse them. . . . Do not repay anyone evil for evil, but consider what is good [*kala*—not 'noble' as in NRSV] before all. If it is possible, as far as it depends on you, live in peace with all. . . . Do not be conquered by evil, but conquer evil with good. Let every person be subordinate to the governing authorities" (Rom. 12:14–13:1 DH). In their texts Peter and Paul do not give us a theory of the providential purpose of secular government or civil order, or of the Christian's responsibility in or for the political order, or of the proper spheres and roles of "church and state."[22] Nor do they provide any mandate whatsoever for Christians or the church to get involved, join the cause of, or become the emperor and his governors; or to aid in defending their sovereignty, policies, or territories against enemies; or to go to war on their behalf—all of which stand in stark contradiction of the gospel of messianic life. Rather, Paul and Peter issue a call to a *messianic, apocalyptic, cruciform* engagement in history, against history, for the sake of history—a call to history making that takes the form

19. Dietrich Bonhoeffer, *Ethics*, trans. Reinhard Krauss, Charles C. West, and Douglas W. Scott, Dietrich Bonhoeffer Works 6 (Minneapolis: Fortress, 2005), 63–64 (emphasis added).

20. Barth, *Epistle to the Romans*, 482 (emphasis original). Here we must note that Dietrich Bonhoeffer, by his participation in the plot to assassinate Hitler, did indeed set what exists against what exists, and thus compromised the truly revolutionary power of his witness.

21. This assumes an Augustinian account of the good as that which *is*, through God's creation, and evil as *privatio boni*, the absence of the good.

22. As Luther, Calvin, and many other commentators suppose. That God may providentially use the ruling powers is a point (perhaps) made by Paul in Rom. 13, and it is not in dispute here. But neither Paul nor Peter is concerned to give us a theology of providence in these texts, as if the long haul of the church in history, and as a player in that same history, is in view. Rather, they are concerned to be clear about the calling of the messianic/apocalyptic people of God, as those who "know what time it is . . . ; the night is far gone, the day is near" (Rom. 13:11–12); as those who know that Christ has already made all powers subject to himself, and that "the end of all things is near" (1 Pet. 3:22; 4:7). Since the truth of the *imminent* arrival of the day has not changed from their time to ours, we no more need a theory of providence for the long haul, vis-à-vis secular government, civil order, and church and state, than did the first readers of these texts, in order to live as the messianic people of God.

of "revolutionary subordination."[23] The chosen Diaspora people of God (1 Pet. 1:1), otherwise known as "aliens and exiles" (2:12), are enlisted in the peaceable and hopeful practice of liberally scattering the seemingly insignificant seeds of the kingdom of God among the nations and letting God himself bring about the growth. Peoples, cities, provinces, and nations may thus be redeemed, not by the manifest or hidden social, political, and economic powers (whether in the church, the state, or the market) inherent in what already exists, but by the revolutionary power of God who, out of his own eternal plenitude apocalypsed in Jesus Christ, raises the dead to life and brings into being that which is not.

Social Revolution (1 Peter 2:18–21)

The strange words "servants [oiketai], subordinate yourselves [hypotassomenoi], in the fear of God [en panti phobō], to the masters" (2:18 DH)[24] run completely against the grain of our normal emancipatory impulses and our modern discourse of human rights and call upon believing servants or slaves to take up their own form of messianic revolution in the social order. Slaves become "a paradigm for the way Christians . . . are to live in the midst of hostile surroundings" (Achtemeier 1996: 194). They are not called to wait passively to be emancipated, whether by their masters or by some external power; nor are they called to attain it themselves through revolt against their oppressors. Rather, *they are already free.* Their freedom is given to them immediately and directly in the gospel word "be subordinate." With the utterance of this word *to the servants themselves as moral agents,*[25] and their obedience to it, they are already made active participants in Jesus Christ and the sociopolitical revolution inaugurated in his own self-subordination and crucifixion. They are now fully free in Christ (2:16) to "do the good" (*agathopoiountes;* 2:20) that Christ himself did and perhaps also, with him and by his grace, to suffer unjustly.

The suffering of slaves is an evil. It is injustice. Neither Peter nor the entire New Testament offers any implicit or explicit justification of the system of masters and slaves, nor any other system of dominance, oppression, or cruelty. Whatever such system may be in place in the wider society, there is in any case never any gospel warrant for such a system being repeated and maintained within the Christian

23. The phrase "revolutionary subordination" is the title of chap. 9 in John Howard Yoder's *The Politics of Jesus: Vicit Agnus Noster,* 2nd ed. (Grand Rapids: Eerdmans, 1994). Chapters 8–10 of that book are decisive for what I have written on 1 Pet. 2:11–3:7.

24. Achtemeier 1996: 194–95 makes the compelling case that *en panti phobō* ("in all fear") refers to fear of God rather than fear of masters.

25. "Here we have a faith that assigns *personal moral responsibility to those who had no legal or moral status* in their culture, and makes of them decision makers. It gives them responsibility for viewing their status in society not as a simple meaningless decree of fate but as their own meaningful witness and ministry, as an issue about which they can make a moral choice" (Yoder, *Politics of Jesus,* 172 [emphasis original]; see also Green 2007: 80).

community, even where the social titles (master, slave) might still be used. Whatever their status in the wider society (and that too is under the judgment of the gospel), *every person* within the messianic social order of the body of Christ is called to conform to and participate in the pattern of Christ's self-offering love as set forth in the gospels, in Phil. 2:5–11, in 1 Pet. 2:21–24, and in many other New Testament texts. That pattern quite simply rules out any form of dominance, oppression, cruelty, or violence. A so-called Christian master who treats a slave (or a husband who treats his wife) in such a manner is simply *unchristian* in the most direct and explicit sense and should be brought under the gospel discipline of the ecclesial community.

Nevertheless, evil and unjust social orders do exist beyond—and even frequently within—the ecclesial community. Peter does not call for a violent revolution against them or for their forceful overthrow. He does not "set what *exists* against what *exists*."[26] All existing social orders, even those regimes established on the constructs of emancipation and human rights, are always only systems of relative justice and injustice. More important, none of them, not even egalitarian liberal democracies, represent the arrival of the new creation.[27] "Be subordinate" is not a call to fit resentfully or happily into a given system, whether hierarchical or egalitarian, nor a call to struggle for a higher place within it. Rather, messianic revolutionaries already live and act as free persons with respect to all existing systems.[28] "Were you a slave when called? Do not be concerned about it. Even if you can gain your freedom, make use of your present condition now more than ever. For whoever was called in the Lord as a slave is a freed person belonging to the Lord, just as whoever was free when called is a slave of Christ. You were bought

26. Barth, *Epistle to the Romans*, 482 (emphasis original).

27. Societies structured according to equality and human rights are certainly in many respects more just than the hierarchical and patriarchal societies of past ages, and are often the products of Christian influence. But they do not finally reflect the true gospel order of the messianic community. For the messianic gospel always creates anew a fundamental *inequality* among humans: I am *always* to regard the other person (of whatever rank) more highly than I regard myself. Therefore the gospel is only truly heard by, for example, kings, rulers, masters, and patriarchs when they, believing, receiving, and following Christ, honor their subjects as more worthy of life, honor, and good than they are—that is, when they themselves hear the word of the gospel—"be subordinate"—and no longer lord it over others as the pagans do. Then and only then are they also free from their bondage to the "desires of the flesh," that is, to seeking their being and identity in the role they occupy, with its attendant power over others, and influence over history. While they might remain in some hollowed-out sense kings, rulers, masters, and patriarchs, they will no longer act like them. For such roles can only now be put to cruciform messianic use. See Giorgio Agamben's illuminating reflections in *The Time That Remains: A Commentary on the Letter to the Romans*, trans. Patricia Dailey (Stanford, CA: Stanford University Press, 2005), 19–43.

28. Here I am certainly echoing Luther's core thesis in *The Freedom of a Christian*: "A Christian is a perfectly free lord of all, subject to none. A Christian is a perfectly dutiful servant of all, subject to all"; Martin Luther, *Three Treatises*, trans. C. M. Jacobs et al. (Philadelphia: Fortress, 1960), 277. However, Luther's doctrines of vocation, station, and the two kingdoms all give a legitimacy to existing social and political orders not found in scripture.

with a price; do not become slaves of human masters. In whatever condition you were called, brothers and sisters, there remain with God" (1 Cor. 7:21–24). "Be subordinate"—serve, love, give oneself, suffer for the other—is the only truly revolutionary political calling and practice because it is itself the worship and obedience of the one Lord and one God (*dia syneidēsin theou* ["being mindful of God"]; 1 Pet. 2:19) and it seeks no other end than sharing in and showing forth God's abundant "grace" (*charis*; 2:20), even toward an oppressive master. As such, it creates a disturbance and a rupture in the system that is far more fundamental than can be humanly imagined. The seeds of the reign of God in history are sown in self-subordinating, self-offering service. Who can predict what the outcome will be?

Peter is not unrealistic about masters, thinking that they will always treat their servants justly. Masters may in fact be oppressive, abusive, cruel, and unjust even to those servants who do good. Their reward is not impunity; their injustice will not go unnoticed by "the one who judges justly" (2:23). Servants can certainly put their trust in that judge. Further, those servants who have taken up the messianic way of doing good, and nevertheless suffer unjustly, are given a very particular "grace" (*charis*; 2:19–20), the grace of following in the steps and participating in the pattern of Christ's suffering—the grace of a messianic revolution in the social order. "If you endure when doing good, and suffer for it, this is grace with God. You were called to this, for Christ also suffered for you" (2:20–21 DH). Goppelt writes: "To bear suffering without wavering is . . . 'grace before God.' Why? . . . Whoever bears unjust affliction from people in the way that Christ did, according to vv. 21ff., participates in his path (4:3), in the path leading to salvation (3:17–22). That is to say, such a person is surrounded and borne along by grace, by God's bestowal of himself, which accepts that person in love (5:12). Grace summoned this person to such conduct (v. 21; cf. Phil. 1:7, 29), and grace brings him or her to its goal (5:10). Even while that person is afflicted by fellow human beings, God is not against but for him or her (3:14; cf. Rom. 8:37–39)."[29] By the grace of being subordinate, and of sharing in the reconciling suffering of Christ, slaves themselves participate in bringing about the new creation in the social order. The whole world is changed (cf. 2 Cor. 5:16–17).

The Original Revolutionary (1 Peter 2:21–25)

In the middle of his instructions to messianic revolutionaries Peter pauses to set before us the "pattern" (*hypogrammon*) and grace of the original revolutionary, Jesus Christ (2:21). *Only as a sharing in the fullness of his life, death, and resurrection is the word "be subordinate" good news* and not another brick in the edifice of the status quo. The Messiah is the one who makes the complete and fundamental

29. Goppelt, *Commentary on 1 Peter*, 199.

break with the sins, lies, threats, abuses, and violence of existing political, social, and familial systems. Rather than repeating them, he bears them and their effects "for us" (*hyper hymōn*; 2:21) and entrusts himself wholly to the judge who renders perfect justice. Christ's death on the cross is both exemplary and vicarious.

Drawing on the portrait of the Suffering Servant in Isa. 53, Peter joins the apostolic testimony to the sinlessness of Jesus (cf. 2 Cor. 5:21; Heb. 4:15; 7:26; 1 John 3:5): "He committed no sin, and no deceit was found in his mouth" (1 Pet. 2:22, quoting Isa. 53:9). Surely this is a testimony to the active moral perfection of Jesus, his total life-act of righteousness and obedience to the Father (cf. Rom. 5:18–19). But the context of 1 Peter leads us to reflect particularly on the sociopolitical aspects of his sinlessness, to which the gospel narratives also bear abundant witness. Jesus engages in a conflict with the totality of temptation and sin, and central to the gospel accounts is the temptation to take up a certain kind of messiahship, patterned in part, it seems, on the achievement of the Maccabean revolt (164 BC)—defeating Israel's enemies, reclaiming the land of Israel from the Roman occupiers, ascending the royal seat in Jerusalem as a descendant of David, and bringing social welfare to the people. In doing so he would have realized the political, social, and economic hopes of a great portion of the Judean population. Those hopes, which he himself surely also harbored as the Messiah for the sake of his people, provided the substance for the devil's temptations in the desert (Matt. 4:1–11; Luke 4:1–13).[30] Peter himself continued to harbor such hopes and gave voice again to them when, at Caesarea Philippi, he confessed that Jesus is the Messiah, but rejected Jesus's prophecy of his own messianic suffering and death.

But Jesus turned decisively away from the temptations of both the devil and Peter ("Get behind me, Satan!" he says to Peter; Matt. 16:23). He did so not because they were expressing sociopolitical hopes in contrast to, say, spiritual ones, but because the normal means (guerrilla warfare, armed revolt, overthrow, territorial control) to those legitimate sociopolitical ends would have required the humiliation, suffering, and death of others (including the Roman masters of the Jewish people). Rather than taking that route—and what reasonable and reasonably powerful political leader would not have seriously considered it? the temptations were real for Jesus—this revolutionary Messiah chose instead to entrust himself wholly to God, to subordinate himself to the unjust governments of Jerusalem and Rome, and, refusing their means, to take upon himself their sins, that is, their socially and politically authorized violence, and the humiliation, suffering, and death that it inflicted upon him. He took up "that strategy of obedience which is no strategy. . . . What Jesus renounced is not first of all violence, but rather *the compulsiveness of purpose* that leads the strong to violate the dignity of others. The point is not that one can attain all of one's legitimate ends without using violent means. It is rather that our readiness to renounce our legitimate ends whenever they cannot be attained by legitimate means itself constitutes our

30. See the reading of the temptations of Jesus in Yoder, *Politics of Jesus*, 24–27.

participation in the triumphant suffering of the Lamb."[31] That is the form of the Messiah's sociopolitical sinlessness; and, just as important, it is his act of setting for us the normative sociopolitical path of subordination toward others and trust and obedience toward God about which Peter has been instructing us.

Peter writes, "When he was abused, he did not return abuse; when he suffered, he did not threaten; but he entrusted himself to the one who judges justly" (1 Pet. 2:23). That God can be trusted to judge justly is crucial to the Messiah's doing of this radically other form of justice and crucial to his call to his followers to do the same. The injustices that messianic revolutionaries are called upon to suffer (as their form of sharing in God's justice) will not be ignored or lightly passed over by God. However God will do it (and we are not sure how, except that it too will be through Jesus Christ; Rom. 2:16), God will judge the world and set things right; justice will be done toward the evildoer. There is no divine haven for those who are cruel, those who oppress, those who ridicule and slander the servants of God (1 Pet. 4:17–18). If there were, neither Jesus nor Peter could justly call us to the way of revolutionary subordination. But because we, with the Messiah, can trust *God* finally to judge justly and to set things right, we *humans* are free to take up the cruciform way of justice revealed in the Messiah.

Thus is the revolutionary Messiah put before us as the true pattern of messianic history making. But he is more than a pattern: he is also our liberating Messiah, who calls us not only to follow him, but also to believe in, share in, delight in, and above all worship him as our God. For he does not leave us in our sins; he delivers us and by the Spirit takes us up into the life that he himself enacts on our behalf and bestows upon us. "He himself bore our sins in his body on the tree, so that, delivered from sins, we might live for justice; by his wound you were healed" (2:24 DH). Jesus Christ is the Suffering Servant of the Lord spoken of in Isa. 53, the servant who not only receives in his body the humiliation, abuse, and violence of our sins, but the one who also for us and for our salvation vicariously takes our sins upon himself and bears them away. He is, as Peter has already said, the one through whose "blood . . . like that of a lamb without defect or blemish" we are "ransomed" from our former futile ways (1:18–19). He is, as Peter will later say, the one who "suffered for sins once for all, the righteous for the unrighteous, in order to bring [us] to God" (3:18). Or, as Paul writes, "For our sake [God] made [Christ] to be sin who knew no sin, so that in him we might become the righteousness of God" (2 Cor. 5:21). Justice for us and for the world is not our achievement. It is God's *gift* freely enacted, given, and received in the death of Christ, in which we are graciously made sharers. The mystery of atonement must therefore fundamentally alter our concept and practice of justice.

The history of theological reflection on the atonement has yielded a rich variety of (sometimes competing) theories about how atonement "works." That variety is testimony to the depth of this mystery, to the many New Testament images and

31. Ibid., 237 (emphasis added).

metaphors of atonement, and to the many contexts in which theories of atonement are intended to clarify and speak the word of the gospel.[32] Peter himself speaks of the atonement in terms of ransom, sacrifice, and substitution. He witnesses to the atonement as the christological and trinitarian mystery in which God takes upon himself, in the divine Word become flesh, the responsibility and penalty for the sin of humanity from which humanity cannot deliver itself. He destroys sin's power over us and in us.

Many forceful human uprisings against existing orders are attempts to overcome a sin of injustice—the sin of the illegitimate or oppressive regime, the sin of the cruel master, the sin of the abusive misogynist—to free oneself from such sin's consequences, and to make the world right. And who would not immediately see the justice in so many of those attempts to undo the injustices of the world? Justice must finally be done, the balance restored, if the whole human struggle for life is not to devolve into an empty striving after the wind. The struggle for justice is what makes us human. But does history not also reveal in all too abundant and horrific detail that that struggle is itself not only the child but also the mother of further injustice? And so it goes. Who shall deliver us from this body of death? Where and how shall justice be done?

The gospel is that *God does justice* in Jesus Christ. God wars against injustice when the divine Son "becomes flesh" and takes "the form of a slave," entering fully into the deepest and broadest realms of injustice, becoming vulnerable to its consequences, absorbing its destructive power, and allowing himself to be conquered by its agents, to be crucified. In this ultimate act of submission to the power of injustice, Christ reveals his ultimate freedom to be just; that is, in his own death, to honor, serve, and forgive the very agents of human injustice that murder him, rather than to inflict their just punishment upon them. The Father receives and honors this ultimate act of life-giving justice by giving life to the just one, raising him from the dead, revealing him as the one in whom alone true justice is eternally enacted. The Holy Spirit draws and binds us to this just one and makes us participants in his justice as we both receive it and do it. We become a people who learn to forsake the false promises, practices, and protections of the rulers of this age and to dwell under the sovereign healing, guidance, and protection of Jesus Christ: "He himself bore our sins in his body on the cross, so that, free from sins, we might live for righteousness; by his wounds you have been healed. For you were going astray like sheep, but now you have returned to the shepherd and guardian of your souls" (1 Pet. 2:24–25). In such a people nations, societies, and families in bondage to injustice might begin to perceive, however dimly, God's justice for all in the Messiah, and to do it.

32. Colin E. Gunton, *The Actuality of Atonement: A Study of Metaphor, Rationality, and the Christian Tradition* (Grand Rapids: Eerdmans, 1999), provides an excellent theological account of the many biblical metaphors of atonement and how they are all needed in order to fully grasp God's work in Jesus Christ.

1 PETER 3

Domestic Revolution (1 Peter 3:1–7)

Having fixed our attention for a time squarely on Jesus Christ, the original revolutionary in whom God's political and social order is enacted and revealed, Peter now turns attention to the relationship between wife and husband. We see immediately that the internal logic of the messianic revolution in the family is no different from that of the revolution in the political and social orders. A single normative form of action pervades every realm: "be subordinate" (*hypotassomenai*; 3:1). Peter is not legitimizing a patriarchal familial regime, whether oppressive or not (→2:18–21). We cannot argue from this text (as some have done) that a wife must remain with her husband even when he abuses her. Nor is the purpose of this text to prescribe a normative domestic order and appoint wives and husbands to roles or stations within it. Peter simply deals with the household regime that exists in his time.[1]

The word of Christ always comes as disruptive grace and plenitude in the midst of what exists, breaking into it and breaking it open for the sake of its own healing. We therefore do well not to think that "be subordinate" is a contextualizing move on Peter's part, a way of making the gospel fit within a particular

---

1. To be sure, what exists in Peter's time with respect to women and wives was a good deal of misogyny. Achtemeier 1996: 206 summarizes the contemporary view: "Dominant among the elite was the notion that the woman was by nature inferior to the man. Because she lacked the capacity for reason that the male had, she was ruled rather by her emotions, and was as a result given to poor judgment, immorality, intemperance, wickedness, avarice; she was untrustworthy, contentious, and as a result, it was her place to obey." Peter's words to the believing wife give no indication that he shared such notions (contra Elliott 2000: 585, who says that 1 Pet. 3:1–7 "presume[s] the inferiority of women"). The woman is exalted in the very fact that Peter instructs her *directly* in the gospel life. Sadly, many commentators on this text in the Christian tradition have more accurately reflected ancient misogyny than gospel life.

(now ancient) political, social, or domestic order by calling upon resident aliens, slaves, and wives to "stay in their place" within it. On the contrary, Peter consistently *contextualizes the orders within the sovereign reign of Jesus Christ.* That is his theological strategy from the very beginning of the letter, and it continues to the end. For special emphasis at this point he places his account of the "original revolutionary" (2:21–25) in the very middle of his instructions to slaves and wives. The true determination of the value, purpose, and action of their lives is precisely *not* to be discerned within the existing social order. It is to be discerned in Christ. The gospel is the power of God for contextualizing! "Be subordinate" is not the gospel adjusting itself to the existing order; rather, it is the gospel itself immediately taking resident aliens, slaves, and wives *beyond* the existing order, locating the truth of their lives *in* the fullness of the crucified and risen Messiah, and radically contextualizing and relativizing the so-called reality of the existing orders within the greater reality of the truth, governance, and care of Jesus Christ. All of God's plenitude dwells in him. He himself is the only true order of all things (cf. Col. 1:15–20). *From there*, participating in and clothed by that greater reality (having "put on the Lord Jesus Christ" in Rom. 13:14), resident aliens, slaves, and wives are called by the gospel to *reappropriate* their place in the existing orders and enact a cruciform life as the means by which the revolutionary power of the gospel is unleashed upon those orders. How that power may finally alter the existing orders is not always obvious, and the temporal outcome of that alteration cannot always be predicted. Hope is the essential virtue. Patience is crucial. But the decisive alteration of history is *already activated* in the cruciform presence and action of the faithful person.

So, again, we hear the word of the gospel, "be subordinate," as that which immediately and directly creates the wife as a person of freedom, a witness to Jesus Christ in the familial relationship, an agent of messianic history. In this case specifically—a believing wife married to an unbelieving husband—her subordination is an enacted sacrament of the revolutionary gospel to a husband who has not yet "obeyed" the messianic "word" or logic (*logos*; 3:1) of freedom. Indeed, the husband, being unbelieving, is likely enslaved to other gods. But the wife's holy and reverent way of life (*anastrophē*; 3:1–2) becomes the unspoken rhetoric that may yet persuade the husband to turn to Jesus Christ, be liberated, and himself take up the logic of revolutionary subordination (→3:1–7 and Paul's word to Christian husbands in Eph. 5:25–33). She declares the truth of the gospel in her free "action void of purpose."[2] The wife's aim is not to manipulate the husband into believing the word—he may finally refuse—rather, she takes up the gracious action of subordination because this is the way of Jesus Christ, and that itself is the end of her action. It is the gospel proclaimed.

2. Karl Barth, *The Epistle to the Romans*, trans. Edwyn C. Hoskyns (Oxford: Oxford University Press, 1933), 483.

Peter contrasts the purposeless purity and grace of being subordinate with "adornment" (*kosmos*; 1 Pet. 3:3; cf. "cosmetic"), the enhancement—for what purpose?—of a woman's physical form through hairstyles, jewelry, clothing, and so on. The point here is not to condemn such adornments as such (though they are not encouraged either), but to draw attention, by contrast, to the "gentle and quiet spirit" (*tou praeōs kai hēsychiou pneumatos*; 3:4) that is the true "cosmetic" of the wife who has put on the Lord Jesus Christ as her beauty. This kind of cosmetic is not a visible physical enhancement intended perhaps to attract the husband's attention or to mask the signs of aging; it is instead "incorruptible" (*aphthartō*), "hidden in the heart of the person" (*ho kryptos tēs kardias anthrōpos*; 3:4), and is visible to God, even if not to humans. For where is there any visible beauty in the crucifixion? "Just as there were many who were astonished at him— so marred was his appearance, beyond human semblance, and his form beyond that of mortals—so shall he startle many nations" (Isa. 52:14–15). The startling beauty of the wife adorned with revolutionary subordination may be as hidden to the ordinary human eye as the beauty of the crucified Lord. Her beauty is the likeness of Christ. "He who is both the head of the man and the beauty of the woman, the husband of the church, Christ Jesus, what sort of crown did he put on, for both male and female? A crown of thorns!" (Tertullian, *On the Crown* 5.14, quoted in Bray 2000: 98). The wife who takes up the calling to participate in the hidden beauty of the crucified Christ does not stand alone and must neither fear nor be intimidated in her witness. She enters into the illustrious company of "the holy women" of old who confidently "hoped in God" and became subordinate to their husbands. She becomes no less than a daughter of Sarah, who proclaimed the same gospel of subordination in her life with Abraham (1 Pet. 3:5–6).

The messianic domestic revolution is not summed up in a wife's subordination. In 3:7 the apostle also addresses believing husbands who, no less than believing wives, are called to live in conformity with the gospel and be liberated by it. Paul writes in Ephesians, "Be subordinate to one another in the fear of Christ: wives to their own husbands as to the Lord . . . ; husbands love your wives as also Christ loved the church and gave himself up for her" (Eph. 5:21–25 DH). Similarly, Peter writes that husbands (and other males), in keeping with their own knowledge of the gospel (*kata gnōsin*), must show "honor" (*timē*) to their wives (and other females in their households; 1 Pet. 3:7).[3] That females may often be physically "weaker" than males cannot be used as an excuse for husbands to dominate or abuse their wives. Rather, they owe them the same honor that they owe to "everyone" and even to "the emperor" (cf. 2:17). For women are "coheirs" (*synklēronomois*) of the "grace of life" (*charitos zōēs*; 3:7). It is this common sharing in the *gift* graciously

3. "While those addressed (οἵ ἄνδρες) surely include husbands, a meaning clearly intended in 3:1, the use of the adjectival substantive 'female' (τῷ γυναικείῳ) instead of the noun 'woman' or 'wife' (τῇ γύνῃ) points to wider meaning, and probably refers to the way males in a household deal with its female members, including of course the man's wife but not limited to her" (Achtemeier 1996: 217).

given, not the *possession* of a superior physical strength, that establishes men in right relationship with women. For grace is how the gospel works. Males who do not acknowledge and live in the reality of that grace are still in bondage to "the desires of the flesh that wage war against the soul" (2:11). The authoritarian husband or domineering male fundamentally fails to understand God and the gospel—so much so that his prayers, which depend from beginning to end on God's grace, may also be "hindered" (3:7). For how can he call upon the grace of God when he refuses to acknowledge that he is a sharer in that grace with women?

Ecclesial Revolution (1 Peter 3:8–12)

Peter now directs his attention, by way of summary, to the whole messianic community and recapitulates for all of its members what he has said specifically to several sectors within it. Five Greek words in 3:8 characterize the life of the community: *homophrones* ("likeminded"), *sympatheis* ("sympathetic"), *philadelphoi* ("brotherly love"), *eusplanchnoi* ("tenderhearted"), *tapeinophrones* ("humble-minded"). With these words Peter joins Paul (Rom. 12:9–18; see the comparison of these two texts in Elliott 2000: 602; see also Phil. 2:1–4) in describing how the church itself displays the life of Christ in the power of the Holy Spirit.

Jesus Christ gathers a people for himself from all of the stations and nations of humankind—"from every tribe and language and people and nation" (Rev. 5:9). Peter's letter addresses the messianic communities in "Pontus, Galatia, Cappadocia, Asia, and Bithynia" (1 Pet. 1:1). Diversity characterizes the body of Christ, in which the rich variety of humankind is embraced and celebrated. And yet "celebration of diversity" is certainly not what draws the people of God together, and it cannot be what binds it together.[4] As Peter has already reminded us in numerous ways, this is a people called, created, set apart, and sent into the world by the very particular God of Israel, who alone is God, whose Son Jesus Christ is of a very particular nature and enacts a very particular way of life, which he both gives to his people and calls forth from them through the very particular Holy Spirit of God. It is not so much that diversity has its limits among this people, as that diversity is held together by a "common object of love," and that object is *commonly identifiable.*[5] The political community called the church is not characterized first by its love of one another ("in all our diversity"), but by its love of the God who has called it into being by his Word and filled it with his Spirit. We know this God. His story can be told. His actions can be traced. The pattern of his life, death, and resurrection can be described. His people can be named, and their common practices specified. Further, to be the people of this God means

---

4. A habit of thinking that is increasingly prevalent in the Protestant churches of the Western world.

5. Oliver O'Donovan, *Common Objects of Love: Moral Reflection and the Shaping of Community* (Grand Rapids: Eerdmans, 2002).

that in good measure we *agree* on the details of the story, the actions, the pattern, the people, and the practices.

We are "likeminded" about them or, perhaps better said, we have a "shared intelligence" (*homophrones*; 3:8). We are able to locate the church as the work of the Holy Spirit through its public agreement on such matters as the canon of scripture, the shape of the liturgy, the creeds and doctrines, the traditions and practices that shape it. And yet, to be likeminded is not to say that the people of God constitutes itself *on the basis of* its common agreements; it is rather to say that it is constituted *from beyond itself* by the one to whom these commonly shared "divine things" truthfully testify as the gifts of the Holy Spirit. As Hütter says, the church "suffers" or receives these gifts: "The salvific-economic mission of the Holy Spirit is thus realized not 'spiritually' in the immediacy of the in-spiration of Spirit into individual religious consciousness, but in the form of concrete church practices which are to be understood as the gift of the Spirit in the service of God's economy."[6] A church that thinks it can do without agreement on canon, liturgy, creeds, traditions, and practices, exchanging such "shared intelligence" for mere diversity of opinion (Greek *hairesis*, "heresy"), cuts itself off from the very source of its life in the triune God and the crucified and risen Messiah. It fails to be the revolutionary political community that testifies to God's act of justice and deliverance in Jesus Christ. Heresy kills, as Peter also makes clear in his second letter (2 Pet. 2).

The church is bound together in a shared intelligence about its common object of love. It is also bound together by a *common love*, a "shared passion" (*sympatheis*) for that object. We do well not to translate this into the usual English sense of "compassion" or "sympathy," the feelings that the members of the body of Christ have for one another. Peter has other words to speak about that. Rather, the members of the messianic community share a common pathos or passion for the one about whom they share a common intelligence. The people of God is that political community that loves the Lord God above all and enacts its life together as the shared act of that love: "Hear, O Israel: The LORD is our God, the LORD alone. You [the people] shall love the LORD your God with all your heart, and with all your soul, and with all your might" (Deut. 6:4–5). "For the love of Christ urges us on" (2 Cor. 5:14). *Homophrones* (shared intelligence about the triune God) and *sympatheis* (shared passion for the triune God) together bind the church into the unified messianic political community. Commenting on Augustine's political theology, O'Donovan writes: "Community has its root in evaluations that we form and hold together, the *common objects of love*. Loving is the corporate function that determines and defines the structure of the political society; it is the key to its coherence and its organization. Loving *things*, not loving *one another*. Augustine also affirmed that members of a community loved one another; but that is a second step. The love that founds the community is not reciprocal, but

6. Reinhard Hütter, *Suffering Divine Things: Theology as Church Practice*, trans. Doug Stott (Grand Rapids: Eerdmans, 2000), 127.

turned outward upon an object."[7] For Peter that "object" for the messianic people of God is the original revolutionary, Jesus the Messiah (→2:21–25). Love of the Messiah determines and defines the messianic community.

The next three terms characterize the relationships of members of the community among one another. *Philadelphoi* ("brotherly love") in the first place acknowledges an objective kinship among the members: they have been made brothers and sisters of one another by being made sharers in Jesus Christ through the Holy Spirit. The love called for in this term does not itself constitute the kinship relation, but is rather what that relation, constituted in Christ, calls for. As with natural brothers and sisters, the members of the messianic community are joined together by a bond that transcends their feelings of mutual affection (which may be present in greater or lesser measure); and yet it is also that bond that generates the recognition, respect, care, and affection for one another appropriate to brothers and sisters. These are "my people" in Christ. We uphold, serve, and look out for one another. We belong together.

More than that, we stand in basic openness to one another; we are "tenderhearted" (*eusplanchnoi*), allowing ourselves to be affected in our "guts" (*splanchna*) by the lives of others, responding from the heart to their joys, sorrows, needs, and affections. Our love for one another in Christ goes beyond recognition and respect, though those are basic; our lives also become bound together with bonds of mutual affection when they are shared with one another in the household of God.

The messianic community is also characterized by humility; we are "humbleminded" (*tapeinophrones*). This goes to the heart of relationships in the messianic community, as set before us in the Messiah in the most startling and concrete way: "Having loved his own who were in the world, he loved them to the end. . . . And during supper Jesus, knowing that the Father had given all things into his hands, and that he had come from God and was going to God, got up from the table, took off his outer robe, and tied a towel around himself. Then he poured water into a basin and began to wash the disciples' feet and to wipe them with the towel" (John 13:1–5; cf. Phil. 2:5–11). Humility is the foundation of all of Peter's instructions to "be subordinate," for it is the attitude and habit in which we esteem others above ourselves (Phil. 2:3), no matter what our station or theirs. We become servants of one another, giving ourselves as gifts to the whole body for its building up.

Perhaps it seems like Peter is being unrealistic, giving the church an impossible ideal to which it is called to aspire but will never attain. And yet the very next sentence looks unflinchingly at the messianic community as a place where "evil" and "abuse" still occur (1 Pet. 3:9). The attention is not here turned toward the outsider; Peter is still speaking to the people of God in their internal relations.[8]

---

7. O'Donovan, *Common Objects of Love*, 25–26 (emphasis original).

8. Elliott 2000: 600, 616 suggests that at 3:9 Peter turns again to write about the relations of Christians with those outside the community. However, as Achtemeier 1996: 221 points out, "There

Bad things are done. One member abuses another. Sin takes hold. Such things threaten to destroy the church from within. The church can neither be blind to these facts of sinful human interaction in its midst nor unaware of the cost of healing the wounds and mending the breaches. There is a powerful natural inclination, even among God's people, to pitch "evil against evil, abuse against abuse," to retaliate, take revenge, pay back. Retaliation seems to make sense; it is straightforward and easy to apply. It evens things out, and we take this as justice. Evil institutes the economy of lack and of the zero sum: we become habituated and enslaved to the stinginess of repayment in kind.

But the messianic community is called to another, revolutionary, way. It is the calling of the church so to discern, enact, and habitually practice another economy that it becomes the new "natural." Just as Jesus the messianic sovereign did not repeat the economy of repaying abuse with abuse, but himself freely bore the sins of the abusers for their own liberation and healing (2:23–24), so it must be among his people: "Repay with a blessing. It was for this that you were called—that you might inherit a blessing" (3:9). The new natural, that which runs with the grain of the new creation and is yet as old as creation itself, is *blessing*. By repaying evil and abuse with blessing we participate already in (i.e., we "inherit") God's economy of blessing. That is neither an easy nor a cheap response to those who would undermine, shame, or attack us. It may cost us much. But it will never cost us more than we have already been given. God's blessing, and our share in it, is that "grace abounding" that ultimately overcomes evil's economy of lack and retribution; it is that overflowing of the fullness of divine life that will bring into being the final (and original) human community. "Owe no one anything, except to love one another; for the one who loves has fulfilled the law" (Rom. 13:8).

The "life," "good days," and "peace" that God's people desire do not come to them in their passivity. Evil has taken hold not only of minds and hearts, but also of bodies. Body parts have been activated in its cause. We *do* evil. That kind of doing must cease. Therefore, says Peter (quoting Ps. 34:13–14), "let them keep their tongues from evil and their lips from speaking deceit; let them turn away from evil" (1 Pet. 3:10–11). It is necessary to abstain from evil; it is essential to refuse to do it. But it is not enough that we cease doing evil. More important, something else altogether must fully enlist, engage, and activate us: "Let them . . . do good; let them seek peace and pursue it" (3:11). The pursuit of the good, of peace, of justice, is our true end. Having been turned toward and activated by that end, and now striving toward it, we see that it is in fact the face of the Lord that we are seeking, the *visio Dei*. He himself is our good, our peace, our justice. We see that his "eyes" and "ears" are already turned toward us in grace (3:12). We may therefore fully entrust ourselves and our prayers to him. However, those who persist in doing evil and repaying evil for evil will see only the angry face of the

is no clear indication in the text of such a shift of focus." I take it that Peter is acknowledging the struggle to overcome evil and retribution even within the Christian community.

Lord. For them the Lord himself appears to be bound up in the economy of lack, in the stingy economy of repayment in kind. They miss the overflowing grace that creates and gives life to the people of God.

Messianic Proclamation (1 Peter 3:13–17)

The people of God proclaim God. As Peter has already said, we have been made "God's own people" in order that we "may proclaim [*exangeilēte*] the mighty acts of him who called you out of darkness into his marvelous light" (2:9). He now shows how the proclamation of the messianic people is a participation in Christ's own act of proclamation.

God's people proclaim by doing good. Peter has laid out the character of that doing, and so too of that proclaiming, in the preceding verses. In an often hostile world, within often unjust and oppressive political and social systems, the messianic people proclaim the gospel by taking up the cruciform way of the Messiah, the way of "being subordinate." Their proclamation therefore often takes the form of suffering.

But who will do evil to those who are "zealots of the good" (*tou agathou zēlōtai*; 3:13)? As we have seen, Peter calls the messianic community to turn away from repaying evil for evil, thereby interrupting the seemingly inexorable cycle of evil. It would seem less likely, then, that they would be the targets of evildoers than those who themselves do evil. But while it may be less likely that they will suffer harm, it is not impossible. Messianic "exiles and aliens" who are subordinate to kings and governors and honor the emperor are sometimes imprisoned, tortured, executed. Messianic slaves who are subordinate to their masters are sometimes mistreated, beaten, killed. Messianic wives who are subordinate to their husbands are sometimes disregarded, dishonored, dismissed. There is no guarantee of a safe and easy life for the people of God. Quite the contrary: many have suffered and will suffer in following the way of messianic justice (*dia dikaiosynēn*, "because of justice"; 3:14). Those, as we have seen, are already blessed, because they suffer according to God's will (3:17), and they share in the life and destiny of their Lord.

The ones who despise, persecute, and harm God's people seem to have all the power and authority; they can do what they like with their subjects. They seem to be in supreme control, exercising their prerogatives freely. But Peter says they are in fact living in and acting out of "fear" (*phobos*; 3:14). How else would we explain their arbitrary and cruel exercise of power over even those subjects who are doing good? It can only be that they fear losing their image, honor, status, authority, and control in the various political, social, and economic orders in which they exercise their rule. They fear their own finitude, which they do not gratefully receive from God as the grace of creatureliness (contrast 4:19). Rather they rebel against their finitude in hubristic efforts to establish a claim against an infinity that they believe is finally empty, indifferent, or hostile to their existence.

Fear is the father of compulsion, of the instinctive drive to survive, conquer, and rule at all costs. There is no freedom in fear.

Here again we see why the call to "be subordinate" is good news. Those who have no worldly image, honor, authority, and rule to gain or lose, to horde or defend, also need not be troubled by or "fear what they [the ones doing harm] fear" (3:14). Freed from such fear, God's people are also freed up for the goodness to which they are called. Having relinquished their own desires and labors toward sovereignty by being subordinate, they make "holy room" (*hagiasate*, "sanctify"; 3:15) in their hearts for only one sovereign, Christ the Lord, who, as Peter repeatedly reminds us, enacted his sovereignty on the cross. He is the one in whom our desires find their end and fulfillment. In him we already share, as much as we allow, in the gracious infinite fullness of the triune God. What more do we need? What is there to fear?

Such a free and revolutionary life as lived by the followers of Christ will surely provoke a host of questions from those who observe it, from those whose hopes, expectations, and habits of thought and practice have been withered and misshapen by the powers of this age: How can a person reasonably follow Christ? How can anyone live such a "subordinate" life? How can it be good, especially if it brings suffering? How can you think that justice is being done in the world by it? How can you turn the other cheek, walk another mile, give your shirt as well as your coat? How can you not desire to wield the power that the rulers and masters do, so that at least *you* can do the good and the justice that they are not doing? How can families, societies, nations, and empires be expected to live in such an anarchic manner? Would that not be the end of the world as we know it?

Indeed!

Jesus Christ is the "hope" (*elpidos*) of the world (3:15). He truly is the end of the world as we know it, since he himself, in his crucifixion and resurrection, cancels the normal expectations and habits of thought and practice that give all of those questions their seemingly obvious power to undermine and cancel the whole messianic project. He brings those questions to naught, and from their ruins he brings about a whole new world. So then, how can we answer such questions? What kind of apologia, what kind of reasonable account, what kind of proof, can we offer for the messianic way of life? Not, surely, one that assumes, works within, and builds on the whole unredeemed rationality presupposed by such questions. Such a realistic and pragmatic apology would only in the end confirm and yield to the fateful order and stability sought by the culture and politics of fear and death. Rather, our word in defense of the hope that we have, our apologia, must be nothing other than the rationality (*logos*) that takes flesh in the life, crucifixion, resurrection, and parousia of the cosmic sovereign, Jesus Christ. That *logos* radically interrupts and destabilizes all conservative, progressive, and revolutionary reasons for hope that the world gives, renders them questionable, puts them in their place. Our apology must be an account of Christ's story, and that account cannot be given apart from the living testimony of the messianic people. The defense that we offer for our hope is nothing other than the story of Christ, which he lived for the sake of the church and the world, and the story of the church itself, to which Christ gives his own life in the Spirit through the sacraments, for the sake of the world. The church's apologia for its hope must take the form of witness to the work of Christ; it is therefore characterized not by proud arguments and clever proofs, but by "humility" (*prautētos*), reverence, and a good conscience (3:16). Therein lies the power of the church's appeal. As Paul writes: "I myself . . . appeal to you by the humility [*prautētos*] and gentleness of Christ. . . . For though we live in the flesh, we do not walk according to the flesh, for the weapons of our warfare are not of the flesh, but are powerful through God to overthrow strongholds. We overthrow worldly rationality [*logismous*] and every vaunted thought [*pan hypsōma*, 'every high thing'] raised up against the knowledge of God, and we take every thought [*noēma*] captive to the obedience of Christ" (2 Cor. 10:1, 3–5 DH).

The Christian theological discipline of apologetics is often tempted to locate the social, cultural, and intellectual strongholds of a given society and then argue from them to the gospel, or assimilate the gospel to them, or render the gospel in their terms, in order to show that the Christian faith is aligned with and supported by, rather than alien to, such strongholds. But that strategy usually amounts to the cancellation of the gospel rather than the defeat of the strongholds. To be sure, when the apostles engage in the task of apologetics they do not refuse the linguistic, cultural, and intellectual coin of their time. They cannot but make use of it. Indeed, they embrace it. But that coin is never simply presupposed as foundational either. The current language, culture, and knowledge are engaged and overthrown by the crucifixion-resurrection logic of the gospel. Only then are they seized, taken captive, and made to serve the proclamation of the good news of Jesus Christ.[9] We can see, for example, how John the Evangelist engages in that kind of apology when he takes the popular philosophical *logos* concept and binds it to the flesh of Jesus Christ whose "glory . . . full of grace and truth" is revealed when Christ is "lifted up," that is, crucified and raised from the dead.

Will such an apology be seen, heard, and believed by the world? There are no guarantees, no surefire ways to secure its hoped-for effects. We do not fight with "fleshly" weapons. Our apologia is finally given over to God and to those who hear and see it, for their judgment. That last phrase, "for their judgment," is deliberately ambiguous.[10] The church's defense of the gospel must always be defenseless, which

---

9. See the larger development of this theme in relation to Paul in my *Paul among the Postliberals: Pauline Theology beyond Christendom and Modernity* (Grand Rapids: Brazos, 2003), 209–54.

10. I am here following the lead of Rowan Williams, "Postmodern Theology and the Judgment of the World," in *Postmodern Theology: Christian Faith in a Pluralist World*, ed. Frederic B. Burnham (San Francisco: Harper & Row, 1989), 92–112, who argues that the phrase "the judgment of the world" reveals a set of complex relations between the church and the world. Relevant also are Chris K. Huebner's important reflections on martyrdom and truth in *A Precarious Peace: Yoderian Explorations on Theology, Knowledge, and Identity* (Waterloo, ON: Herald, 2006), 133–44.

is intrinsic to the very character of the gospel being proclaimed. Such defenseless-ness is exactly for the sake of the societies in which the defense is being offered. As we have seen, the truth of Christ is made manifest in the lives of believers in their very act of being subordinate, of self-dispossession, of free relinquishment of control over the outcome of their witness to Christ. The judgment of the world is all that is left. And we cannot predict how this will go. The "Gentiles" may judge that the "good way of life in Christ" (*agathēn en Christō anastrophēn*; 1 Pet. 3:16 DH) is in fact the very truth they must see, hear, and believe, and welcome these messianic "exiles of the Diaspora" in their midst. Then God's judgment comes as the healing and blessing of the Gentiles. On the other hand the Gentiles may judge the witnesses' vulnerable apologia as irrational, ridiculous, unrealistic, perhaps even dangerous and subversive of the taken-for-granted systems of family, society, and nation; in which case they may "malign" or "abuse" the messianic witnesses or subject them to suffering. But then the world's humiliation of the witnesses will in fact be its own shame in the coming judgment of God, when cross and resurrection are revealed to all as the logic of "the way things are," when the Lamb who was slain is alone able to unlock the book of history.

Crucial in all of this, though, as Peter makes clear in these verses, is that the church itself must truly be displaying the "good way of life in Christ" and not "doing evil" (3:17). It is for the sake of the world that the church offers its gra-cious, vulnerable, cruciform witness. But if the church participates in the very ways of the world that the gospel reveals as evil (manipulation, coercion, lying, mastery, abuse, revenge, violence, war), will not the judgment of the world upon the church, in the form of the world's refusal of the church's message, itself be the form of God's judgment upon a church that has forgotten the true, cruci-form scandal of the gospel? As Peter says later, God's judgment begins with the household of God (4:17).

We might pause briefly at this point to show that Peter's thoughts here correspond exactly to Jesus's teaching on the judgment of the nations in Matt. 25:31–46. That text is unfortunately almost always taken as an exhortation to *Christian* activism toward social and political transformation with respect to the poor, the homeless, and the imprisoned. But this text is not (directly) about Christian discipleship, nor is it directed to the Christian community. Jesus is clear that he is speaking of the "nations" (*panta ta ethnē*; 25:32) gathered before the throne of the Son of Man. It is they—rather than Christians, or just people in general—who are separated one from another in the judgment, and the criterion of their judgment is how they have received "these my brothers" (*toutōn tōn adelphōn*; 25:40 DH)—that is, Christ's disciples—in their midst. For Christ's disciples are sent—sown—among the nations (as they were sent in Israel in Matt. 10) in exilic vulnerability—without money, without food, without extra clothing, without protection, indeed, even without an apologia ready to hand (10:9–10, 19).[11] This very exilic vulnerability

---

11. Luther 1967: 108 makes a connection between Matt. 10:19–20 and 1 Pet. 3:16.

is the power of their proclamation of God's gracious gospel to the nations: "You received without payment; give without payment" (10:8). Not coincidentally, it is also, then, the form of their solidarity and fellowship with the poor, the homeless, the imprisoned in the world. It cannot be otherwise with messianic *exiles*, who as such will often find themselves living and working among and with those on the margins of the social, political, and economic power centers of society. But how will the nations receive the exilic messianic witnesses, the disciples of Jesus? Will they welcome them, care for them, feed, clothe, and protect them? Then they have also done all of those things not only to the witnesses but to Jesus Christ himself, and their judgment is that they receive blessing. Or, will the nations refuse, turn away from, dishonor, despise, and neglect these messianic witnesses whose exilic vulnerability is the very vulnerability of the Messiah? Then those nations will be "accursed" and assigned to eternal punishment. Matthew 25:31–46 is not an exhortation to powerful, perhaps even coercive Christian intervention in the political and economic machinations of the nations for the sake of the poor and oppressed. Quite the contrary: it assumes that Christian disciples are themselves the poor and oppressed, that is, the dispossessed, messianic, political witnesses that Peter calls us to be in his letter. *That* existence *is* the critical and fundamental sociopolitical proclamation of Jesus Christ that the church has to offer to the nations. It is that royal-priestly presence and practice of the church (1 Pet. 2:9) in the light of which the nations will be judged, for their blessing or for their condemnation.

Messiah's Proclamation (1 Peter 3:18–22)

The church's vulnerability and suffering among the nations proclaims its participation in Christ. "For Christ also suffered for sins once for all, the righteous for the unrighteous, in order to bring you to God" (3:18). This is the gospel! There is no messianic community or witness without it. The church is a body of the ungodly who have been justified. It does not have it *in itself* to bring itself to God, let alone to bring the nations to God. It is brought to God only through Christ's singular (*hapax*, "once for all") substitutionary suffering for sins. That particular suffering cannot be imitated by the church; it is rather "the objective ground and cause of salvation" (Achtemeier 1996: 251) that brings the church into being. It can only be believed, participated in, witnessed to by the church.

The church often finds itself participating in the world's struggles for justice. And who can deny that many relative social, economic, cultural, and political goods have come about through ecclesial and Christian influence in the wider world: care of the unborn, orphans, infirm, and elderly; universal education; hospitals; abolition of slavery; religious freedom; perhaps even participatory democracy?[12]

12. Baptists often (rightly) claim a good measure of credit for the establishment of religious freedom (Roger Williams) in the United States and worldwide. The conversations over "radical

When the seeds of the gospel are sown among the nations in the lives of messianic Diaspora people, should we not expect that God will cause them to grow? Nevertheless, tempted then by the thought that what the nations really need and what it can best offer is its effective contribution to "working for peace and justice"—that is, its support of, participation in, and influence upon conservative, progressive, radical, or revolutionary political means of establishing, enforcing, and defending a just national and world order—the church has also often become a coperpetrator of injustice among the nations.[13] What the nations in the first place really need from the church is not its contribution to their own means and ends, but its faithful witness to the divine messianic justice graciously *given* in the gospel. The gospel is the revelation of the new world order in the midst of "the present evil age" (Gal. 1:4), an order founded in the self-offering of "the just for the unjust," which happens in Christ alone. The church proclaims and enacts primary justice among the nations to the extent that it participates in, lives by, and witnesses to the justice done in Christ's substitutionary suffering, an act vindicated by the Father through the life-giving power of the Holy Spirit. As Peter writes, Christ's being "put to death by flesh" was met, not with more death dealing "for the sake of the greater good," but with an excess of divine goodness, with resurrection, with being "made alive by the Spirit" (3:18).[14] Therein the new world order comes into

---

democracy" by Stanley Hauerwas and Romand Coles in *Christianity, Democracy, and the Radical Ordinary: Conversations between a Radical Democrat and a Christian* (Eugene, OR: Cascade, 2008), building on pregnant suggestions in the work of John Howard Yoder, yield up a multifaceted, open-textured, sometimes tensive participation of the church in the practices of radical democracy. Such democracy, however, is usually practiced "below the radar" of the usual instruments of the reigning economies and political orders. (I am grateful to R. R. Reno for helping me to think through the issues in this paragraph.)

13. In democracies Christians are often urged to be good citizens, to get out and vote as their sacred democratic duty, to be involved in worldly political processes, to become leaders of political parties, cities, states, and nations to bring about good for the nation and the world. These various modes of participation in worldly politics are deemed to be the primary and essential forms of Christian political witness; see, for example, from different ends of the American political spectrum, Jim Wallis, *God's Politics: A New Vision for Faith and Politics in America* (San Francisco: Harper, 2005); and Charles J. Chaput, *Render unto Caesar: Serving Our Nation by Living Our Catholic Beliefs in Political Life* (New York: Doubleday, 2008). But that view finds little warrant in 1 Peter, or in the New Testament as whole. For alternative perspectives on the church's political witness see John Howard Yoder, *Body Politics: Five Practices of the Christian Community before the Watching World* (Nashville: Discipleship Resources, 1992); idem, *The Politics of Jesus: Vicit Agnus Noster*, 2nd ed. (Grand Rapids: Eerdmans, 1994); idem, *For the Nations: Essays Public and Evangelical* (Grand Rapids: Eerdmans, 1997); idem, *The Christian Witness to the State* (Eugene, OR: Wipf & Stock, 1998); Daniel M. Bell Jr., *Liberation Theology after the End of History* (London/New York: Routledge, 2001); William T. Cavanaugh, *Theopolitical Imagination* (London/New York: Clark, 2002); and Ted Lewis, ed., *Electing Not to Vote: Christian Reflections on Reasons for Not Voting* (Eugene, OR: Cascade, 2008).

14. I follow the translation of this phrase by Achtemeier 1996: 239, who argues (250): "It is hard to see how Christ could die 'by means of the flesh' so long as 'flesh' is understood either as Christ's own flesh or as a description of his human life. Yet the passive form of θανατωθείς ['having been put to death'] indicates something done to Christ by others, and if one understands σάρξ ['flesh']

being. Messianic self-offering, resurrection, and life in the Spirit is God's way of making the world right. That is the gospel of God's justice.

"In the" (*en hō*) Spirit, Peter says, Christ "also" (*kai*) "went" (*poreutheis*) and "preached" (*ekēryxen*) "to the spirits in prison" (*tois en phylakē pneumasin*; 3:19) who were disobedient in the days of Noah.[15] Peter here does not write about an event that took place in hell or in the realm of the dead in the time between Christ's crucifixion and resurrection.[16] Rather, he reveals how the risen and ascending Christ announced God's judgment on spiritual powers in rebellion against God who cause evil. That leads up to Peter's final declaration that all "angels, authorities,

---

to stand here for humanity as it does in 1:24, then it names the agency of Christ's death. In that case, it means that Christ was put to death by humans but raised by (God's) Spirit. The contrast between the human and divine attitude to Christ spelled out by our author in 2:6–8 is thus here carried forward to its final outcome: Christ put to death by unbelieving humanity, but raised by (God's) Spirit. Such a construal has the advantage of allowing us to understand Christ's resurrection in the second member of the parallel phrase in its normal form, as a bodily resurrection, since the resurrection is being described in terms of the one who brought it about (Spirit), not in terms of the sphere within which it occurred (spirit)."

15. 1 Pet. 3:19–20 is, by almost unanimous consent, one of the most difficult texts of the entire New Testament. For a variety of patristic interpretations, including the theme of Christ's "descent into hell," see Bray 2000: 106–14. Luther 1967: 113 writes: "This is a strange text and certainly a more obscure passage than any other passage in the New Testament. I still do not know for sure what the apostle means." He then allows for more than one interpretation. Achtemeier 1996: 252 writes: "This verse [3:19] is one of the shorter, but surely the most problematic, in this letter, if not in the NT canon as a whole, and eludes any agreement on its precise meaning." Modern scholarship has helped a little to clear up the puzzles in this text. Achtemeier 1996: 244–46 and Elliott 2000: 648–50 each summarize the various interpretive options and provide extensive bibliography. In an important move, Achtemeier argues for separating the exegesis of this text from that of 4:6. I follow Achtemeier 1996: 253 in taking *en hō*, together with *kai* (in 3:19), as "designating the second act in a series instigated by the Spirit, the first being Christ's resurrection, the second his proclamation." The verb *poreutheis* ("went") does not necessarily bear the meaning of a descending movement; in 3:22 it bears the meaning of an ascending movement (see Achtemeier 1996: 256–58).

16. This means, then, that I do not take the text to indicate that Christ "descended into hell" in the time between his crucifixion and resurrection and made a proclamation to souls imprisoned there. The phrase "descended into hell" in the Apostles' Creed may have been based on 1 Pet. 3:19 (together with 4:6) as well as other texts (Acts 2:31; Rom. 10:7; Eph. 4:9), perhaps reflecting an early tradition about the "harrowing of hell" by Christ upon his crucifixion; see the accounts of the development of this tradition in Elliott 2000: 706–10 and Jobes 2005: 247–51. Jared Wicks, "Christ's Saving Descent to the Dead: Early Witnesses from Ignatius of Antioch to Origen," *Pro ecclesia* 17, no. 3 (2008): 281–309, provides an account of the *descensus* in early Christian theology. But 1 Pet. 3:19 need not be taken in that direction, and indeed the grammar strongly suggests that the event occurring in 3:19 is an act of the risen Christ (so Achtemeier, Elliott, Jobes, and Senior; Goppelt and Green defend the *descensus ad inferos* interpretation). The other New Testament texts noted above do not indicate a saving journey into hell by the crucified Christ either. They emphasize the reality of his death. He truly died! He truly shared the destiny of all human beings who die. Yet death did not finally triumph over him. So the Apostles' Creed may be read, "He was crucified, died, and was buried. He entered fully into the reality of death. On the third day he rose again from the dead." It is important to note that the descent into hell does not appear in the Nicene-Constantinopolitan Creed (AD 381).

and powers" have been subjected to Christ (3:22). In making this argument, Peter draws on Jewish traditions about "the days of Noah."[17]

In New Testament times the pseudonymous Jewish writing known as 1 Enoch was highly regarded as a testament written by the character Enoch from Gen. 5:21–24, who "walked with God; then he was no more, because God took him" (5:24). According to 1 Enoch 12:1–2, "when Enoch was taken away from the earth, he went to dwell with 'the Watchers and the holy ones'"—the Watchers being the legendary "sons of God" who took the "the daughters of men" and had children by them, as told in the story in Gen. 6:1–4 (Jobes 2005: 243). According to 1 Enoch, the children born of this illicit union of fallen angels (the Watchers) and human women were giants, and from them came evil spirits (1 Enoch 15:9) who have led and will continue to lead people into corruption until the end of the age. As the story goes:

> The Watchers appeal to Enoch to intercede with God on behalf of themselves and the evil progeny they have produced. Enoch obliges and returns with God's proclamation to the Watchers: "[you will] not be able to ascend into heaven unto all eternity, but you shall remain inside the earth, imprisoned all the days of eternity." Moreover, the Watchers would see the destruction of their sons (referred to as "the spirits") because the petitions for themselves and for their sons (the spirits) will not be heard by God (14:5–6). These "spirits" that came from the bodies of the giants fathered by the Watchers through human women were the cause of the human evil that led to the great flood during the time of Enoch's grandson, Noah. (Jobes 2005: 244)

The story of the origin of these spirits and God's judgment upon them as told in 1 Enoch seems to lie behind 1 Pet. 3:19–20. Jobes writes:

> If this is the assumed tradition behind 1 Pet. 3:19, then the spirits to whom Christ preached should be understood as fallen angels and/or demonic spirits. Their imprisonment represents in spatial terms God's restraining power over them, and the message Christ preached to them is the confirmation that "the day of the great conclusion," first announced by the flood, is now upon them. Christ's ascension itself may have been the proclamation of their defeat. . . . In other words, the apostle Peter is identifying Jesus Christ as the victor over all evil in both the spirit and the human worlds forevermore. (Jobes 2005: 244)

By referring to this tradition about "the days of Noah," Peter is declaring that Christ's "proclamation to the spirits in prison" is a clear sign that he has authority over all of the powers of evil that might oppress the messianic community either from within or without, a point Peter makes more clearly in 1 Pet. 3:22.

In the days of Noah God "waited patiently" while Noah constructed the ark of salvation for the "eight souls" who were saved "through water" (*di' hydatos*; 3:20).

17. For what follows, I am indebted to the discussion in Jobes 2005: 242–51.

The ark with its eight souls is a figure of the messianic community amid the nations of the world, nations that have succumbed to evil powers that hold them in bondage and incite them to bring persecution and suffering upon God's people. Baptism is the salvation of God's messianic community, not because baptismal water itself is effective ("not as a removal of dirt from the body"; 3:21), but because in baptism we receive our salvation "through the resurrection [*di' anastaseōs*] of Jesus Christ." Risen from the dead, ascending above all evil powers, Christ pronounces their final doom and removes their power to destroy God's people. Baptism seals our participation in the victory of Christ over the powers through his crucifixion and resurrection (cf. Rom. 6). Baptism then is also "a pledge of a good conscience toward God" (1 Pet. 3:21 DH), for in our baptism we renounce all the powers of evil, give thanks to God for our rescue from destruction, and declare our allegiance, trust, and love toward God and his Messiah alone.

The community formed in the Messiah testifies in baptism to the resurrection, exaltation, and cosmic sovereignty of Jesus the Messiah, "who has gone into heaven, and is at the right hand of God, with angels, authorities, and powers made subject to him" (3:22). The "good conscience" of the messianic community, its hopeful and fearless witness to God's new order, comes not from its ability to control its own destiny, but from its confidence in the divine sovereignty of the Messiah. God has overcome and subjugated to Christ those powers that enslave humans to their false claims to sovereignty and false promises of well-being. But what are the "angels," "authorities" (*exousiai*), and "powers" (*dynameis*) of which Peter writes? Peter joins Paul (Rom. 8:38; 1 Cor. 2:6–8; Gal. 4:3; Eph. 1:21; 2:2; 6:12; Col. 2:8) in using these terms to designate all of those creaturely powers, whether personal or impersonal, whether beneficent or malevolent, whether spiritual, cosmic, or earthly, that would "separate us from the love of God in Christ Jesus our Lord" (Rom. 8:39). Barth helps us to grasp their significance:

> We have to speak about these powers. We have to do so because we see them and know them and know about them and have to take their reality and efficacy into account. We have to do so because in all their strangeness they *are* real and efficacious. World history, being the history of man and humanity, of Adamic humanity which has fallen from God, is also the history of innumerable absolutisms of different kinds, of forces that are truly and properly man's own but that have won a certain autonomy, independence, and even superiority in relation to him. There they are, powerful enough in and in spite of their impotence to be too much for the one who can and should be their lord and to take him to task, to master him who should master them, influencing, determining, and controlling his thought and speech and also his purposes and enterprises for himself and in his common life with others. If they are only pseudo-objective realities, strangely enough they are still powerful realities which make a fine display of their lying objectivity. If their power is only a usurped and creaturely one, and therefore relative and limited, nevertheless even in its relativity and limitation it is a highly effective one in its outward penetration and expansion. If they work only "as if" they were legitimate, this "as if" is clear

and convincing and even forceful enough to fill man with respect for them and continually to deliver him up to their authority. No adjuring of human freedom, no overlooking, forgetting, or denying, is of any help here. They are not just the supports but the motors of society. They are the secret guarantee of man's great and small conventions, customs, habits, traditions, and institutions. They are the hidden wirepullers in man's great and small enterprises, movements, achievements, and revolutions. They are not just the potencies but the real factors and agents of human progress, regress, and stagnation in politics, economics, scholarship, technology, and art, and also of the evolutions and retardations in all the personal life of the individual. It is not really people who do things, whether leaders or the masses. Through mankind's fault, things are invisibly done without and above man, even above the human individual in all his uniqueness, by the host of absolutisms, of powers that seek to be lordless and that make an impressive enough attempt to exhibit and present themselves as such.[18]

We can discern these "lordless" powers and their effect upon human life and history by asking ourselves some probing questions. Who or what would claim our highest allegiance, for whom or what do we give our bodies as sacrifices or, more determinative, the bodies of our own and others' children—a king, queen, emperor, the people; a city, nation, empire; an ideal such as law, justice, freedom, democracy? In whom or what do we put our trust and hope, who will save us—commanders-in-chief and armies, the global economy and the market, education and opportunity, science and technology, doctors and medicine? What is the criterion in terms of which we judge truth, beauty, and goodness—scientific reason, esthetic sense, political or pragmatic realism, personal choice? What end fuels our most dedicated labors—pleasure, wealth, fame, power, victory, defiance, oblivion? The answers to these questions begin to name the "angels, authorities, and powers" that exercise spiritual, political, and material sovereignty over peoples, cultures, societies, institutions, individuals. There are indeed "many gods and many lords" in this world to which we have become "accustomed" through our habitual loyalty and service to them (1 Cor. 8:5, 7). How gripped with fear do we become when those objects of our loyalty, hope, and labor begin to show weakness or threaten to collapse? To answer that question, as, for example, America and other nations recently did following 9/11, is to reveal the depth of their power over us and our enslavement to them.

Nevertheless, "elect exiles of the Diaspora," followers of the crucified, risen, and sovereign Messiah, have been delivered through him from slavery to those powers. They now forswear looking to anyone or anything other than him as the final object of their allegiance, hope, and labor. He is Lord of all powers. Refusing allegiance to the powers, the people of this Lord find themselves as "strangers and aliens" among those for whom the various "gods and lords" hold the keys to

18. Karl Barth, *The Christian Life: Church Dogmatics*, vol. 4/4: *Lecture Fragments*, trans. Geoffrey W. Bromiley (Grand Rapids: Eerdmans, 1981), 216 (emphasis original).

the cosmos and human well-being within it. Separating themselves from, indeed, rejecting the sacred objects, shrines, and centers of pseudodivine power, the followers of Christ become objects of suspicion, threats to the taken-for-granted sacred religio-political order, outcasts from the sacred society. Their strange worship of one deemed a shameful criminal alienates them from the sacred law and order. They now begin to look like atheists, unbelievers with respect to all of those powers that are deemed necessary to sustain "life as we know it."

To whom then shall the messianic people turn, when the real world effectively sustained by the angels, authorities, and powers turns against them and they are subjected to marginalization, disdain, persecution, suffering, even death? How shall these exiles sustain a good conscience in the face of all of that and not succumb again to the powers through carelessness, cowardice, compromise, or capitulation? Peter's answer is straightforward: despite their claims and appearances, none of those powers holds final sway, none has the last word, none is anything other than a finite creature subject to the authority of the infinite creator, and therefore none is worthy of our fear, our ultimate allegiance, or our final hope. All of them have been conquered, all "have been subordinated" (*hypotagentōn*) to Jesus Christ who alone reigns "at the right hand of God" over all of them (1 Pet. 3:22). As Paul also writes, "God put [his] power to work in Christ when he raised him from the dead and seated him at his right hand in the heavenly places, far above all rule and authority and power and dominion, and above every name that is named, not only in this age but also in the age to come. And he has put all things under his feet and has made him the head over all things for the church, which is his body, the fullness of him who fills all in all" (Eph. 1:20–23). The spiritual, cosmic, political sovereignty of the triune God alone evokes and sustains the free and joyful existence of the church, the body of Christ, the "ark" of God, constituted through baptism "in the name of the Father, the Son, and the Holy Spirit," which endures the storm of God's judgment upon "the present evil age."

1 PETER 4

What Was (1 Peter 4:1–6)

Messianic people are called to an exilic, diasporic existence in their natural home-lands. Those are not homelands defined by physical geography, but by who rules, and what the rules are, that is, by spiritual, political, and cultural forces and forms of life. We have just seen how all rule—spiritual, cosmic, political—has been made subject to Jesus Christ through his crucifixion, resurrection, and ascension to "the right hand of God" (3:22). Having come through faith and baptism to acknowl-edge and share in the rule of God and his Messiah, we become "homeless" in the homelands of "the rulers of this age." Far from accepting the messianic life revealed in Jesus, those rulers revealed their true intentions by conspiring to have "the Lord of glory" tortured, shamed, and killed on a cross—the powerful symbol of their "authority" rooted in greed, domination, and violence (1 Cor. 2:8). The people of God are not at home among the nations to the extent that they no longer live according to the rules that the powers of this age lay down for their subjects. While those powers "are doomed to perish" (2:6), as we have just seen (→3:18–22), they nonetheless continue to claim and receive the allegiance and service of nations, societies, and individuals, who in turn are also at times all too willing to oppose and oppress the servants of the Lord of glory. To embrace messianic life, Peter says, is to become an exile and therefore to anticipate suffering.

With a rather startling image, Peter calls upon messianic militants to "arm" themselves: "Since therefore Christ suffered in the flesh [*sarki*], arm yourselves [*hoplisasthe*] also with the same intention" (4:1). With an even more startling image, he calls upon them to arm themselves with the "thought" or "intent" (*en-noian*) of *suffering* even as Christ himself suffered. It is a strange warfare we are called to fight, and a strange weapon that is placed in our hands. If Peter, together with the whole New Testament, espouses a messianic pacifism, he never espouses passivism. Militant messianic warfare is necessary, whether engaged by the Messiah himself (Luke 11:21–22) or by his people, armed to the teeth with the messianic weapons of war (2 Cor. 6:7; 10:3–5; Eph. 6:11–17). "For since the Lord steps to the front in the fray, how much more should His servants rejoice to step forward" (Luther 1967: 118).

Our warfare is not against other flesh-and-blood humans, but against the powers of sin and death that seek to enslave us. For it is those powers that lay vigorous claim to fleshly bodies, demanding that we offer our bodies in the service of their persuasive promises of life and salvation. Empires and nation-states claim bodies for torturing, killing, and dying, promising peace and security; global markets claim them for producing and consuming, promising success and satisfaction; global entertainment industries claim them for competing and copulating, promising fame and fulfillment; technology and medicine claim them for engineering and experimenting, promising freedom and immortality. And not only our own (North American) bodies, but the innumerable host of human bodies around the world that are also co-opted, conscripted, or enslaved in service of those claims and promises. In the midst of this, how are we prepared instead to offer our bodies to God as "living sacrifices, holy and acceptable to God, which is our rational worship"? How do we resist being "conformed to [the false promises of] this world," being instead "transformed by the renewing of [our] minds" in Christ and made capable of discerning the will of God (Rom. 12:1–2 DH)? How do we embrace messianic homelessness in a world in which destructive powers define our citizenship and sin defends the borders? How are we "finished with sin"?

Peter says: "For whoever has suffered in the flesh [*sarki*] has finished with sin" (1 Pet. 4:1). In the very act of refusing to give our bodies to the rulers of this age, we arm ourselves with the intent to suffer. For where the powers of our age name and control the means and meanings of peace, justice, security, success, health, fulfillment, enjoyment, freedom, and so on, our refusal of those means and meanings sometimes sets us outside the bounds of the benefaction and protection of the powers and at odds with their aims. When we refuse to trade our messianic loyalty to the cross for the anthems and flags of the nations, suffering is nearby. When we refuse to assert our rights for justice and liberation in the face of domestic, social, and political inequities, suffering is nearby. When we refuse to entrust our economic well-being to "the wealth of nations" and "the invisible hand," suffering is nearby.[1] Peter does not have just any old suffering in mind

1. The early Christians' nonparticipation in the cultural, religious, and political practices prevalent in the cities of Asia Minor often led to suspicion, charges of treason, and persecution. "Pliny (*Ep.* 10.96) notes that where Christians were numerous, temples were deserted, sacred festivals were no longer observed, sacrificial animals were no longer purchased. Minucius Felix (*Octavian* 12) reports that Christians are chided for 'refraining from proper pleasure,' under which are included attending the theater, taking part in processions, public banquets, sacred games, and food and drink offered to the gods; Tertullian admits he does not participate in such festivals as Saturnalia and Liberalia, does not wear a garland on his head, does not attend games, and does not buy incense for sacrifice (*Apol.* 42), nor do Christians cover doorposts with laurels nor light lamps for festivals (*Apol.* 35). . . . The more the Christian communities consolidated themselves, the more

here, but specifically that suffering that comes about because loyalty to Christ and his way comes into conflict with a world that rules him out. We prepare for such suffering and accept it, if it should come, not because it is "good for us," but because it is ingredient in following Christ, which puts us into a nonviolent struggle with sin and the powers. Christ won the war against the sin, injustice, and violence of humankind by making himself subject to, putting himself at the mercy of, those enslaved by the powers of darkness. He did not fight the way the powers fight, by inciting human revolt, warfare, cruelty, violence, and death. Though human rulers sinned most grievously in torturing and crucifying him, he himself did not sin, but absorbed their sin and its effects "in the flesh." Thus sin comes to a dead end in his bodily suffering and death. When he is broken, he breaks sin's back. It is finished!

God's people are enlisted in Christ's battle with sin, and they defeat it the same way he did—by living the gospel of subordination and self-offering (2:13–3:7), by being armed with the intent to suffer "in the flesh" when they are either opposed or tempted by the strong forces of sin. By suffering, Christ did "the will of God" (*thelēmati theou*) and prevailed against "the lusts [*epithymiais*] of men," that is, against the political greed, fear, and grasping that nailed him to the cross (4:2). Christ enacts the will of God: what God does, he does; what he does, God does. We do God's will by trusting Christ and sharing in his death and resurrection through baptism, in which we receive the Holy Spirit who liberates us from destructive lusts. In "the time remaining" to us to live "in the flesh" (*en sarki biōsai chronon*; 4:2)—in "ordinary time" we might say—we learn to live for God through receiving and participating in Christ's life as the Holy Spirit works in us through the church and sacraments. Peter reminds us that our battle with sin and the powers of evil is always waged on the sites of our ordinary human flesh and our everyday human desires. Christ won that battle for us through suffering "in the flesh." Sharing in him, we are now prepared to do the same. As Paul wrote to the Colossians: "I am now rejoicing in my sufferings for your sake, and in my flesh [*en tē sarki mou*] I am completing what is lacking in Christ's afflictions for the sake of his body, that is, the church" (Col. 1:24).

> Any of the saints who has subjected his body to the violence of the persecutors for martyrdom has without doubt kept from sinning to the end of his life, as far as this is humanly possible. For how could anyone who is affixed to wood or surrounded by blows from stones or exposed to the nibbling of beasts or set on flames of fire or flayed by the excruciating lash or weakened by any other kind of punishment think about committing sin, about bodily desires; what could he turn over in his

---

they will have been obvious in their 'antisocial' behavior. That that process of consolidation was already under way when our letter [1 Peter] was written is evident precisely from 4:4" (Achtemeier 1996: 285n122).

mind except the will of God? He was compelled to desire this alone, when with the contest over he would receive the crown of life.[2]

Besides, Peter writes, we have already spent more than enough time, "lost time" (*ho parelēlythōs chronos*), sharing in the "the will of the Gentiles" (*to boulēma tōn ethnōn*) and doing what they like to do (1 Pet. 4:3). Goppelt notes that the will of the Gentiles "manifests itself especially in those forms of social and religious [and political] custom that become requirements through the power of habit and the pressure for conformity."[3] "Doing what the Gentiles like to do" (4:3) is not obviously sinful; it is just normal life. The social, political, cultural, and moral homeland or habitat in which we dwell is created and sustained in seemingly natural and naturalizing ways—we become conformed and accustomed to a form of life, to habits of believing, thinking, and doing that seem as ordinary and fitting as the clothes we don each morning. As "Gentiles" (even as Christian Gentiles) we learn to accept political, social, and personal sin as ingredient to the fabric of everyday life, necessary for the common good of our nation, part of "the way things are." Greed is normal. War is normal. Torture is normal.[4] Violence is normal. Execution of criminals is normal. Acquiring and using weapons "in self-defense" is normal. Abortion is normal. Sexual deviance, promiscuity, and pornography are normal. Divorce is normal. Disproportionate wealth is normal. Poverty is normal. Homelessness is normal. Opulence and indulgence are normal. Environmental destruction is normal. Nihilism is normal. All such things sooner or later merge into the even tone of "life as we know it." This is the real world. We are suspicious of apocalyptic alarmists (such as Peter) who, wild-eyed, interrupt the smooth flow of life and call attention to the brutality of the ordinary.

So, would the Gentiles even recognize themselves in the pejorative words and phrases that Peter uses to sum up their way of life: "licentiousness, passions, drunkenness, revels, carousing, and lawless idolatry" (4:3)? Would we have recognized ourselves in such words when we were at home in our unbelief?[5] Would

2. Bede the Venerable, *The Commentary on the Seven Catholic Epistles*, Cistercian Studies Series 82 (Kalamazoo, MI: Cistercian Publications, 1985), 107–8.
3. Leonhard Goppelt, *A Commentary on 1 Peter*, ed. Ferdinand Hahn, trans. John E. Alsup (Grand Rapids: Eerdmans, 1993), 284.
4. In the years following September 11, 2001, the torture of persons, whether through extraordinary rendition or at the notorious Guantánamo Bay detention unit, was increasingly normalized as necessary to homeland security in the United States and even in some measure in Canada. The case of Omar Khadr, a fifteen-year-old Canadian citizen wounded in Afghanistan, arrested as a terrorist and spy, detained without trial at Guantánamo Bay (for seven years at the time of writing), and tortured in many ways over the years in that facility and previously in a U.S. military hospital in Afghanistan, and now awaiting a military trial—all with no word of protest from the Canadian government—is only one of the atrocities committed by the United States and Canada. More disturbing, virtually no public protest has been raised in either nation. Illegal detainment and torture threaten to become part of the fabric of North American life.
5. We must not assume that this short list of sins covers all the sins of the Gentiles, or that all Gentiles are engaged in all of these vices. Calvin 1963: 300 writes: "Indeed we know that some

they—would we—not simply reckon such ways as the natural form of life, necessary (though perhaps sometimes unsavory) aspects of the exuberant pursuit of life, liberty, and happiness?

The burning light of the gospel reveals the truth of the matter: the habits and practices of the normal are the manifestations of "lost time," time given over to nothing. But Peter does not focus on the larger and more obvious structural sins of the Gentiles—war, injustice, slavery, and so on. Rather, he turns our attention to places where everyday greed, violence, and nihilism are hidden—and revealed—in the shear pointlessness of some of the Gentile habits and practices. "Licentiousness" (*aselgeiais*; 4:3) is an omnibus word meaning to give unrestricted rein to the fulfillment of desires, primarily but not only sexual. In late-capitalist liberal democratic societies we know this as "freedom." For example, in our time in North America we "freely" consume sexual experiences without regard for covenant, procreation, or social order. Achtemeier notes that "in classical Greek ἀσελγείαις meant 'brutality'" (1996: 282). Philosopher Slavoj Žižek exposes the brutality in "free" sex: "Here is the dark side of 1960s 'sexual liberation': the full commodification of sexuality. . . . The morning-after of the Sexual Revolution [is] the sterility of a universe dominated by the superego injunction to enjoy. . . . Sex is an absolute necessity, to renounce it is to wither away, so love cannot flourish without sex; simultaneously, however, love is impossible precisely because of sex; sex which 'proliferates as the epitome of late capitalism's dominance, has permanently stained human relationships as inevitable reproductions of the dehumanizing nature of liberal society; it has, essentially, ruined love.'"[6] "Passions" (*epithymiais*, "selfish cravings"; Elliott 2000: 722) are pursued with no *telos* beyond their own immediate gratification; war, abortion clinics, addiction programs, and fitness centers offer solutions to the problems we create. "Drunkenness, revels, carousing"—alcohol, food, bodies, goods, and property are consumed, cast off, or destroyed without regard for consequences or the common good. "Lawless idolatry"—not even the gods and religions represent a final nonconsumable good beyond all consumables that might limit and qualify what, how, and how much we consume. In late-capitalist liberal democracies religion (or spirituality) above

---

among the Gentiles lived honorably and without any taint of infamy. . . . Peter does not attribute these vices to the Gentiles with the purpose of charging every individual with all of them, but because we are by nature inclined to all these evils, and not only so, but that we are so much under the power of depravity that these fruits which he specifies necessarily proceed from an evil root. There is no one who has not within him the seed of all vices, but they do not germinate and grow up in every individual. Yet the contagion is so spread and scattered through the whole human race, that the whole community appears infected with innumerable evils, and no member is free or pure from the common corruption." Calvin rightly attunes us to the spiritual, personal, and social dimensions of our bondage to sin, while not suggesting that every Gentile sins equally egregiously.

6. Slavoj Žižek, *Violence: Six Sideways Reflections* (New York: Verso, 2008), 35–36. The embedded comment is from Nicholas Sabloff, "Of Filth and Frozen Dinners," *Common Review* (Winter 2007): 50–51. I was alerted to this Žižek quotation by Halden Doerge's blog, Inhabitatio Dei, Sept. 8, 2008.

all is a consumable item, designed to meet the need for a final meaning. Marketers and profiteers love religion. Everyone has a right to choose one (and its accompanying paraphernalia) and use it in the privacy of their own heart or home. All may freely choose their household gods (Jesus too), hold on to them, shape them at will according to self-defined needs, desires, and goals, so long as they make no claim upon our bodies as citizens in public space and time—so long, that is, as they do not press upon us any criterion of public accountability that might name an end beyond what we define, market, and consume. Liberal democratic governments establish departments of Homeland Security and invade and bomb other nations in order to protect or establish the right to consume gods at will ("religious freedom")—along with all other consumable items.

The gospel reveals that time spent "doing what the Gentiles like to do," consuming without end, is lost time, the time of death. It hears no call. It participates in nothing beyond itself. It is consumed and comes to an end in itself. It becomes merely *what was*, without remainder. "So with us; while we were minors, we were enslaved to the elemental spirits of the world" (Gal. 4:3). But the messianic community is called to live by another time, the time of Jesus Christ, the time of the end that comes, cancels, redeems, surrounds, sustains, and fulfills *chronos* in the flesh. "But when the fullness of time had come, God sent his Son" (4:4). In Christ the messianic community is delivered from consuming without end, from dead time, by first *being consumed* by an end beyond itself, by being interrupted, arrested, and taken up into God's judgment and reconciliation in the cross, and by *receiving* in Christ the living food and water that fills our hunger and thirst for God's righteousness. Thus delivered, the messianic community becomes a stranger to greed and violence.

The Gentiles, "thinking it strange/foreign" (*xenizontai*) that messianic people are not consumed by insatiable consuming, have no response except to make another empty gesture in lost time: they "blaspheme" and malign God's people (4:4). They ridicule, reduce, and seek to restrain this foreign element among them, or urge or impose conformity upon it, or else extradite it altogether. "It is no light temptation," writes Calvin, "when those among whom we live charge us that our life is out of conformity with that of mankind in general. A new world (they say) must be made for people like that, who differ from all mankind. So they accuse the children of God, as though they are trying to engineer a split in the world" (1963: 301). And indeed they are! But no engineering is necessary. The cross has already engineered the fundamental "split in the world." The "present evil age" has already been interrupted, invaded, defeated. A new world order is already coming upon us. For the messianic community, "the end of all things has drawn near" (4:7 DH). It is this end that draws them. It is to this end that they are accountable.

But the Gentiles too, despite themselves, are accountable to an end beyond themselves. While they spend their time in "excesses of dissipation" (4:4) without reference to a final transcendent end, there is nevertheless the inconsumable one "who stands ready to judge the living and the dead" (4:5). Merely thinking that there is nothing beyond human desires and their temporal fulfillment does not make it so. Those who consume without end, and blaspheme those who do not, will not escape the final judgment. They too must give an account, in the end, *to* an end, which is God himself, the final good, who measures our economies of desiring and consuming in the light of his own economy of self-emptying, servanthood, and sacrifice in Jesus Christ. God's judgment even of the Gentiles is always by the criterion of the gospel (cf. 4:17). But Gentiles render their malignant judgments against God's people because they judge "according to [their own] human standards" (*kata anthrōpous*; following Achtemeier 1996: 287–88 and Elliott 2000: 736–37).[7] Indeed, some of God's people have died under such human judgment and perhaps even because of persecution and martyrdom. Are those dead believers, then, not proof to the Gentiles, and perhaps even to some living believers, that the world's judgment has won the day, that indeed the messianic intention—to suffer in the flesh as Christ did (4:1) rather than to continue with the Gentiles in their passions, excesses, brutality, and idolatry—itself amounts to "lost time"? The judgment of the Gentiles upon those believers seems to be right: they were fools. They gave up the pleasures of this world for nothing. And now they are dead.

But Peter reminds us that "good news" (*euēngelisthē*) was in fact preached even to these now dead believers (4:6). God's people, living and dead, can trust the judge of all because, as Peter has already said, he "judges justly" (2:23). The martyrs' faith in the gospel and their trust in God are not pointless or foolish. To be sure, while they were alive "in the flesh" they were judged and condemned by the same distorted human standards (*kata anthrōpous*) that crucified the Lord of glory. But now, beyond death, having been judged justly according to God's standards (*kata theon*), they are alive in the Spirit, sharing already in God's own glorious "eternal life" (*zōsi . . . pneumati*; 4:6). Those who have died in Christ are vindicated in the justice of God.[8] This is the good news that sustains the hope of all who have armed themselves with the intent to suffer and enables them to live faithfully, even joyfully, in the face of persecution and death.

For "the elect exiles of the Diaspora" (1:1) still living among unbelieving and sometimes hostile nations, there are two important implications here. First, God's just judgment is precisely the basis of their hope as they take up the difficult task

---

7. "The phrases *kata anthrōpous . . . kata theon* describe contrary standards of reckoning, that of the Gentiles versus that of God. . . . The phrase *kata anthrōpous* emphasizes that the deceased Christians were faulted by the Gentiles according to Gentile standards (and, by implication of what follows, not according to God's standards)" (Elliott 2000: 737).

8. Following Achtemeier, Elliott, Jobes, Senior, and others, I do not take 4:6 (or 3:19–20) as an account of Christ's descent to the realm of the dead to preach the gospel to the dead. For a defense of that reading see, e.g., Green 2007: 118–34. See also Jared Wicks, "Christ's Saving Descent to the Dead: Early Witnesses from Ignatius of Antioch to Origen," *Pro ecclesia* 17, no. 3 (2008): 281–309, who shows how the doctrine of the descent to the dead was worked out in early Christian theology.

of often living at odds with a wider economy, culture, and politics characterized by dissipation, idolatry, and death. They may fully entrust their vulnerable exilic lives in Christ to God. Second, the same God who renders just judgment upon his own people, for life, will also justly judge the Gentiles who continue in their deadly ways and sometimes deal out death to God's people. God's justice will surely be done. Therefore, God's people may, indeed must, leave the judgment of the Gentiles to God (cf. Rom. 12:19–21). It is not their task to see that God's justice is done upon their persecutors. Rather, it is their task, as Peter says (1 Pet. 4:1), to "arm [themselves] . . . with the intention" of suffering in the flesh, as Christ himself did. That is, they have only the one undivided task: to witness among the Gentiles with their own lives, and perhaps deaths, to the cruciform way, truth, and life of Jesus Christ.

What Is (1 Peter 4:7–11)

We must clarify the meaning of *telos* ("end, goal") in 4:7: "For the end of all things has drawn near" (*pantōn de to telos ēngiken*) (DH). First, it is not in any significant sense simply the final point in the cosmic or historical temporal sequence. It is not the end as midnight is the end of a twenty-four-hour day, nor is it near in the sense that midnight is near to 11:59 PM. It is not the next or last thing, but the *goal* of all things, a goal that subsumes the temporal but cannot be summed up by it. Second, the *telos* here is not immanent in or intrinsic to the being of all things, something given a priori and awaiting discovery and realization. It is not a possession or potential. It is *other*; it is fundamentally *beyond*; it is present in its *coming*. Third, the *telos* of all things does not merely beckon from beyond and await our approach; it *draws near*; it *gives itself* as an end; it *transforms* the present. It gives itself in *apokalypsis*, which is not only God's self-revelation, but also his invasion, liberation, and transformation of all things. The *telos* of all things ("the end of times"; 1:20 DH) of which Peter writes has *already* been revealed in the death and resurrection of Christ, and it is "*ready to be* revealed in the last time" (1:5); it is here and it is coming. The crucifixion of Christ spells the end of all purely immanent *teloi* ("ends")—Paul calls them "the elemental spirits of this world" (*ta stoicheia tou kosmou*; Gal. 4:3)—to which we were formerly enslaved. The resurrection of Christ is the radically other *telos*, the eternal life of the triune God that has already invaded the realm of sin and death with the promise of new life. In the coming of the Holy Spirit upon the church, the end is already given as a "foretaste"; in the church's calling upon "Abba, Father," the end is already given in prayer; in the Eucharist the end is already enacted and proclaimed. The drawing near of the triune end constitutes the messianic community by interrupting and unsettling the stable *chronos* and *kosmos* of Jews and Gentiles and creating them as the new humanity taken up into the gravitational orbit of the divine life.

The fullness of "time" (*kairos*) comes upon the people of God; a new "creation" (*ktisis*) is on the way.[9]

Dwelling now in the nearness of the end, the messianic community is called to "be sober minded" (*sōphronēsate*) and "be vigilant" (*nēpsate*) (1 Pet. 4:7). Peter calls us to this heightened state of awareness because there is always the temptation to fall back again into the life of the Gentiles, which, as we have seen, is characterized by a kind of sleepwalking in lost time, a steady state of intoxication with the normal that renders us incapable of assessing the danger that the normal poses and the damage that it does. "Elect exiles of the Diaspora" (1:1) often feel the strong pull of assimilation back into the citizenship of the normal. Paul saw this tendency among the Galatians: "Formerly, when you did not know God, you were enslaved to beings that by nature are not gods. Now, however, that you have come to know God, or rather to be known by God, how can you turn back again to the weak and beggarly elemental spirits [*stoicheia*]? How can you want to be enslaved again" (Gal. 4:8–9; cf. 4:3). The *stoicheia* are the core principles of the normal, the assumed religious, social, economic, and political sureties that give order and stability to life. The way of the cross is disruptive. Holiness is difficult. But that is why Peter immediately sets the messianic life within the greater gravitational force of "the end of all things" that "has drawn near." Messianic faithfulness is rendered possible by the power of the end. We are called not so much to attend critically to the dead time from which we have been delivered, as to be vigilantly aware and alert to the time of the end to which we have been called—an end that in any case is not far off, but has drawn near, so near we can taste it in bread and wine. As Paul writes, "But you, beloved, are not in darkness, for that day [of the Lord] to surprise you like a thief; for you are all children of light and children of the day; we are not of the night or of darkness. So then let us not fall asleep as others do, but let us keep awake and be sober; for those who sleep sleep at night, and those who are drunk get drunk at night. But since we belong to the day, let us be sober" (1 Thess. 5:4–7).[10] Jesus says, "Stay awake and pray that you may not come into the time of trial; the spirit is willing, but the flesh is weak" (Matt. 26:41). To be sober minded and vigilant is thus to be constantly "in prayer(s)" (*eis proseuchas*; 1 Pet. 4:7), that is, to be continually calling upon the Father who has drawn near to us in the Son and Holy Spirit, asking that he make his kingdom come and his will be done on earth as it is in heaven.

9. Oecumenius (sixth century) displays a fine sense for this text: "The end of all things means their completion and consummation. Perhaps this means that the end of all the prophecies is near, for that refers to Christ who is in himself the consummation of all things. This is very different from Epicurus, who said that pleasure is the end of all things, or other Greeks, who said the end is wisdom or contemplation or virtue" (from *Commentary on 1 Peter*, quoted in Bray 2000: 116). Oecumenius's contrast of the gospel *telos* with the understandings of "other Greeks" clarifies that the *telos* of which Peter writes is not in the first place something for which we strive, but something that comes to us.

10. Most commentators also note the close thematic similarity between 1 Pet. 4:7–11 and Rom. 12.

"The end of all things has drawn near" is, further, the reality that generates and sustains the life of the messianic community in its exile. Freed from the deadly power of Gentile normal (4:3), God's people are graciously given time to shape a new form of social, political, and economic life conformed to the life of Jesus Christ. Therefore the core and chief characteristic of the community ("above all," *pro pantōn*) is "constant love [*agapēn*] for one another" (4:8).[11] By contrast to the kind of consuming and exploiting love that we once knew and practiced among the Gentiles, this is a love that always honors and seeks the good of the other. In fact, this is a "love [that] covers a multitude of sins" (*agapē kalyptei plēthos hamartiōn*; 4:8). Going beyond the kind of love that sees the good in others, this love unflinchingly acknowledges the sins of others and yet, absorbing the cost, "covers" those sins over and over again ("seventy times seven"; Matt. 18:21–22 NRSV margin) with grace and forgiveness, the same grace and forgiveness with which one's own sins are covered by the sacrifice of Jesus Christ, who "bore our sins in his body on the cross" (1 Pet. 2:24). Such radical, sin-covering love must be the rule of the community of Christ: "Love is patient; love is kind; love is not envious or boastful or arrogant or rude. It does not insist on its own way; it is not irritable or resentful; it does not rejoice in wrongdoing, but rejoices in the truth. It bears all things, believes all things, hopes all things, endures all things" (1 Cor. 13:4–7). Paul concludes his hymn in praise of love with the words: "Love never ends." Love never ends, because love—the triune love that God himself both is and gives—*love itself is the end of all things*. The end of all things draws near to the messianic community, indeed, *comes* among it, in the self-offering, sin-covering love of Christ for the church and of its members for one another. In this the kingdom of the Father comes, and his will is done on earth as in heaven.

The messianic community is also characterized by "hospitality" (*philoxenoi*, "friendship with strangers"; 1 Pet. 4:9). Mutual welcome and friendship in the messianic community, in particular toward the "strangers" (*xenoi*) among God's people, is crucial in creating and sustaining the new political reality of the church. Such hospitality is never abstract: it is enacted concretely in the sharing of food and home "without complaining," as Peter says. Hospitality is the practice of open hearts, open homes, and open hands. It moves beyond fear to openness and the risk of being used and abused, or worse. It therefore requires and enacts a fundamental trust in God for protection and provision. Peace takes shape in the messianic body politic when *philoxenoi* overcomes xenophobia. The fear of the stranger is one of the chief causes of violence and war in the world. When the members of the messianic community show hospitality to the strangers in their midst, they in some small measure enact among themselves the coming peace of God and bear witness to that peace as they dwell among the nations.

11. Achtemeier 1996: 294 notes that the "phrase with which this verse [4:8] begins (πρὸ πάντων) reflects the opening word of v. 7 (πάντων) in what is probably a rhetorical play on words: since the end of *all things* is at hand . . . one should, *above all* else, cultivate love within the Christian community" (emphasis original).

So near is the end among the people of God that it generates an economy of "grace" (*charitas*) and "gift" (*charisma*) (4:10). Peter is explicit that this is the fundamental economic character of the messianic community: the members of the community are each to understand themselves as "economic stewards" (*oikonomoi*) of "the manifold grace of God," entrusted with the task of wisely administering (*diakonountes*) the gifts that they have received. This is a radical departure from the greed, hoarding, and consuming that characterizes the economy of scarcity among "the Gentiles" and that is so often the root cause of envy, theft, and violence—as well as condescending benevolence—that destroys human communities. God's economy is one of abundance. His grace is always "superabounding" to sinful beggars (Rom. 5), his riches are always inexhaustibly being given, his giving is never-ending. When we acknowledge that everything we have is a gift given from "the manifold grace of God," and is always more than enough, we are liberated from the greed that once consumed us and are instead employed as faithful stewards in "the eschatological economy" of God's coming kingdom.[12] The great model of such an economy is given for the church's contemplation and corresponding practice in the church of Jerusalem (Acts 2:41–47; 4:32–25).

"The end of all things has drawn near." So near is the end—so near and attractive and effective is the reign and power of God—that messianic speaking and serving are already participating in the life of God. "If anyone speaks, let it be as though it were the very oracles of God [*hōs logia theou*]; if anyone administers [*diakonei*], let it be as by the strength that God supplies" (1 Pet. 4:11 DH). The power of the end takes hold of the messianic people, such that their life is now taken up into God's life, their speaking into God's speaking, their working into God's working. This is indeed the form of life in the messianic age, the end-time reality that comes upon the people of God when they are fully given over to their end, caught up by and into the love of the Father, Son, and Holy Spirit. Now, when one member speaks, the others hear God speaking. Now, when one member administers, the others receive the ministry of God.[13]

In the messianic community that Peter envisages in 4:7–11, the glory of God begins to shine through in "all things" (*en pasin*), for the whole life of the community is now clearly displaying the reign of Jesus the Messiah in its midst. Christ himself is taking social, economic, and political form among his people, in the midst of the nations—and Christ himself is the very form and glory of God. The

---

12. The phrase "the eschatological economy" is borrowed from Douglas H. Knight, *The Eschatological Economy: Time and the Hospitality of God* (Grand Rapids: Eerdmans, 2006). God's economy of abundance is explored in Frances Young and David Ford, *Meaning and Truth in 2 Corinthians* (Grand Rapids: Eerdmans, 1987), 166–85; and William T. Cavanaugh, *Being Consumed: Economics and Christian Desire* (Grand Rapids: Eerdmans, 2008). For an account of economy and stewardship that resonates most deeply with 1 Peter, Kelly S. Johnson's *The Fear of Beggars: Stewardship and Poverty in Christian Ethics* (Grand Rapids: Eerdmans, 2007) is essential reading. Luther 1967: 123–24, unfortunately, spiritualizes this text and thereby leaves the existing economy intact.

13. Luther and Calvin are inclined to apply 4:11 to the preaching, teaching, and diaconal offices of the church. While it surely applies there, Peter does not limit his instruction to specific offices.

revelation of God's glory and power through the Messiah and *in his people* evokes a hymn of doxology—which is itself the primary human act constituting the people of God: "To him belong the glory and the power forever and ever. Amen."

What Is to Come (1 Peter 4:12–19)

It is no accident that, immediately following his description of the life of the messianic community and the declaration that all glory and power belong to Jesus Christ, Peter returns to the conflict between this community and the world around it. The "beloved" (*agapētoi*; 4:12) messianic community has been chosen by God, drawn out from the Gentile nations and their lawless idolatry, greedy economics, violent politics, and dissolute way of life, and created anew to declare by their life together and their doxological praise that the true order of things comes into being through the worship of God and Jesus the Messiah. Should there be any surprise then (*mē xenizesthe*, "do not think it strange" [DH]) at the "fiery ordeal" that now befalls them at the hands of their neighbors and fellow citizens? It is not "a strange thing" (*xenou*) that is happening to them. Suspicion, ridicule, perhaps persecution, may become *the new normal* for those who have been estranged (cf. *xenizontai* in 4:4) from the wider sociopolitical order because of their obedience to and imitation of Jesus. To take up the cruciform way of the Messiah, to live by the gospel, is already to enter into the "fiery ordeal," the purifying trial (*pyrōsei pros peirasmon hymin*; 4:12) of the final judgment, which for "the household of God" begins now (4:17). It is to enter with Jesus into the garden of Gethsemane and to stay awake with him as he confronts the final messianic temptation to rise up in violent revolt against the enemies of his people. It is to endure with him the dire consequences of refusing that temptation—rejection by his own people, the shame of ridicule, and even the pain of execution. It is no wonder that Jesus himself instructs us to pray, "Do not bring us to the time of trial" (Luke 11:4), because the decision to keep following him is a difficult one, and the question whether we will even endure the trial cannot be answered in advance. Peter himself denied Jesus in the time of trial. So we must also pray, "Deliver us from the evil one," and "Forgive us our sins."

Nevertheless, Peter does not depict the trial of God's people as merely a time of temptation, terror, and torment. Exactly the contrary! "Rejoice!" "Be glad!" he says (1 Pet. 4:13), echoing Jesus's words: "Blessed are you when people revile you and persecute you and utter all kinds of evil against you falsely on my account. Rejoice and be glad, for your reward is great in heaven, for in the same way they persecuted the prophets who were before you" (Matt. 5:11–12).[14] But how is that different from sheer masochism? Do Christians enjoy suffering? Do they seek it

14. Green 2007: 156 notes a number of significant verbal connections between Jesus's beatitude in Matt. 5:10–12 and 1 Pet. 4:12–19.

out with some warped notion of suffering's pleasure or good purpose? Is it "good for them"? Everything depends on the conditional clause: "insofar as you share in the sufferings of Christ" (1 Pet. 4:13). "The joy in suffering discussed here is … unrelated to anything inherent in suffering as such: that it builds character, makes one sensitive to others, or provides an uplifting example" (Achtemeier 1996: 307). Rather, messianic joy in suffering comes about because we have entered into and now share in the very truth of life—the Messiah himself, who is nonetheless opposed by the powers of falsehood. Joy in suffering comes about because we have been taken up into God's way of making things right, which is nevertheless opposed by the powers of injustice. Participation in Christ, sharing even now in the coming kingdom of truth and justice, is at one and the same time the source of messianic joy, because the kingdom is so near and palpable, and is also the reason why God's people may suffer, because there are those who vigorously and often violently oppose the witnesses of the kingdom.

But more, God's people may be joyful in suffering with the Messiah because they are anticipating the revelation of the Messiah's glory: "So that you may also be glad and shout for joy when his glory is revealed [*en tē apokalypsei tēs doxēs autou*]" (4:13). That coming *apokalypsis* already shines glorious light on the present darkness, such that that light becomes the greater reality in which we live and, if necessary, endure suffering. Paul makes the same point in Rom. 8:18: "I consider that the sufferings of this present time are not worth comparing with the glory about to be revealed to us." At the same time, the glory of the *apokalypsis* of Christ is not something simply to be awaited, but also something that rests upon those Christians who suffer in Christ now. In them, or upon them, God's blessing and glory has already come in the Holy Spirit. "If you are reviled for the name of Christ, you are blessed, because the spirit of glory, which is the Spirit of God [*to tēs doxēs kai to tou theou pneuma*], is resting on you" (1 Pet. 4:14). According to the Gospel of John, the hour of Jesus's trial and crucifixion is simultaneously the hour in which he is glorified in the world and in which he glorifies God (John 13:31–32; 17:1–5). He does not await the resurrection for his glory to be manifest. His glory *is* his obedience through trial to the very end. The glory that Christ manifests in his resurrection is inseparable from the glory that he manifests in the crucifixion; thus the wounds of crucifixion remain visible and touchable even in his glorious resurrected body. We might also note that when Stephen is stoned to death (Acts 7:54–60) he is at that very moment filled with the Holy Spirit, the promised eschatological blessing, and given a vision of the glory of God. The point is this: God's blessing and glory—God's Holy Spirit—comes in special measure upon the followers of Christ in the moment of their most radical obedience, when they endure the trials of ridicule, suffering, and even martyrdom in the name of Christ. Such sufferings are not the miserable means to a distant end of glory (which nevertheless will come); they are themselves the *very site of God's glory* manifest in the present. Therefore, we may take joy even in times of messianic trial, since these themselves are moments when the glorious reality of God is also clearly manifested to us and through us.

> She [the church] was white before in the works of the brethren; now she has become purple [i.e., royal] in the blood of the martyrs. Among her flowers are wanting neither roses nor lilies. Now let each one strive for the largest dignity of either honor. Let them receive crowns, either white, as of labors, or purple, as of suffering. In the heavenly camp both peace and strife have their own flowers, with which the soldier of Christ may be crowned for glory.[15]

Everything depends upon the trial and suffering being truly *messianic*, that is, occurring for the reason that the Messiah himself was tried, suffered, and was executed. There are conceivably many nonmessianic reasons to be reviled, put on trial, and perhaps executed. Peter names a few: for being "a murderer, a thief, a criminal, or even . . . a mischief maker" (4:15). Such reasons for incurring suffering do not count as messianic, and there is no glory in them. Three were crucified on Golgotha; only one was the Messiah. As Peter has already said (2:14), when people suffer because they murder, steal, commit crimes, or otherwise interfere in the lives of others, they may well be suffering punishment from God, meted out through the instrumentality of the governing authorities. Our suffering is messianic—we are martyrs, witnesses—when we are utterly loyal to Jesus Christ the crucified Lord, when we refuse to worship the gods and powers of this world, including their earthly agents, refuse to participate in the ordinary brutality of the normal or the extraordinary brutality of war, refuse to participate in the empty practices and pleasures of lost time (4:3–4). To the wider world we appear as dangerous sectarians and engender suspicion and fear—and name-calling.

"But if any one [suffers] as a Christian [*christianos*, a 'messianic'], let that one not be ashamed, but let him glorify God by that name" (4:16 DH). In Peter's time there was no glory in being called a *christianos*. It was a name likely invented by outsiders (cf. Acts 11:26; 26:28) to label the followers of the crucified Jew, Jesus, who called him *ho christos* ("the Messiah"). Because this Jew was crucified, *christianos* was also a name that bore the reproach of his well-known shameful form of public execution. The ridiculousness of worshiping and serving a crucified Messiah was worthy of the ridicule of name-calling. The shame was in the name, and the name itself was a means of segregating and derogating the early Jesus movement. Just to be labeled with it was to suffer social and perhaps political opprobrium.[16]

15. Cyprian, *Epistle* 8, quoted in Tripp York, *The Purple Crown: The Politics of Martyrdom* (Scottdale, PA: Herald, 2007), 47.

16. Some years after Peter's letter the Roman governor Pliny wrote these words: "I have never been present at an examination of Christians. Consequently I do not know the nature or the extent of the punishments usually meted out to them, nor the grounds for starting an investigation and how far it should be pressed. Nor am I at all sure . . . whether a pardon ought to be granted to anyone retracting his beliefs, or if he has once professed Christianity, he shall gain nothing by renouncing it; and whether it is the mere name of Christian which is punishable, even if innocent of crime, or

It makes sense that the early Christians would have been ashamed of it. But Peter finds here another opportunity to "glorify God," precisely because the name itself immediately identifies those who are labeled with it with the one from whom the name is derived. The name itself clarifies the witness of those who bear it—they are those whose way and truth and life are given fundamental shape and character by the one who was crucified. Peter and the other apostles, we read in Acts 5:40–41, "rejoiced" after a flogging because "they were considered worthy to suffer dishonor for the sake of the name [of Jesus]." Not only Christians themselves, but everyone around them, should expect that their lives will conform and testify to the one by whose name they are now being called, the crucified Christ.

Name-calling is but one aspect of the inauguration of the "time [*kairos*] . . . of judgment [*krima*]" that "begin[s] with the household of God" (1 Pet. 4:17). The trial of the witnesses is not something that takes place only in the future, before the throne of God. It is also already underway through the ridicule, social exclusion, and other kinds of harm that many of God's people among the nations experience. It is also already underway through the softer temptations that many more of God's people experience, to fall asleep, to give up the difficult way, to blend in smoothly again into the bland and brutal ordinary, to return again to the principles and powers that make enslaved life look safe, normal, even desirable (cf. Exod. 14:11–12; 16:3). "Elect exiles of the Diaspora" may all too easily return home and become again natural citizens of the nations and cultures out of which they were chosen and called to be God's royal priesthood and holy nation. The roads of return are many, and nicely paved; the path of the Messiah is narrow and difficult. There is never a moment when the church is not in the time of eschatological judgment, never a moment when it is not called and directed to its true end in Christ, in which it is constituted in its being as "elect exiles of the Diaspora." There is never a moment in which the church, as it proves faithful in the face of temptation or persecution, has not already both received and reflected the Spirit of glory, which is the Spirit of God.

Peter's words about suffering and judgment in this chapter are not written to frighten the church with the prospect of its possible failure and damnation, but to impress upon the church the gravity of today, the day in which it must "obey the gospel of God" (1 Pet. 4:17), or find itself aligned with those who do not. For all are judged finally by the same standard, the same criterion of the good—the faithful life, crucifixion, and vindication of the Messiah Jesus. This "gospel of

---

rather the crimes associated with the name. For the moment this is the line I have taken with all persons brought before me on the charge of being Christians. I have asked them in person if they are Christians, and if they admit it, I repeat the question a second and third time, with a warning of the punishment awaiting them. If they persist, I order them to be led away for execution; for, whatever the nature of their admission, I am convinced that their stubbornness and unshakeable obstinacy ought not to go unpunished" (Pliny, *Letters* 10.96, quoted in David L. Bartlett, "The First Letter of Peter: Introduction, Commentary, and Reflections," in *The New Interpreter's Bible*, ed. Leander E. Keck [Nashville: Abingdon, 1998], 12.311).

God" is the end of all things that has drawn near; it is the criterion of judgment for the nations as well as for the people of God. Therefore everything depends for the nations upon having in their midst a visible sign of the messianic end in the life of God's people, which is not only exilic, but also diasporic, sown abroad for the sake of the nations. The salvation or destruction of the nations depends upon it. Thus Peter writes that "the time has come for judgment to begin with the household of God," so that the church's witness might be purified through suffering, not only for its own sake, but also for the sake of those who are now disobedient. "If it [i.e., God's judgment according to Christ] begins with us, what will be the end [*telos*] for those who do not obey the gospel of God?" The Gentiles are not without hope, but it is a very difficult hope indeed, since they have already set themselves against the witnesses of the Messiah. Will they believe and obey that gospel that is for them, "the ungodly and the sinners," just as it is for us (4:18)? "For while we were still weak, at the right time Christ died for the ungodly. . . . God proves his love for us in that while we were still sinners Christ died for us" (Rom. 5:6, 8).

"It is hard for the righteous to be saved" (1 Pet. 4:18). Will the household of God endure the "fiery ordeal"? Or will they be overwhelmed in the test of messianic suffering? That apocalyptic question confronts the church in every moment of its vulnerable existence as "elect exiles of the Diaspora." In every moment there is only one way forward: the righteous will be saved in the trial only by God's grace through faith and obedience. As Peter says, "let those suffering in accordance with God's will entrust themselves to a faithful Creator, while continuing to do good" (4:19). The way of the Messiah, while difficult, is not complicated: he entrusted himself to "a faithful Creator" and set out on the road from Nazareth to Jerusalem where, as he well knew, violent opposition and execution awaited him. He continued to do good in the midst of enmity and suffering. He himself is the very form and content of the good. He does the good that we must do. We are called to do the good in him and through him.

1 PETER 5

Messianic Leadership (1 Peter 5:1–5)

"The time has come for judgment to begin with the household of God" (4:17), in order that God's people might be purified of all that contradicts the gospel and mars its witness among the nations. Does the common life and order of the messianic community correspond to and reflect the cruciform life and order of the Messiah? Or do its internal affairs more nearly mirror the envy, competition, and coercion of the wider Gentile society? The apostle Paul was troubled that the latter was prevalently the case in the church of God in Corinth and wrote his letter, 1 Corinthians, to try to correct the situation. Peter writes this section of his letter to warn against it. For the messianic community cannot "embody one set of standards outside the community (so that we can make sense of our marginal status in a world set against us) only to adopt a different set of standards inside the community (so that we can marginalize other believers)" (Green 2007: 163).

Christ did not leave the church without leaders to teach, guide, and protect it. In fact, Peter himself receives a very particular commissioning from the risen Christ to "tend" and "feed" the flock of Christ (John 21:15–17), taking up the shepherding work of Christ himself (10:1–18). Leadership is graciously given by the Holy Spirit to guide and guard the church. In Paul's final speech to the elders of the church in Ephesus (Acts 20:17–35) he instructs them to "keep watch over yourselves and over all the flock [*poimniō*], of which the Holy Spirit has made you overseers [*episkopous*], to shepherd [*poimainein*] the church of God that he obtained with the blood of his own Son. I know that after I have gone, savage wolves will come in among you, not sparing the flock" (20:28–29). The New Testament recognizes both informal charismatic leadership and more formally ordered leadership—we read of elders, bishops, and deacons in 1 Tim. 3 and Titus 1. Leadership can be a contentious issue in the church, with great potential for the abuse of prerogative and power. With good reason there is often considerable suspicion about church leadership, especially if it takes official or hierarchical form. But the point is not that there should not be leaders in the church, or that its leadership must be informal or even nonhierarchical in structure. It is rather that leadership in the messianic community must be conducted according to the pattern of the Messiah's leadership.

Therefore Peter writes to "exhort" (*parakalō*; 1 Pet. 5:1) his fellow elders on the manner of their leadership. He describes his authority to do so in three ways: he is a coelder with other elders, he is a "witness" of Christ's sufferings, and he is a "partaker" (*koinōnos*) in "the glory about to be revealed."

Writing now in the first person (5:1), Peter addresses the "elders" (*presbyterous*) of the churches as a "coelder" (*sympresbyteros*), a sharer in the common ministry of shepherding and overseeing (*episkopountes*; 5:2).[1] If there is any sense in which Peter might be "first" among the leaders of the churches, he does not indicate it here; rather, he locates himself among them as a partner.[2] As Calvin notes, "If he had the right of primacy he would have claimed it, and this would have been most suitable on the present occasion, but although he was an apostle, he knew that authority over his colleagues was by no means delegated to him, but that on the contrary he was joined with the others in the sharing of the same office" (1963: 315).[3] Whether "office" is the right word, or whether *presbyteros* is not yet in Peter's time a formal office as such (cf. Achtemeier 1996: 323 and Elliott 2000: 813–16), it is church leaders that Peter addresses, and he calls them in particular, in all times and places, and whether in formal offices or not, to a way of "shepherding" the "flock" (5:2) that reflects the character and manner of leadership of the "chief shepherd" (*archipoimenos*; 5:4), Jesus Christ.

It is no accident, then, that Peter further roots his authority in his being a "witness" (*martys*) of Christ's sufferings (5:1). *Martys* has more than one meaning here. It surely means that Peter was a witness of the events leading up to the crucifixion of Christ—although in the end he was able to follow Jesus only "at a distance" (Mark 14:54), and when the shepherd was stricken, Peter too was scattered with the rest of the sheep (14:27). The Gospels nowhere indicate that Peter witnessed the crucifixion itself. But Peter became a *martys* of Christ's sufferings

1. The word *episkopountes*—cf. *episkopos* ("overseer"), from which the word "bishop" is derived—has a checkered textual history in this verse, with it being absent from some manuscripts. Nevertheless, the weight of textual criticism is on the side of its inclusion (Achtemeier 1996: 320; Elliott 2000: 824n665).

2. *Sympresbyteros* ("coelder") is unique to Peter, among all Greek literature to his time (Elliott 2000: 816–17); clearly Peter is taking pains to emphasize his collegiality among the elders.

3. See also Luther 1967: 133: "And here St. Peter humbles himself. He does not say that he is an overlord, although he could have done so, since he was an apostle of Christ. He calls himself not only a fellow elder but also 'a witness of the sufferings of Christ.' It is as if he were saying: I not only preach, but I am also one of the Christians who must suffer. In this way he points out that where there are Christians, they must suffer and be persecuted. This is a true apostle. If there were a pope or a bishop of this kind today who also bore this title, we would be glad to kiss his feet." Of course, both before and after Luther there were many such popes and bishops.

in another, more difficult sense: he himself suffered for the name of Christ as he boldly testified (i.e., "witnessed") to Christ's crucifixion and resurrection in his preaching (Acts 5:40–41; 12:3–4). Finally, according to Jesus's prophecy, Peter was bound and led to execution, suffering "the kind of death by which he would glorify God" (John 21:19)—that is, probably (according to tradition), crucifixion. Peter did, and would ultimately, rightly bear the name of *martys* not only because he faithfully preached the sufferings of Christ, but also because he was "considered worthy to suffer dishonor for the sake of the name" of Jesus (Acts 5:41). He is able to instruct the elders in the way of messianic leadership because he himself bears the marks of the Messiah in his own body. His own leadership is cruciform.

Further, Peter says he is a "partaker" (*koinōnos*) in "the glory about to be revealed" (*tēs mellousēs apokalyptesthai doxēs*; 1 Pet. 5:1). This clause too bears more than one meaning. Surely it must mean, as we read in 4:13–14, that Peter participates in "the spirit of glory, which is the Spirit of God" because he has been "reviled for the name of Christ." That is, his being a witness to Christ's sufferings and a partaker in the coming glory in this sense coincide; they are one and the same thing. He himself is able to rejoice in his sufferings because of that, and he urges us to do the same. In addition, when we receive the Holy Spirit of glory in our suffering, we are granted therein a foretaste of the final glory that is the hope of all the saints—sharing fully in the eternal life and light of the Holy Trinity. That glory is "about to be apocalypsed," but it is so near when God's people suffer that it is already palpable; we are already "participants" (*koinōnos*) in it, and it is the reality for which we and all creation groan together in the Spirit—a symphony of yearning for the final revelation of God's glory (Rom. 8:17–27).[4] There is perhaps still another dimension to Peter's claim that he is a sharer of the glory about to be revealed. Bede intriguingly takes this clause to refer to the transfiguration and the resurrection appearances: "When he saw the heavenly glory of His countenance on the holy mountain with James and John, or when he saw the power of His resurrection and ascension with the other disciples who were present."[5] Peter also recalls the transfiguration in →2 Pet. 1:16–18 and there emphasizes that that event was the apocalypse of Christ in his ultimate divine glory, as it will be revealed to all when he comes again. Peter, James, and John received at the transfiguration an anticipatory participation in Christ's glory—one that they had great difficulty coping with: they hid their faces.

Thus drawing his fellow elders into the truth and authority of his own extraordinary life in the Messiah, Peter instructs them in the way of messianic leadership. They are "to tend [*poimanate*, 'shepherd'] the flock [*poimnion*] of God that is in [their] charge" (5:2). In their shepherding, church leaders are sharing in the very work of God, the great shepherd of the flock of Israel (Ps. 80:1). Isaiah writes

4. The logic of suffering and glory in Rom. 8:17–18 is very close to Peter's, and Paul's words in 8:18—*tēn mellousan doxan apokalypsthēnai*—are almost identical to 1 Pet. 5:1.
5. Bede the Venerable, *The Commentary on the Seven Catholic Epistles*, Cistercian Studies Series 82 (Kalamazoo, MI: Cistercian Publications, 1985), 114.

that God "will feed his flock like a shepherd; he will gather the lambs in his arms, and carry them in his bosom, and gently lead the mother sheep" (Isa. 40:11). The psalmist declares that "the LORD is my shepherd" (Ps. 23:1). When the leaders of Israel fail to shepherd God's people, but rather scatter and destroy them, God himself takes up the work of the shepherd and gathers his people, the sheep, back into the fold, where they need no longer fear or be dismayed (Jer. 23:1–4). That is what Jesus also does when he declares, "I am the good shepherd" (John 10:11, 14; cf. Heb. 13:20) who gathers and guards his flock. However, Jesus is the good shepherd in the most radical sense: "The good shepherd lays down his life for the sheep" (John 10:11). It is hard to imagine an ordinary shepherd doing that for the flock; but in fact Jesus says that that is what distinguishes a true shepherd from a mere hired hand (10:12–13).

When Peter speaks of church leaders as shepherds, he is assimilating their work into the work of God and his Son Jesus Christ, the "chief shepherd" (1 Pet. 5:4). They are willingly to "exercise the oversight" (*episkopountes*) of the people as true shepherds—"not under compulsion . . . not for sordid gain" (5:2)—that is, not as hired hands who grudgingly do the bare minimum required to get a paycheck. Rather, they are to tend their flocks "as God would have you do it" (*kata theon*). Jesus Christ himself is the divine and human model for church leaders, for he is, as Peter has already said, the one who gathers the sheep who were "going astray" and is now "the shepherd [*poimena*] and guardian [*episkopon*] of [their] souls" (2:25). All of that is to say that messianic church leadership must bear the image of Christ the shepherd, and that means above all that church leaders (in whatever informal or formal capacity) must continually be seeking the good of their churches and members at all costs—including the cost, if necessary, of their own livelihoods or lives. Just as discipleship is costly, messianic leadership is costly. Our "willingness" (*ekousiōs*) and "eagerness" (*prothymōs*) (5:2) to assume leadership in the church should be nothing other than our willingness and eagerness to suffer with Christ. Sadly, that is in stark contrast to the intention and practice of too many priests, pastors, teachers, and bishops of the church throughout the centuries, who have been, and are, sometimes more concerned about salaries, prestige, power, career stability, and advancement in status than they are about the well-being of the people of God.

The demise of the church as an honored social institution in Western societies, together with the concomitant decline of honor for the village vicar and the diocesan bishop, may have the good effect of discouraging Christians from taking up church leadership for the sake of public prestige and power. Nevertheless, there is still plenty of opportunity *within* the church for its leaders to act as hired hands, rather than as true shepherds after the model of the "chief shepherd" (*archipoimenos*; 5:4). There is the persistent temptation to use authority and power in the church for one's own ends—the quest, perhaps, for a "crown of glory" among the people. Peter continues his instruction to the elders by addressing this very issue: "Do not lord it over [*katakyrieuontes*] those in your charge, but be examples [*typoi*] to the flock" (5:3). Peter no doubt has Christ's own saying in his mind when he writes this. "You know that among the Gentiles those whom they recognize as their rulers lord it over [*katakyrieuousin*] them, and their great ones are tyrants over them. But it is not so among you; but whoever wished to become great among you must be your servant, and whoever wishes to be first among you must be slave of all. For the Son of Man came not to be served but to serve, and to give his life a ransom for many" (Mark 10:42–45). The leaders of God's people possess only one kind of authentic authority—the authority of serving the flock by giving their lives for it. They must display in their messianic leadership exactly the kind of servant lordship that the Messiah himself displayed, so that the members of the flock might in fact see in them a "type" (*typos*) after which they themselves might pattern their lives. Only in this way, but also precisely in this way, is the church leader truly a vicar of Christ, a vicarious representative or proxy of the "chief shepherd." That same chief shepherd will soon come or "appear" (*phanerōthentos*; 1 Pet. 5:4)—that is, make himself visible in his own true cruciform lordly reality. He will then *bestow* the unfading "crown of glory" upon those leaders who have, like Peter, become witnesses of the sufferings of Christ. The crown of glory cannot be seized.

Peter instructs "the younger" (*neōteroi*) members of the flock (i.e., those who are not leaders) to "likewise [*homoiōs*] . . . be subordinate [*hypotagēte*] to the elders" (5:5 DH). The word "likewise" is significant, both for the younger members and for the elders/leaders. First, it invites *leaders* in the church to reflect again upon their own role in the messianic community and to see it now also in terms of the instruction to "be subordinate." In a radical inversion of earthly Gentile authority, to be subordinate is in fact the very form of messianic authority: it is submission and service, indeed it is being "slave of all" (Mark 10:43); to "be subordinate" as an elder (as "likewise" implies, but does not directly state) is itself a living proclamation in the church of the cruciform lordship of the Messiah. "Be subject [*hypotassomenoi*] to one another out of reverence for Christ" (Eph. 5:21). But, while church leaders are implicated in the instruction to "be subordinate," it is directed explicitly to the "younger" nonleading members of the community. They are to acknowledge and honor Christ's cruciform rule in the church through the cruciform authority of the church leaders, who have the well-being of the messianic flock at heart. The practice of the cross is always this concrete: it is always learning to be subordinate to the specific person with whom I have to do in a particular relationship. We have already seen that the practice of subordination is exactly the sociopolitical form that the gospel takes in the relationships Christians have with those outside the messianic community, whether emperors or presidents, masters or employers, husbands or wives (1 Pet. 2:13–3:7). The form of the gospel *within* the messianic community must have the character of *mutual* subordination, for this community is to be a sign before the watching world of how God actually heals and orders social and political life through the crucifixion and resurrection of Christ and the gifts of the Holy Spirit.[6]

The Holy Spirit raises up messianic leaders to serve the church. When lay members of the messianic community take up the call to "be subordinate" to their leaders, they are simply participating in their own way in the social order of the new creation taking shape in their midst. For the new creation is finally not characterized by the pride of authority, or the envy of authority, or competition for authority, or even the equal distribution of authority (e.g., who has the right to be ordained). All of those are the marks of a community still under the power of sin and threatened with self-destruction. The gospel brings about the new creation by calling and ordering "all" (*pantes*) members of the community to "humility" (*tapeinophrosynē*) toward one another (5:5). Humility is the common clothing with which all in the messianic community must "clothe" themselves (*enkombōsasthe*). "The verb itself (ἐνκομβώσασθε) appears to derive from a word (ἐνκόμβωμα) probably identifying a garment or apron a slave tied over other garments in order to perform certain menial tasks" (Achtemeier 1996: 332–33).[7] The clothing is in fact the Christ garment that we receive in our baptism, in which our old ways of parsing up people and portioning out power have been brought to an end (Gal. 3:27–28). Rich and poor get the same clothes; men and women get the same clothes; old and young get the same clothes; the powerful and the weak get the same clothes; the educated and the illiterate get the same clothes. Each member bows to the other. Each member lifts the other up in honor. This is the pattern that is to govern the whole of the messianic community, according to the mind of the Messiah himself: "Do nothing from selfish ambition or conceit, but in humility regard others as better than yourselves. . . . Let the same mind be in you that was in Christ Jesus. . . . Taking the form of a slave . . . he humbled himself" (Phil. 2:3–8). "Love one another with mutual affection; outdo one another in showing honor" (Rom. 12:10). This is the practice of messianic social order according to God's own gracious wisdom: "God opposes the proud, but gives grace to the humble" (Prov. 3:34 LXX, quoted in 1 Pet. 5:5). In practicing Christlike humility in its midst the messianic community makes its primary witness to the peace of all creation. "All ranks in society have to look after the whole body, and this cannot be done unless all the members are joined together by the bond of mutual subjection" (Calvin 1963: 318). "If this were done, we would have good peace, and things would go well on earth" (Luther 1967: 139).

6. This point is developed powerfully by John Howard Yoder, *Body Politics: Five Practices of the Christian Community before the Watching World* (Nashville: Discipleship Resources, 1992); and idem, *The Royal Priesthood: Essays Ecclesiological and Ecumenical*, ed. Michael Cartwright (Grand Rapids: Eerdmans, 1994).

7. Achtemeier 1996: 333 writes further: "What is to be put on as this garment is humble-mindedness (ταπεινοφροσύνη), a word whose root in the Greek world meant an attitude expected of slaves but unworthy of free people."

The Power of God for Messianic Life (1 Peter 5:6–11)

Among the "elect exiles of the Diaspora" humility toward one another in the community is grounded most fundamentally in our relationship with God. In all things the triune God is the source, power, and end of the messianic life. As Peter now comes to the end of his letter he again acknowledges the exilic vulnerability of the messianic community, which is so often under attack and therefore subject to anxiety and suffering. He calls the community to live its life within the gracious care of God.

Peter's point in saying "humble yourselves therefore under the mighty hand of God" (5:6) is not to "put us in our place" before God, but rather to call us to entrust ourselves to God's care in the most radical sense. The messianic life is possible only under this condition—that we trust God absolutely in every circumstance. Only such trust will free us from the constant and normal temptations to assert our own power in circumstances, to take down the enemy or oppressor, to seek our own good, to establish our own rights, to attain our own position of honor, or, most basically, simply to defend ourselves and secure our own safety. Without humble trust in "the mighty hand of God," how would we be able to follow the way of the Messiah, who did not do any of those things, but rather, "entrust[ing] himself to the one who judges justly" (2:23), walked the journey from divine glory to the cross? All messianic life must, therefore, be other than a mere imitation of Christ carried out by the sheer power of human will. It must be a *participation in Christ* whose own life of trust (which is the root of his sinlessness) precedes, defines, bears, and completes ours. The Messiah is the Alpha and Omega of the messianic life. *He* humbled himself under the mighty hand of God, entrusted himself radically into God's hand, and endured shame, suffering, and death, in order that *in him* we might also humble ourselves and trust God.

Peter assures us that our vindication will come, but it will come *from God* according to *God's time*: God will "exalt you in due time [*en kairō*]" (5:6). "He humbled himself.... Therefore God also highly exalted him" (Phil. 2:8–9). Clearly evoking the pattern of Christ's humiliation and exaltation set forth in Phil. 2:6–11—and in each of the canonical gospels—Peter locates the messianic life right at the crux of that pattern. The "mighty hand of God" under which we now live in humility with one another is not the hand that oppresses; it is, rather, the hand that is even now ready to deliver and exalt God's cruciform people, and that will happen *en kairō*, in the time coming that has already been made near and palpable in the transfiguration, resurrection, and exaltation of Jesus. God's mighty hand thus revealed evokes trust from his people, not fear. For it is the powerful, protecting hand that dispels all fear, the kind of fear that would cause us to hesitate or defect in the face of messianic suffering or to be tempted again to return to worldly ways of coping with the vulnerability of the messianic-exilic way of life. Such fear is dispelled only by throwing it into God's hand and letting God himself carry it on our behalf: "Cast all your anxiety on him, because he cares for you" (1 Pet. 5:7).

Trusting in God does not mean slipping into a state of relaxed passivity. Being freed from anxiety does not mean being freed from danger. Peter immediately utters two staccato imperatives: "Be sober [*nēpsate*]! Stay awake [*grēgorēsate*]!" (5:8 DH). As the reality of God's final victory (the *kairos*) approaches, a high state of alert is called for, because in this very time the enemy steps up the intensity of his opposition to the rule of God and his Messiah. God's messianic people find themselves on the front, facing a formidable foe: "Like a roaring lion your adversary the devil prowls around, looking for someone to devour" (5:8). But if this ravenous enemy prowls around roaring, why would we need to be on high alert? Are his presence and intent not simply obvious—and then too the nature of the warfare against him? Yes, and no.

Yes, in one sense the enemy seems to be all too obvious: it is the various religious, cultural, social, and political realities that press upon the small pocket of messianic exiles on all sides (including from within), now tempting, now coercing them to accommodate, conform, or convert back to their former life among the Gentiles. Perhaps even more concretely and obviously, the enemy is a particular group of Gentiles, or even just one of them, who is in some form or other ridiculing, pressuring, or attacking the messianic community.

But, no, Peter does not allow us to look at the obvious flesh-and-blood enemies and engage in that mode of warfare against them that seems most natural to us. While the Gentiles are indeed often the human agents of opposition, and their religious, cultural, social, legal, and political practices and institutions are often the forms that their opposition takes, these are not themselves the adversary, and a normal warfare waged (in whatever form) against them would miss the target and fail. Not only would it miss the target, but it would be the very means and mode by which the adversary himself would pounce upon and devour God's people. In our efforts to triumph over the apparent flesh-and-blood enemies, we would miss the sneak attack of the real adversary—the devil—the one who has already devoured "them" and now seeks to devour "us," exactly by setting us in warfare against them. The defeat of the messianic people would be total, because the very messianic character that defines them would precisely disappear. A wholly other kind of warfare and a wholly other set of armor and weapons are required (Eph. 6:10–17).

The militant revolt demanded of Christians—and this distinguishes it from all kinds of other revolts—is not directed *against* any people: not even against the host of unbelievers, false believers, and the superstitious whom, for lack of the knowledge of God which they themselves have been given, they see taking totally different and corrupt and fatal paths, nor even, very generally, against the wicked on account of their wickedness and oppression or on account of what Christians have to suffer at their hands in coarser or more refined forms. . . .

In terms of their commission—even though they will sometimes clash with all kinds of people in discharging it—they rebel and fight *for* all men, even, and in the last resort precisely, for those with whom they may clash. Their cause—the problem of the *militia Christi* and therefore of the *ecclesia militans*—is the cause of man precisely because it is the cause of God.[8]

The devilish danger to which the messianic community must be ever alert is real and voracious and must be resisted. The devil will try to devour us not only through our inclinations toward pride, lust, envy, anger, and so on, but also, more subtly, through our very desires and actions for justice, good order, peace, and progress. What evil "must" we do that these good things might come? "Resist him," Peter urges. That resistance can only take one form: remaining "firm in the faith" (*stereoi tē pistei*; 1 Pet. 5:9 DH). Peter has made clear throughout the letter that messianic "faith" (*pistis*) has a very particular content and shape: the content is the Messiah himself, and its shape is suffering. "Since therefore Christ suffered in the flesh, *arm yourselves* also with the same intention (for whoever has suffered in the flesh has finished with sin)" (4:1). *Pistis* is remaining loyal to this one and this way. *Pistis* is believing that Christ already rules over the "angels, authorities, and powers" (3:22). *Pistis* is leaving behind the deadly ways and habits of "the Gentiles" (4:3–4). *Pistis* is "being subordinate" even to those who might oppress. *Pistis* is trusting in "the one who judges justly" (2:23). *Pistis* is humbly waiting for the "mighty hand of God" to bring about justice for God's people and the wider world. Firm in this *pistis*, this faith in its very specific content and form, we resist the dangerous power of the devil to persuade us that there are better ways to triumph over evil than through the sufferings of Christ.

To encourage God's people in such faith Peter reminds us that our "brothers and sisters in all the world [*en tō kosmō*] are undergoing the same kinds of suffering" (5:9). God's messianic communities in many places are small, weak, and vulnerable. But all of them share commonly in the one Messiah, and all are called to the common task of participating in and witnessing to his sufferings by their own sufferings. They have the same hope and share in the same Spirit of glory when they participate in Christ's suffering. When they do so, they resist the devil and are finished with sin.

Further, those who suffer in Christ never do so apart from "the God of all grace, who has called you to his eternal glory in Christ" (5:10). With this, Peter sums up the source, power, and end of the messianic life and locates the being of the messianic community right in the midst of it. God's grace creates the messianic community in the mercy by which he chooses and sets apart a people for his name, to be the recipients of his blessing and the means by which his blessing is shed abroad among the nations (1:1–2). God's grace reconciles, redeems, and heals the church through the Messiah who "bore our sins in his body on the cross" (2:24). God's grace sustains and builds up the church through the Holy Spirit, who creates unity, gives gifts, activates preaching and the sacraments, and comes in glory upon

8. Karl Barth, *The Christian Life: Church Dogmatics*, vol. 4/4: *Lecture Fragments*, trans. Geoffrey W. Bromiley (Grand Rapids: Eerdmans, 1981), 210 (emphasis original).

those who suffer for the name of Christ (4:16). God's grace completes the church by providing strength and faith in the time of trial and judgment that "begin[s] with the household of God" for its own purification. This God is indeed "the God of *all* grace" in whom the messianic community lives and moves and has its being. This same God calls the church "[in]to his eternal glory in Christ." Christ stands among us, and beyond us, in his risen and transfigured glorious body, as the end to which we are beckoned as his now suffering body. The church is called to an eternal and glorious end in which God will "restore, support, strengthen, and establish" (5:10) the marred and martyred body of Christ as it comes to share in the healing power of God's own triune life. In relation to this "eternal" (*aiōnion*) and glorious end, the present time of suffering for the church will seem "short" (*oligon*) indeed.

Rightly then, Peter brings the body of his letter to its only proper end, the end of all things, which is doxology: "To him"—to the God of all grace who calls us into his eternal glory in Christ—"to him the dominion [*kratos*] belongs forever and ever. Amen" (5:11 DH).

Final Greetings (1 Peter 5:12–14)

Peter begins his farewell by identifying the messenger by whom it is sent: Silvanus, "a faithful brother" (5:12). This is likely the same Silvanus (Silas) who was the bearer of the apostolic letter sent out to the church in Antioch after the council in Jerusalem (see Elliott 2000: 871–74 for discussion). Peter sends Silvanus as more than a mail carrier, however. In Acts, Silas and Judas not only deliver the apostolic letter, but also, as "leaders among the brothers" (Acts 15:22) and as "prophets themselves," they both read the letter in Antioch and "said much to encourage and strengthen the believers" (15:32). Additionally, for at least some time Silvanus is a partner in Paul's mission to the nations (2 Cor. 1:19; 1 Thess. 1:1; 2 Thess. 1:1).[9] Silvanus, as a "faithful brother," carries Peter's letter to the various churches in Asia Minor bearing the commission of Peter himself and the authority to read it and expound it in those congregations in the power of the Holy Spirit.

Peter also reiterates that everything he has written in the "short letter" has been for the sake of our encouragement and to "testify" (*epimartyrōn*) to us "that this is the true grace of God." By "this" he means the entire content of the letter. Whatever he has written, as we have just noted (→5:6–11), is written not as an imposing and burdensome "exhortation to martyrdom," but as an explication of God's manifold grace, of which martyrdom itself—sharing in the sufferings of

9. The connections between Peter, Silvanus, Mark, and Paul indicated in 5:12–13, together with their apparently spending time together in Rome (before the martyrdom of Peter and Paul), goes a long way toward accounting for the evidently Pauline character of 1 Peter.

Christ—may be a joyful manifestation. The whole of the messianic life is given as God's grace, and so Peter exhorts the messianic-exilic communities to "stand fast in it" (5:12). Stand fast in the very grace of God that enables us to stand.

Peter sends greetings to the churches from "she [who is] in Babylon" (*hē en Babylōni*; 5:13 DH). With this cryptic designation Peter indicates that he is sending the letter from the church ("she") in Rome, for which "Babylon" was frequently a figure in the early church. Whether there were security reasons for this metaphorical reference is hard to determine. What is more likely is that Peter takes us with this reference back to the very first words of address in the letter: "to the elect exiles of the Diaspora." With that phrase (→1:1b) Peter sets forth the ecclesiology that undergirds the entire letter. Babylon is, of course, both the reality and the great symbol of exilic existence in scripture. Merely to mention the name here again reminds us that not only the churches in Asia Minor, but also the church in Rome (perhaps paradigmatically), and the church everywhere is always in exile, always qualitatively homeless in a world that does not confess Jesus the Messiah of God—that confession that constitutes the fundamental character of the messianic community in its witness among the nations. This church "in Babylon," Peter says, is "chosen together [*syneklektē*] with you." Again Peter takes us back to his opening greeting; being the chosen people of God is constitutive of the nature of the messianic community.

Peter includes greetings from his "son Mark." This is not likely Peter's natural son, but his "son" in Christ, as Silvanus is his "brother" in Christ. Mark is likely John Mark, the apostolic associate mentioned in Acts 12 and Acts 15 and in some of Paul's letters (see Elliott 2000: 887–89). According to tradition this Mark became a close associate of Peter and was commissioned by Peter to write the canonical Gospel of Mark on Peter's behalf. If so, Peter ensured thereby that the original apostolic witness to the Messiah's sufferings was handed on faithfully to the next generation of leaders in the messianic community, in order that the witness of the church might be sustained in its participation in the Messiah's suffering.

Peter concludes his letter with the instruction to "greet one another with a kiss of love" (5:14). The kiss of love in the messianic community is a concrete bodily symbol of their communion in the Messiah, with whom and in whom also they are at peace with one another.

2 PETER

2 PETER 1

Simeon Peter (2 Peter 1:1a)

Peter identifies himself as "servant and apostle of Jesus Christ" (1:1; →1 Pet. 1:1a). As a servant (*doulos*, "slave"), Peter puts himself fully at the disposal of the Lord who claims and commissions him to write these words. As an apostle of Jesus Christ he receives his commission and message from the one whom he serves. Writing and sending letters (and gospels) to the churches is an activity intrinsic to the divine calling and commission of at least some of the apostles. Therefore we attend to apostolic letters not only, or even primarily, as historical documents of long-dead authors, but as the living word of Jesus Christ that we must hear and obey in our time. Commentary on those letters aims to clarify and communicate the word of Christ spoken through these letters to the church in another generation.

Receiving Faith through God's Justice (2 Peter 1:1b–2)

Peter addresses his letter to "those who have received, with us, a faith of equal content and value because of the justice of our God and Savior Jesus Christ" (1:1b DH). He declares that it is nothing less than a matter of the active "justice" (*dikaiosynē*) of Jesus Christ that we find ourselves sharing the apostles' faith with them, a faith that is of the same content and quality (*isotimon*) as that which Peter and the other apostles have.[1] It is a modern habit to construe the content of the

---

1. This point is made by Kraftchick 2002: 86–87 and stands behind my translation of the sentence. See also Duane Watson, "The Second Letter of Peter," in *The New Interpreter's Bible* (Nashville: Abingdon, 1998), 12.334: the faith received is "of the same kind and precious caliber." Note that Peter does not speak for himself alone: "with us" (*hēmin*) certainly indicates the other apostles.

apostles' message as their human response to the life, death, and resurrection of Jesus Christ. Christ is thought of as the passive object of a variety of merely human "interpretations" by the apostolic witnesses. But Peter asserts that Christ is anything but passive in the apostolic witness and our reception of it. "If the apostles, and men and women after them by way of their word, have a knowledge of Jesus's identity, it is because Jesus, in the power of God's act, shares it with them. This means that they can neither gain it from themselves nor at any time exercise control over it."[2] The content and continuity of the apostolic message, together with its faithful reception in the church in other times and places, is in the first place a matter of God working in the church to preserve the apostolic testimony through scripture, creed, and tradition. God reveals his righteousness in that. As we shall see, human faithfulness to the reliable testimony of the prophets and apostles is a matter of crucial concern in this letter. Peter's chief task is to "remind" his readers (1:12) and to "refresh [their] memory" (1:13), so that when he is gone they "may be able at any time to recall" (1:15) the teaching they have received, and remain faithful to it, as well as to discern and reject false teachings. Peter's readers have received the apostolic faith, but they are also in imminent danger of losing it. In this context the first thing Peter does is not to warn against defection or exhort to faithfulness, but to testify to the saving power of Jesus Christ, who himself is at one and the same time both the content of our faith and the one who, because he is righteous, guarantees that the saving gospel will not ultimately be lost.

This letter as a whole raises the question of what will preserve the church from "destructive heresies" (2:1 DH) or (in Paul's phrase) "another gospel." The answer to that question arises in the first verse of the letter: the church will be preserved in the truth of the gospel by the righteous act of our God and Savior Jesus Christ. Thus, while theologians and preachers in the church are rightly concerned—as Peter is—to refute false teachings that distort or erode the truth of the gospel, our final confidence that the apostolic message will endure does not rest in our own power of formulation, critique, or persuasion, but in the divine power of Jesus Christ who sees to it as a matter of his own justice toward us. Theologians and other erstwhile defenders of the faith have frequently succumbed to the thought that it is they who both define the truth and secure the continuity of the apostolic message. Peter reminds us that Jesus Christ himself is not only the truth, but also the power of truth through time.

Peter includes in his greeting a reference to "our God and Savior Jesus Christ" (1:1). Here he introduces the central theme of his letter: the acknowledgement of the divine identity and divine power of Jesus Christ. In the very next sentence (1:2) Peter makes a distinction between God and Jesus Christ, but then in the following sentence (1:3) he again ascribes "divine power" to Jesus Christ (the nearest

2. David E. Demson, *Hans Frei and Karl Barth: Different Ways of Reading Scripture* (Grand Rapids: Eerdmans, 1997), 83. Demson is here summarizing an aspect of Barth's theology.

antecedent of the personal pronoun *autou*, "his").[3] The transcendent divine glory of Jesus Christ is a theme that pervades the letter, coming to a climax first in the account of the transfiguration of Jesus in 1:16–18. We know Christ rightly when we know him sharing fully in the divinity, majesty, and glory of the God of Israel, whose beloved Son he is. To recognize this here is crucial, so that when we come to 1:4 we will be able to get an appropriate sense of how Christians themselves are given a share, with Christ, in "the divine nature."

Peter's use of the title "Savior" is also significant: it occurs five times in the letter (1:1, 11; 2:20; 3:2, 18), whereas, as a title, it is used infrequently in the rest of the New Testament. The title would be very familiar to Peter's first readers from other contexts. The gods of the Gentiles were often believed to be saviors. The Roman emperor was regularly hailed as "god and savior" by his subjects.[4] He was divinized and exalted as the great deliverer from Rome's enemies and the bringer of a tangibly better world—the global rule of the Roman Empire, which certainly brought significant benefits, including peace and security, for all loyal Roman citizens. As such, the emperor was the object of faith and hope (Harrington 2003: 242). In this context, Peter's declaration that *Jesus Christ* is "God and Savior" is first of all a reminder to honor the first commandment: "You shall have no other gods before me" (Exod. 20:3). To ascribe the title "God and Savior" to any other, and thereby put our ultimate faith and hope in any other, is idolatry. The divine glory and majesty that belongs to Jesus Christ as revealed in his transfiguration belongs to him *alone* as the one Son of the Father: we give our worship and loyalty to Jesus Christ as our primary act of exclusive devotion to the one God of Israel. In Exodus the first commandment is not uttered apart from God's declaration of his great deed of deliverance for his people: "I am the LORD your God, who brought you out of the land of Egypt, out of the house of slavery" (Exod. 20:2). Jesus's title "God and Savior" is likewise a declaration that real deliverance from our bondages and corruptions comes only from the one God, creator of the heavens and the earth, and not from any worldly (or otherworldly) powers, no matter how majestically and gloriously they present themselves and their accomplishments. As mere creatures, the emperors, rulers, presidents, and prime ministers of this age cannot save, despite their persistent claims and promises to do so, for they are incapable of bringing about a *new creation* in which "righteousness is at home" (2 Pet. 3:13).[5] Only God the creator

---

3. But James M. Starr, *Sharers in Divine Nature: 2 Peter 1:4 in Its Hellenistic Context*, Coniectanea Biblica, New Testament Series 33 (Stockholm: Almqvist & Wiksell, 2000), 39, notes that "in 1:2 Christ and God are not practically distinguishable" since no distinct activities are attributed to the one and the other. Thus in 1:3 "his divine power" may refer to "Jesus our Lord" (the nearest individual antecedent) or to "God-and-Jesus-our-Lord" as in some sense a single divine entity.

4. Ralph P. Martin, "The Theology of Jude, 1 Peter, and 2 Peter," in *New Testament Theology: The Theology of the Letters of James, Peter, and Jude*, by Andrew Chester and Ralph P. Martin (Cambridge: Cambridge University Press, 1994), 159.

5. William T. Cavanaugh, *Theopolitical Imagination* (London/New York: Clark, 2002), shows how the right worship of the triune God is for Christians the primary political act and how

and re-creator can do so. Jesus is able to deliver us, save us, because he himself is God—the one to whom God the Father says: "This is my Son, my Beloved, with whom I am well pleased" (1:17). Jesus Christ saves us by joining us to himself, by making us, with the apostles, witnesses of and sharers in his divine glory, power, freedom, and incorruptibility.

Those who wait (whether after fifty years or two thousand years) for the final arrival of the divine deliverer, Jesus Christ, clearly need the reminders that Peter gives here. In our time of waiting, when all things seem to "continue as they were from the beginning of creation" (3:4), the great temptation for Christians and the church to turn to other gods and saviors continually presses upon us. Idolatrously we turn our faith and hope toward the immanent powers of technology, medicine, economic security, powerful leaders, military might, and the global rule of our empire to bring about the new world we hope for. The church in North America, living with the benefits and freedoms of the global reign of the capitalist market and the American empire, all too readily succumbs to just this temptation. But in so doing it finds itself more deeply enslaved and corrupted by the powers of the present evil age, subject to God's judgment, and threatened with destruction. The one hope of the church, Peter declares, is to confess that Jesus Christ alone is God and Savior. He is "the one Word of God which we have to hear and which we have to trust and obey in life and in death."[6]

In the blessing Peter affirms that just as by God's act of justice we receive the apostolic faith, so also through "the knowledge [*epignōsis*] of God and of Jesus our Lord" (1:2) we receive God's abundant grace and peace. *Epignōsis* in 2 Peter (1:2, 3, 8; 2:20) and in other New Testament texts (Heb. 10:26; 1 Tim. 2:4; 2 Tim. 2:25; 3:7; Titus 1:1) bears the meaning "the knowledge gained in conversion," that is, the knowledge that comes through our hearing, believing, and participating in the gospel (Bauckham 1983: 169). But it is certainly also more than that: it is the "knowledge that decisively alters one's life" (Kraftchick 2002: 88). That is not knowledge that we gain once for all, like a fact, but is a unique form of knowledge as an ever deeper participation, by faith, in the reality of God. Such knowledge is given only through a transformative journey in which, as Gregory of Nyssa writes of Abraham's journey of faith, we find ourselves always stretching forward to what is ahead. "[Abraham] always considered what he had achieved by his own power as smaller than what he still looked for. In his conceptions about God he went beyond every thought which might be derived from considering his name; he

the politics of the secular state stands over against this as an "alternative soteriology," a parody of God's salvation accomplished through the crucifixion and resurrection of Jesus Christ celebrated in the Christian liturgy.

6. This is the famous first article of the 1934 Barmen Declaration: confessed in a context in which the church was all too ready to "trust and obey" the social and political mandates of the ruling Nazi regime. The exclusive claim of Christ, which Barmen declares, is necessary even (or especially) when the church is living its life under an apparently friendly and benign regime—which of course, from a certain ecclesiastical perspective, the Nazi regime also appeared to be.

purified his reasoning of all such ideas and so embraced a faith, unmixed and free of every such conception [*ennoia*]. This he laid down as an infallible and clear sign that we know God—the conviction that God is superior to, and higher than, every semantic marker." In other words, Abraham's knowledge of God cannot finally be, despite Abraham's constant striving, a human achievement, but comes as a gift of God himself, given in Abraham's faith: "The law of faith becomes [Abraham's] rule of life. By means of his own story he instructs those who would approach God that there is no other way of drawing close to God except through the medium of faith, that of itself knits together into one the searching mind and the incomprehensible nature." In the end, "Abraham left behind him the vain search for knowledge." Instead, he believed God and thereby participated in God: "Faith makes our own that which exceeds the grasp of our minds."[7]

As we shall discover, it is precisely this knowledge given in faith (or the lack of it) that is at stake in Peter's response to those who preach another gospel. Where heretical teachings and disobedient practices undermine or distort the original, life-altering, and life-giving personal knowledge of "God and Jesus our Lord," the abundant flow of grace and peace given in the gospel is also cut off. For that reason, heresy is cruel. "If a teaching is wrong opinion rather than right opinion the consequences are cruel, the Christian faith is distorted, and people who follow these teachings are hurt."[8] This fact accounts for the vituperative rhetoric we find in the second chapter of this letter. There Peter passionately warns us against being persuaded and destroyed by a cruel, destructive message (2:1), delivered by those who distort or forsake the knowledge of "the way of righteousness" (2:21) that they once learned in Christ.

Sharing in Divine Nature (2 Peter 1:3–4)

The theological center of gravity of the letter's message is 1:3–18, with its emphasis on God's gift, promise, call, and election; with its claim that we might become "sharers of the divine nature"; with its list of virtues extending from faith to love; and with its account of the transfiguration of Jesus. Peter's purpose in 2 Pet. 1, with respect to the letter as a whole, is clear: he is concerned to equip us to stand firm in our faith against the arguments, attacks, and enticements of false teachers. His first step (1:3–4), however, is not to provide arguments against false teachers or to attack their errors. Instead, he reminds us of what we already have been given, of where we already stand, of what we are already promised, and for what we have already been called and chosen. He reminds us, in brief, of God's gracious work on our behalf and of our share in God's very own life.

7. Gregory of Nyssa, *Against Eunomius* 2.89–93, in Anthony Meredith, *Gregory of Nyssa* (London/New York: Routledge, 1999), 90–91.

8. C. FitzSimons Allison, *The Cruelty of Heresy: An Affirmation of Christian Orthodoxy* (Harrisburg, PA: Morehouse, 1994), 20.

Peter begins by rooting our life in the divine power, grace, and calling of Jesus
Christ. The "divine power" (*theias dynameōs*) of Jesus Christ has given us "everything needed for life and godliness" (1:3). Peter is not reluctant later to exhort
us to "make every effort" (1:15) to take up the way of virtue and moral action,
but that is not where he begins. He begins by declaring that the power to live a
godly life does not reside within us, but in Jesus Christ and his gifts. A Christian
lives to God as one who already shares in God's power and grace given in Jesus
Christ. Peter's astonishing claim in the next sentence, that we may become "sharers of the divine nature" (1:4), begins with this prior claim that we are recipients
of God's outpouring of glory and goodness in Jesus Christ. "[Peter] refers to the
boundless goodness of God which they had already experienced, so that they
may place a greater reliance on Him in the future. . . . God has fully unfolded the
vast resources of His power" (Calvin 1963: 328). Further, these abundant gifts
of God's power are not, as Calvin rightly notes, the "varied gifts of nature," but
are in fact "the special gifts of the new spiritual life which take their origin from
the kingdom of Christ. . . . By claiming the whole total of godliness and all the
helps to salvation as originating in the divine power of Christ, Peter here removes
them from the common nature of man, thereby leaving us without the merest
scrap of virtue" (1963: 329). Given that a few verses later Peter does indeed call
us to pursue vigorously a life of virtue, Calvin makes an important point. The
godly life of the Christian is originally constituted not in our own striving for
"excellence" or "virtue" (*aretē*), but in the "glory and excellence"—or "glorious
excellence"—of Jesus Christ himself.[9] Christ's divine power has given us everything
necessary "through the knowledge of him who called us by [or to] his own glory
[*doxa*] and excellence [*aretē*]" (1:3 DH). The glory of Christ as the beloved Son
is bestowed upon him directly from God the Father, who himself is the "Majestic
[Magnificent, Sublime] Glory," as Peter calls God in 1:17. Christ's glory consists
in his sharing fully in the Father's divine nature and sovereignty. In 1:3, then, Peter
already anticipates his account of the transfiguration, the revelation of Christ's full
divine-human reality shining forth with the very "beauty of the infinite,"[10] as the
event that most clearly reveals and persuades us about the truth and transcendent
reality of Christ (1:16–18). Thus we must say that it is the sheer *attractive and
compelling beauty, glory, and authority of Christ's own being and life* that comes to
us, calls us, draws us irresistibly to him, and elicits from us a corresponding life of
godliness and excellence.[11] This provides us with a clue to the passion of Peter in

9. Peter often makes use of hendiadys (Bauckham 1983: 178), the use of two nouns together
to convey one meaning: e.g., "life and godliness" may also be translated "godly life"; "glory and
excellence" may well be translated "glorious excellence," though with this latter example we should
note that the word "glory" (*doxa*) itself plays an important role in the letter.
10. A phrase borrowed from the title of David Bentley Hart's *The Beauty of the Infinite: The
Aesthetics of Christian Truth* (Grand Rapids: Eerdmans, 2003).
11. Cf. the following comment, which, however, draws the meaning of Christ's glory and
virtue not from the transfiguration, but from his life, death, and resurrection: "The Lord Christ

this letter: it seems inconceivable to him that someone who was once seized by and made a sharer in the overwhelming glory, excellence, and beauty of Christ would later abandon that *epignōsis*, that original and life-altering knowledge in which our own life is conformed to Christ's, and trade it for something else.

As if Christ giving us "everything needed for life and godliness" were not enough, Peter goes on to say that Christ has, out of his own glorious excellence, also given us "his precious and very great promises" (1:4). Peter thus draws us further into the heart of his message, where we discover that it is exactly those promises that are now being doubted by his readers and dismissed by the false teachers. The core promise around which the others are gathered is the "coming in power of our Lord Jesus Christ" (1:16 DH) to bring about the "new heavens and a new earth" (3:8–13). It is the promise of this radical, apocalyptic, world-dissolving, and world-constituting act of God that Peter passionately affirms, promotes, and defends throughout the letter. Literally everything depends on it.

Peter has much more to say about Christ's coming in power later in the letter; here he states that through the promises Christ has given we "may become sharers of divine nature, having escaped the corruption that is in the world because of sinful desire" (DH).[12]

The world suffers "corruption" (*phthora*). This word is best understood as the mortality or perishability of all things (cf. 1 Cor. 15:42, 50–54). The apostle Paul speaks of the creation being "subjected to futility [or vanity]" (Rom. 8:20) and of its "bondage to decay [*phthora*]" (8:21), from which it awaits God's deliverance. Existential concern over the perishability, transitoriness, or fleetingness of the world and of human life is a common theme in the literature of peoples throughout history. It also has deep roots in the Hebrew world of thought. The entire book of Ecclesiastes, for example, is an extended reflection on the transitory, vaporlike character (Hebrew *hebel*, "mist, vanity") of all things and human life itself. Isaiah 40:6–8 declares that all flesh is as grass; it is like a flower that withers and fades. Genesis 2–3 reveals that humans are made from the dust of the earth and because of their disobedience are destined to return to the dust. In 2 Peter's Hellenistic context it would be common to believe that corruption, decay, and perishability are *intrinsic* to the creation as such, inherent in the nature of all things physical, material, and bodily; salvation would then be understood as escape from this world

---

first revealed heaven and all heaven's blessings, then he invited men to draw near and receive those blessings. How did he invite them? By words alone? By words indeed, but not only by words; by glory and virtue. By glory: that is by his glorious Resurrection; by virtue: that is, by his wonderful service and suffering. By these he has invited us to receive 'the exceedingly great promises' that, by them, we may partake of God's nature" (Nikolai Velimirović, quoted in Johanna Manley, ed., *The Bible and the Holy Fathers for Orthodox* [Crestwood, NY: St. Vladimir's Seminary Press, 2003], 663).

12. I am following the translation of Bauckham 1983: 179, 182; and Kraftchick 2002: 93, rendering the aorist participle *apophygontes* ("having escaped") as an event that precedes the sharing in the divine nature. An indispensable study for understanding 1:4 and its significance in the letter is Starr's *Sharers in Divine Nature*.

to a sphere of incorruptible and immortal spiritual existence uncontaminated and unhindered by the limits of the body and the earth.

It is tempting to read Peter's language in 1:4 in this Hellenistic way, as many Christians have done through the centuries, since he himself also speaks of "escape" from the corruption of the world to sharing in the divine nature.[13] But we must note that it is the *corruption* of the world that we escape and not the creation itself. Peter makes the subtle but important point in 1:4 that the *phthora* in the world is the result of "desire" or "lust" (*en epithymia*). The corruption in the world is not intrinsic to its character as created, but enters the world because of disordered human desire. Peter speaks more clearly about this in 2:19–20, where he writes how the false teachers are "slaves of corruption" who at one time had "escaped the defilements [*miasmata*] of the world through the knowledge of our Lord and Savior Jesus Christ." The problem with creatureliness is not its finitude and contingency but its sinfulness and bondage. In 2 Pet. 3 any seemingly Hellenistic motifs are ultimately transformed by being caught up into a Jewish apocalyptic vision in which the goal of human life is not flight from finitude, matter, body, and the world, but life in a new, transfigured creation "where righteousness is at home" (3:13), brought into being by the creating, judging, and redeeming God. Creation and creatures look forward not to escape from creatureliness, but to this final transfiguration and sharing in God's life. Through our participation in Jesus Christ, we are granted a share in the nature and destiny of the one who did not lead his followers on a gnostic journey *out of the world*, but who himself was *visibly and bodily* transfigured and glorified by God *in the world*, on "the holy mountain," in the presence and sight of Peter and the two other apostles. As Jesus shares *bodily* in the Father's glory, so also will those who know Jesus Christ share bodily in his glory through his transforming power: Christ "will transform the body of our humiliation that it may be conformed to the body of his glory, by the power that also enables him to subdue everything to himself" (Phil. 3:21 DH). As Paul argues in 1 Cor. 15, the perishable body "puts on" imperishability, the mortal body "puts on" immortality, through the resurrection of the *body* by the life-giving Spirit of Jesus Christ, not through a flight of the soul or spirit from the body. With the rest of scripture, Peter enables us to resist the many spiritualizing, world-denying and body-denying understandings of our final destiny that continue to be common among Christians, as well as in other contemporary and new age gnosticisms that all too frequently influence our understanding of Christian faith.

To participate fully, personally, and bodily in the divine glory and eternity of Jesus Christ is the meaning of becoming "sharers in divine nature" in 2 Pet. 1:4. It is the final destiny of the Christian life. This phrase, *theias koinōnoi physeōs*, is unique in the Bible, found only in this relatively obscure letter of the New Testament; yet it

---

13. Ernst Käsemann, "An Apologia for Primitive Christian Eschatology," in his *Essays on New Testament Themes*, trans. W. J. Montague (Philadelphia: Fortress, 1982), 180, takes 1:4 as primary evidence that 2 Peter is thoroughly immersed in Hellenistic dualism. Käsemann is finally unpersuasive; see the critique in Bauckham 1983: 183–84.

has become a text of great significance in the history of theology, most particularly and centrally in the Orthodox tradition, with its doctrine of "deification," "divinization," or *theōsis*.[14] The great early Greek theologians—Athanasius (ca. 296–373), Gregory of Nyssa (ca. 330–ca. 395), Maximus the Confessor (ca. 580–662), Simeon the New Theologian (949–1022), and Gregory Palamas (ca. 1296–1359)—all developed careful, complex, and sophisticated accounts of *theōsis* that are nonetheless often confusing to the Western theological mind because they work within a conceptual universe very different from that of the West.[15] While 1:4 is not the only biblical text upon which the doctrine of *theōsis* is built, the doctrine intends to take Peter's startling claim that we are made "sharers of divine nature" with full and radical seriousness.[16]

Taking Ps. 82:6 ("I said, 'You are "gods"; you are all sons of the Most High'" [NIV]) and its reiteration by Jesus in John 10:34–36 as a reference to human beings, Orthodox theologians understand these three passages as declaring that all human beings, created in the image of God, are called to become divine in some sense: "As human beings we each have this one, unique calling, to achieve theosis. In other words, we are each destined to become a god, to be like God himself, to be united with him. The apostle Peter describes with total clarity the

14. David L. O. Balás, "Participation," in *Encyclopedia of Early Christianity*, ed. Everett Ferguson, 2nd ed. (New York: Garland, 1997), 2.692–95.

15. The indispensable source on this theme in Greek patristic theology is Norman Russell, *The Doctrine of Deification in the Greek Patristic Tradition* (Oxford/New York: Oxford University Press, 2004). Other helpful accounts of *theōsis* may be found in Michael J. Christensen and Jeffery A. Wittung, ed., *Partakers of the Divine Nature: The History and Development of Deification in the Christian Tradition* (Grand Rapids: Baker Academic, 2008); Daniel B. Clendenin, *Eastern Orthodox Theology: A Contemporary Reader* (Grand Rapids: Baker Academic, 1995), 183–92; Nonna Verna Harrison, "Theosis as Salvation: An Orthodox Perspective," *Pro ecclesia* 6 (1997): 429–43; and Veli-Matti Kärkkäinen, *One with God: Salvation as Deification and Justification* (Collegeville, MN: Liturgical Press, 2004), who not only provides an introduction to the doctrine of deification in Eastern Orthodoxy (17–36) but also shows its use in some Western traditions, including Luther (37–66) and later Protestantism (67–86).

16. *Theōsis* is "the defining principle of the doctrine of salvation in Eastern theology" (Kärkkäinen, *One with God*, 29). While the theme of sharing in the divine nature was frequently explored and affirmed in pre-Reformation Western theology by the likes of Augustine, Pseudo-Dionysius, Thomas Aquinas, and some of the mystical theologians (e.g., Meister Eckhardt), Protestant theology has often been cautious in its use of the concept of deification. But there is growing openness to the language and thought of *theōsis* as Protestant theologians more frequently explore the promising discourse generated by the language of 1:4. On Western theological uses of *theōsis*, see Christensen and Wittung, *Partakers of the Divine Nature*, 163–229; Kärkkäinen, *One with God*, 87–137; Tuomo Mannermaa, *Christ Present in Faith: Luther's View of Justification* (Minneapolis: Fortress, 2005), for a reading of Luther as a theologian of *theōsis*; Thomas N. Finger, *A Contemporary Anabaptist Theology: Biblical, Historical, Constructive* (Downers Grove, IL: InterVarsity, 2004), 109–56, for the proposal that divinization is an important theme in authentic Anabaptist soteriology; Robert W. Jenson, *Systematic Theology*, vol. 1: *The Triune God* (New York: Oxford University Press, 1997), 224–36; idem, *Systematic Theology*, vol. 2: *The Works of God* (New York: Oxford University Press, 1999), 340–46, for a Lutheran appropriation of the *theōsis* doctrine.

purpose of life: we are to become partakers of divine nature (2 Pet. 1:4)."[17] Stav-ropoulos's claim is bold, yet flirts with theological danger—as, perhaps, Peter's phrase itself does.[18] In general, Eastern theologians are careful to guard against the potential misunderstanding of this idea—related especially to the language of 2 Pet. 1:4—as a claim that human nature becomes somehow dissolved by, absorbed into, or identical with the divine nature; that is, that humans actually are or become God *by nature*. For example, Gregory Palamas, in writing of deification, makes an important distinction: "Thus to our human nature He has given the glory of the Godhead, but not the divine nature; for the nature of God is one thing, His glory another, even though they be inseparable from one another."[19] What then of the word "nature" (*physis*) in a text like 2 Pet. 1:4? According to Meyendorff, for Palamas "there is no question of identifying the word 'nature' . . . as used in the New Testament with the Patristic conception of 'nature'; all that the Apostle [Peter] wished to express was the *reality* of our participation in the *very* life of God."[20]

However, in a classic statement on *theōsis* from Maximus the Confessor, the distinctions are perhaps not quite so clear. In an exegesis of 1 Cor. 10:11, Maximus first describes *theōsis* as that movement of humanity in the divine economy that follows after the incarnation:

> For if [God] has brought to completion his mystical work of becoming human, having become like us in every way save without sin (cf. Heb. 4:15), and even descended into the lower regions of the earth where the tyranny of sin compelled humanity, then God will also completely fulfill the goal of his mystical work of deifying humanity in every respect, of course, short of an identity of essence with God; and he will assimilate humanity to himself and elevate us to a position above all the heavens. It is to this exalted position that the natural magnitude of God's grace summons lowly humanity, out of a goodness that is infinite.[21]

Here Maximus makes two important points about *theōsis*. First, he guards against thinking that in deification humans will be given an "identity of essence with God." Second, *theōsis* is deification by grace, not by any potential in human nature. Still,

17. Christoforos Stavropoulos, "Partakers of Divine Nature," quoted in Clendenin, *Eastern Orthodox Theology*, 184.

18. The language of each human being becoming "a god" is confusing, bordering on idolatry. We always only share *as human creatures* in God's triune life. Recognizing such danger, Harrison, "Theosis as Salvation," 431, writes: "The language of deification is easily misunderstood, and perhaps it should not be used in popular preaching with careful explanation, if at all."

19. *The Triads* 2.3.15, in Gregory Palamas, *The Triads*, ed. John Meyendorff, trans. Nicholas Gendle (New York: Paulist Press, 1983), 60.

20. John Meyendorff, *A Study of Gregory Palamas* (Crestwood, NY: St. Vladimir's Seminary Press, 1998), 178 (emphasis original).

21. *Ad Thalassium* 22, in Maximus the Confessor, *On the Cosmic Mystery of Jesus Christ*, trans. Paul M. Blowers and Robert Louis Wilkins (Crestwood, NY: St. Vladimir's Seminary Press, 2003), 116.

when Maximus further elaborates the meaning of *theōsis*, it seems that human *creatureliness* (in any meaningful sense) gets lost:

> Existing here and now, we arrive at the *end of the ages* as active agents and reach the end of the exertion of our power and activity. But in the ages to come we shall undergo by grace the transformation unto deification and no longer be active but passive; and for this reason we shall not cease from being deified. At that point our passion will be supernatural, and there will be no principle restrictive of the divine activity in infinitely deifying those who are passive to it. . . . When in the future we are rendered passive (in deification), and have fully transcended the principles of beings created out of nothing, we will unwittingly enter into the true Cause of existent beings and terminate our proper faculties along with everything in our nature that has reached completion. We shall become that which in no way results from our natural ability, since our nature has no faculty for grasping what transcends nature. For nothing created is by its nature capable of inducing deification, since it is incapable of comprehending God. Intrinsically it is only by the grace of God that deification is bestowed proportionately on created beings. Grace alone illuminates human nature with supernatural light, and, by the superiority of its glory, elevates our nature above its proper limits in excess of glory.[22]

Maximus is surely right to emphasize the profound change that must be wrought by God on the human creature in order for humanity to participate in God's eternal life. And he fully acknowledges that deification is "bestowed proportionately on created beings." But if finally in *theōsis* we "have fully transcended the principles of being created out of nothing," does creatureliness itself remain? Or are human beings endowed (by grace, to be sure), beyond creatureliness, with the uncreated divine nature? It is not clear in this text from Maximus, or in Palamas. Explicating Palamas, Meyendorff writes: "It is not by their own efforts that Christians become 'eternal' and 'uncreated'; it is the divine life, which they only possess through grace, which gives them that character."[23] This notion of deification also seems to blur the distinction between the creature and creator, insofar as glorified human beings *become* "eternal" or "uncreated."

If we are to accept the language of *theōsis* or deification (which itself remains a question),[24] we must seek a definition governed by biblical teaching and orthodox doctrine regarding the triune God, the uncompromised ontological distinction of creator and creature, humankind as created in the image and likeness of God, union with Christ, and the life-giving presence and power of the Holy Spirit. Another more circumspect definition is preferable: "*Theosis* is the mystery of human

---

22. Ibid., 117–18.

23. Meyendorff, *Study of Gregory Palamas*, 177.

24. Bruce McCormack, "Participation in God, Yes, Deification, No: Two Modern Protestant Responses to Ancient Questions," in *Denkwürdiges Geheimnes: Beiträge zur Gotteslehre: Festschrift für Eberhard Jüngel zum 70. Geburtstag*, ed. Ingolf U. Dalferth, Johannes Fischer, and Hans-Peter Grosshans (Tübingen: Mohr Siebeck, 2004), 345–74.

nature's perfection in Christ, not its alteration or destruction, because *theosis* is the mystery of eternal life in communion with God in the divine Logos."[25] This statement points us toward clarifying the meaning of *theōsis* christologically and pneumatologically. First, a christological clarification: only the Son of God is divine by very nature, that is, is God in the strict sense. Peter himself is clear that God's declaration of Jesus's sonship and sharing in the divine majesty at the transfiguration is *unique*—Peter and the other apostles are "eyewitnesses" of it, not themselves recipients of the declaration (1:16–18). If other human beings become "sons of God," it is because they do so through divine grace and participation in Christ, by having their creaturely humanity united with his through baptismal and eucharistic incorporation into the body of Christ, the church.[26] They are "adopted" as sons (to use Paul's language) and made to share *by grace* in the sonship that Christ has by nature—as Maximus the Confessor and Gregory Palamas surely emphasize. Jenson provides three important christological clarifications of the concept of deification:[27] (1) "Because we become God,[28] we do not cease to be creatures; we will be those creatures who are indissolubly one with the creature God the Son is." (2) "The God who becomes what we are is the God-man; what he becomes is what we actually are, 'fallen and passible man, condemned to death'; and we become what he is, humans so united with God as to 'receive and bear God'" (quoting Irenaeus). (3) "The God-man becomes one of us, but the redeemed do not become additional God-humans. Rather they become participants in the one God-man, members of the *totus Christus*; they are God-bearers communally and not otherwise." Jenson's clarifications enable us to see that "sharing in the divine nature" comes about because our human nature is purified and taken up, through our participation in Christ's humanity (and through his in ours), into the divine life and fulfilled *in its humanity*, through that participation.[29]

25. Kärkkäinen, *One with God*, 25. Kraftchick 2002: 94 clarifies that Peter "does not argue that humans can become divine, or discover their divine nature. Rather, only by God's initiative are human beings *made* participants in the divine nature" (emphasis original). Other New Testament witnesses may also be read in support of a carefully qualified doctrine of *theōsis*. Paul's language of being "in Christ," particularly as it is explicated at length in Eph. 1:3–2:10, might certainly be understood along these lines, as well as some of the language and concepts in the Johannine writings. Starr, *Sharers in Divine Nature*, 167–216, provides an extensive and valuable discussion of each phrase in 2 Pet. 1:3–4 in relation to Pauline theology, detecting "the specific influence of Paul's letters on the author of 2 Peter" (216).

26. Palamas, *Triads*, 82–83, is emphatic that deification is utterly gracious. Humans have no natural capacity or faculty for receiving it.

27. Jenson, *Systematic Theology*, 2.341.

28. This phrase in Jenson is, I believe, incautious and inconsistent with what he goes on to say, and it is fundamentally misleading.

29. For a Protestant proposal, based in the theologies of Barth and Jüngel, that humans participate really in God's essence—understood as God's being realized in the history of Jesus Christ, in which humanity is elected to share—see the important essay by McCormack, who proposes a more radical *participation* in God than the Orthodox tradition does, while rejecting the notion of deification. Much depends, however, on whether one accepts McCormack's historicization of

A pneumatological clarification is also important: Christians are made to share in Christ's divine sonship only through the grace and power of the life-giving Holy Spirit. It is by the Holy Spirit that we are enabled, in Christ and in the communion of the saints, to call out as Christ did, "Abba, Father!" Through Christ, in the Holy Spirit, the community of God's people is caught up into God's own triune life, given a share in the eternal communion that is the Father, Son, and Holy Spirit.[30] While Peter's language and concepts are not identical to those of the Greek theologians, Peter does nonetheless express "the *reality* of our participation in the *very* life of God."[31]

The apostle Peter declares that the purpose of Christ's divine power and of "his precious and very great promises" is that we might become "sharers of divine nature," having escaped the decay and corruption of this world. He draws attention to our saving union with "our God and Savior Jesus Christ" through our "knowledge" (*epignōsis*) of him—a knowledge that is itself fully personal and participatory. As we will see, by being taken up into the life of virtue the whole person is given over to this saving knowledge and compellingly attracted to the all-surpassing glory and excellence of Jesus Christ revealed in the transfiguration. We thus come to share in his glory and excellence and therefore also his incorruptibility.

Faithful Virtues (2 Peter 1:5–7)

To this point Peter has taken us into the heart of the gospel by showing us that our lives have been drawn into a world where Jesus Christ, himself glorious and good, gives us everything we need for a godly life through his divine power. He also gives us the great promise of his powerful coming in which we will be made sharers in his glorious and indestructible life. Christ is thus the origin, power, and goal of the Christian life. Now we learn that all of that evokes from us a vigorous effort of our own toward a life of virtue, not that we might secure or add to what Christ has already given us, but that, living from his promise, power, and gifts, we might become ever more deeply engaged in our knowledge of him, our contemplation of his glorious divine reality, and our participation in the divine life. As Maximus says, "It is evident that every person who participates in virtue as a matter of habit participates in God, the substance of the virtues."[32]

God's triune being, based in a contested reading of the theology of Barth. Nonetheless, the title of McCormack's essay, "Participation in God, Yes, Deification, No," finally strikes me as exactly right. In the end it seems that the language of deification itself is problematic.

30. It is perhaps significant that Peter uses the word *koinōneō*, which suggests participation as communion, rather than *metechō*, which may suggest sharing ontic substance, although Bauckham 1983: 181 minimizes the difference in meaning.

31. To reiterate Meyendorff on Palamas; see Meyendorff, *Study of Gregory Palamas*, 178 (emphasis original).

32. *Ambiguum* 7, in Maximus the Confessor, *On the Cosmic Mystery of Jesus Christ*, 58.

Having set before us the vision of our being delivered from corruption and sharing in divine nature, "for this very reason" (1:5) Peter calls us to *strive* ("bring to bear every effort"; Harrington 2003: 244) toward a godly life. He describes that life by means of a list of virtues, those qualities of character that both derive from and sustain the habits and practices of goodness. Peter's list is in fact a common teaching device for moral instruction in the Hellenistic world,[33] and such lists are also used by other New Testament writers (2 Cor. 6:6; Gal. 5:22–23; 1 Tim. 4:12; 6:11; 2 Tim. 2:22; 3:10; 1 Pet. 3:8). Peter lists eight virtues: "Six virtues stem from common Hellenistic moral instruction. Two others [faith and love], rich with Christian overtones, frame them" (Kraftchick 2002: 95).

Christian theologians through the centuries (though not all of them in equal measure; compare Thomas Aquinas) have sometimes expressed reservations about "virtue ethics" and their pagan provenance. Augustine writes:

> Thus the virtues which the mind imagines it possesses, by means of which it rules the body and the vicious elements, are themselves vices rather than virtues, if the mind does not bring them into relation with God in order to achieve anything whatsoever and to maintain that achievement. For although the virtues are reckoned by some people to be genuine and honorable when they are related only to themselves and are sought for no other end, even then they are puffed up and proud, and so are to be accounted vices rather than virtues. (*City of God* 19.25 [trans. Henry Bettenson])

Echoing Augustine, Hauerwas and Pinches write that "to defend virtue itself is a dangerous thing for Christians to do, for they may discover that the defense inevitably yields a set of virtues that are vicious—that is, vicious according to the Christian gospel. . . . Greek accounts of the virtues are there to be *used* by Christians, not *built upon*."[34] Wilson cautions: "Because the language of virtue is almost entirely missing from the New Testament, and because virtue often, though not necessarily, tends to place undue emphasis on human ability to achieve the good apart from God's grace, the language of virtue needs to be transfigured for the church's use."[35] But Peter's account of the virtues displays just the kind of

33. J. Daryl Charles, "2 Peter, Jude," in *Believers Church Bible Commentary: 1–2 Peter, Jude*, ed. Erland Waltner and J. Daryl Charles (Scottdale, PA/Waterloo, ON: Herald, 1999), 263–65.

34. Stanley Hauerwas and Charles Pinches, *Christians among the Virtues: Theological Conversations with Ancient and Modern Ethics* (Notre Dame, IN: University of Notre Dame Press, 1997), 55, 68.

35. Jonathan R. Wilson, *Living Faithfully in a Fragmented World: Lessons for the Church from MacIntyre's "After Virtue"* (Harrisburg, PA: Trinity, 1997), 64. Wilson's claim that virtue language is "almost entirely missing from the New Testament" is overstated. We find virtue lists in Rom. 5:3–5; Jas. 1:3–4; and Gal. 5:22–23 (the last is rather lengthy). Peter H. Davids, *The Letters of 2 Peter and Jude*, Pillar New Testament Commentaries (Grand Rapids: Eerdmans, 2006), 177–78, provides comparison of 2 Pet. 1:5–7 with those lists, as well as with lists from Philo, Wisdom of Solomon, and Qumran.

gospel transfiguration that Augustine, Hauerwas and Pinches, and Wilson think is necessary.[36]

Peter's string of virtues begins with "faith" (*pistis*), here understood as "the specifically Christian 'faith' in the gospel which is the basis of all Christian life" (Bauckham 1983: 185). In this sense the word "faith" draws upon everything that Peter has written thus far, which is a brief summary of the gospel. By being enlisted in the cause of *this* gospel faith, the virtues that follow, most of them common in Hellenistic ethics, are thus appropriated from the Greco-Roman world and assimilated into the world in which Jesus Christ is Lord, the divine power of the virtuous life. "Faith is the root out of which all virtues grow. It is not supplemented with virtue, but develops into virtue" (Bauckham 1990: 57). Christian virtues spring from the *pistis* or loyalty and devotion that Christians give to Jesus Christ. While an educated Roman citizen of Peter's time would certainly recognize most of the virtues in Peter's list, the new purpose to which he puts them would be quite foreign to such a citizen, not least because the world order within which Peter makes his appeal is one in which Jesus Christ, rather than the Caesar or other gods, is confessed as "God and Savior" (1:1); one in which the *telos* of the virtues is not the salvation and glory of the hero in the Greek polis, but life in the new creation "where righteousness is at home"; and one in which the virtues are not personal achievements, but the power and promise of Christ at work in believers and the church.

It is therefore important to note that Peter does not, as some commentators suggest, adopt a language and idiom simply for the purpose of communicating with a Hellenistic audience. We do well not to think of this list as an example of "theological inculturation" (Harrington 2003: 248) according to which the gospel message is exported and in some measure translated into the language and shape of a foreign "host" culture (Bauckham 1983: 185, 187, 192; 1990: 48–49). The procedure in Peter runs in the other direction. By beginning with faith, Peter seizes the familiar Hellenistic virtue language and takes it up *into the service of the gospel*, thereby bending and molding the language and concepts into shapes and meanings consistent with the character of the new world order created by the gospel (1990: 58).[37] Thus the goal of taking up these virtues is to bring about greater effectiveness and fruitfulness in the knowledge of Jesus Christ (1:8)—that is, deeper participation in the life of God.

---

36. For a full theological account of the virtues, thus transfigured, *Christians among the Virtues* by Hauerwas and Pinches is indispensable. See also Jonathan R. Wilson, *Gospel Virtues: Practicing Faith, Hope, and Love in Uncertain Times* (Downers Grove, IL: InterVarsity, 1998). Markus Bockmuehl shows how Paul transfigures Hellenistic virtue language by conforming it to the gospel; *Jewish Law in Gentile Churches: Halakkah and the Beginning of Christian Public Ethics* (Edinburgh: Clark, 2000), 137–40.

37. See my *Paul among the Postliberals: Pauline Theology beyond Christendom and Modernity* (Grand Rapids: Brazos, 2003), 209–54, for how Paul accomplishes this task.

The radical transfiguration of pagan virtues by gospel faith is clearly evident in the next virtue, *aretē* ("excellence, goodness"; 1:5), which follows faith. Peter has already drawn attention to the "glorious excellence" (*doxa kai aretē*) of Jesus Christ, by which we are called into the sphere of his life and authority (1:3). So the meaning of *aretē* cannot in any sense be determined from the typical Hellenistic usage, in which the term indicates originally the personal and moral strength by which the hero conquers foes in battle. Rather, even before we come to the list of virtues, *aretē* is *defined by Peter with direct reference to Jesus Christ*. The language of "virtue" or "excellence" is thereby thoroughly assimilated to and transfigured by the gospel—excellence, *aretē*, is what we see in Jesus Christ himself, and it is *his* excellence that has both called us and is that to which we are called. Peter does not in this letter, as he does in 1 Peter, spell out for us the specific shape of the excellence of Jesus Christ by giving us a description of his deeds and character. But we have an abundance of instruction in that regard in the rest of the New Testament, in which 2 Peter is only one witness: we have the gospel narratives of Jesus (which Peter and his first readers surely knew; 1:16–19), and Paul's letters (which Peter and his readers also certainly knew; 3:15), in which we learn that the primary shape of Jesus's *aretē* is the power of his self-giving service and sacrifice for others, culminating finally in the cross—the revelation of his *cruciform* virtue. This is the unique and revolutionary *aretē* toward which we are to strive and as such is the overturning and undoing of the usual antique notions of *aretē*.

The next virtue, *gnōsis* ("knowledge"; 1:5), is likewise not an independent concept. Peter uses the language of knowledge often, already twice before its appearance in the virtue list and then again following the list, each time indicating our primary relation to Jesus Christ with the word *epignōsis*. In 3:18 he speaks of the *gnōsis* of Jesus Christ. So we are not called here to seek a merely intellectual knowledge for its own sake, as if that in itself could set us on the path to goodness and holiness, but to strive after the life-transforming personal knowledge in which we participate ever more deeply in the mystery and majesty of our God and Savior Jesus Christ and learn to walk in the way of godliness. Peter tells us that this kind of knowledge is given in "the words spoken in the past by the holy prophets, and the commandment of the Lord and Savior spoken through your apostles" (3:2), including what is written by the apostle Paul, even though it is difficult to understand (3:16). In other words, our knowledge of Jesus Christ comes through the testimony of the prophets and apostles in the scriptures of the Old and New Testaments as they faithfully bear witness to his divine sovereignty and the promise of his coming on the "day of God" (3:12).

The following two virtues (1:6), "self-control" (*enkrateia*) and "patience" or "steadfastness" (*hypomonē*), are particularly related to the purpose of 2 Peter. In 2 Pet. 2, Peter engages in a strongly worded criticism of those who had forsaken their original knowledge of Jesus Christ and the promise of his coming. In their impatience over his seeming failure to come as promised, they had also rejected Christ's moral claim on their lives. And so they became self-indulgent. Self-control, as the mastery of one's sinful impulses and desires, is intrinsic to being set free from the corruption of the world "through sinful desire" (1:4). Patience or steadfastness is in Christian life the virtue of a sure hope in God, particularly in the promise of the powerful arrival of Jesus Christ to judge the world and create a new heaven and a new earth (Bauckham 1983: 186; cf. Jas. 5:7–8).[38] As Peter makes clear in 2 Pet. 3:11–12, patience is not displayed in indifferent passivity, but rather is enacted in our striving after "holiness and godliness," whereby we "wait for and hasten the coming day of God." Patience is, in Paul's words, our "eager longing" for the promised redemption of God's children and of the whole of creation (Rom. 8:18–25).

To the virtues of self-control and patience, Peter adds "godliness" (*eusebeia*; 2 Pet. 1:6), repeating a word he uses earlier in 1:3. There he makes the point that Jesus Christ by his divine power has already given us everything necessary to live a godly life. So in the midst of this list of virtues, where Peter urges us to strive after them, he nonetheless reminds us that we do not strive toward these virtues out of our own resources and strength; rather we strive for them out of the fullness of the gifts that God has already so generously given us in Christ. The godly life is genuinely *achieved* as God *gives it* out of his own power. As Paul puts it: "Work out your own salvation with fear and trembling; for it is God who is at work in you, enabling you both to will and to work for his good pleasure" (Phil. 2:12–13).

The final two virtues (2 Pet. 1:7), "mutual affection" or "brotherly love" (*Philadelphia*) and "love" (*agapē*), turn our attention to our relationships with neighbors, saints, and God. The virtuous life might all too easily be construed as merely an exercise in individual self-improvement, apart from the gospel test of virtue being how we live with our brothers and sisters in the body of Christ, sharing our gifts with one another for the care and building up of the Christian community. In this Peter accords with the teaching of Jesus, the testimony of Paul (1 Cor. 12), and the wisdom of James (Jas. 2:1–7). In drawing this list to a penultimate conclusion with *philadelphia*, Peter again thoroughly assimilates the virtues to a Christian purpose and gives them Christian shape. That is even more the case with *agapē*, the virtue with which the list concludes and which as such sums up all the rest and infuses them with its own significance, just as "faith," which stands at the head of the list, roots the virtues deeply in the knowledge of Jesus Christ (Bauckham 1990: 58). Love, as Paul testifies in 1 Cor. 13, is the sustained and difficult task of suffering others, that is, of finding one's own life shaped and ordered and constituted in the presence of, and for the sake of, those with whom we are destined or called to live our lives: the other as God, and the others as our neighbors. "I give you a new commandment, that you love one another. Just as I have loved you, you also

38. Jerome H. Neyrey, *2 Peter, Jude: A New Translation with Introduction and Commentary*, Anchor Bible 37C (New York: Doubleday, 1993), 154–55, proposes that *hypomonē*, as steadfastness, is Peter's word for "hope"; thus Peter repeats the three theological virtues—faith, hope, and love—that we find consistently in Paul's letters (Rom. 5:1–5; 1 Cor. 13; and elsewhere).

should love one another. By this everyone will know that you are my disciples, if you have love for one another" (John 13:34–35). Love is the basic grammar of the gospel. Therefore, when Peter concludes his list of virtues with *agapē*, he assimilates the meaning of all of the virtues into the gospel-shaped life: they are now no longer the praiseworthy achievements of a heroic self-sufficient rational male citizen of the Greek polis; nor are they self-improvement guidelines for an autonomous individual in the modern Western world. "For Christians, attaining virtue is not fundamentally a victory, as it is for the Greeks. In that sense, Christianity is not a continuation of the Greek understanding of the virtues, but rather the inauguration of a new tradition that sets the virtues within an entirely different telos in community."[39] We learn from Peter that the virtues are the dispositions and practices by which the members of the body of Christ are assimilated, through God's power, into the saving knowledge of Jesus Christ as God and Savior, freed from the corruption of the world, transformed by the power of Christ's glory, and made to share in his incorruptibility and immortality.

Growing in Grace (2 Peter 1:8–11)

Our striving after the virtues increasingly conforms our life in the world to the divine glory and promise of Jesus Christ and frees us to be productive and fruitful in our knowledge of him ("neither unproductive nor unfruitful"; 1:8 DH). Peter envisages genuine growth in the Christian life and knowledge of God through the practice of the virtues. Conversely, those who fail to strive after the virtues are "blind," "nearsighted," and "forgetful" (1:9). Here we see the close relationship between the practice of virtue and the ability to see the truth: the practice of the Christian life and the right apprehension of the reality of God and Jesus Christ are intrinsic to one another, completely inseparable. There is no divorce between ethics and theology. Having once been "established in the truth" (1:12), our failure to grow in Christian virtue will lead to a fundamental spiritual blindness, an inability rightly to grasp the truth of the glory of Jesus Christ and the promise of his coming. As Peter makes abundantly clear in 2 Pet. 2, this is precisely what happened with the "false prophets"—and we are not sure which came first, their doubts and denials of Christ's coming in power or their own culpable moral failure (Bauckham 1990: 51).[40] Either way, because of them the "way of truth" is now maligned.

Peter also says that failure to strive after the virtues is the result of being "forgetful of the cleansing of past sins" (1:9), failing to remember our baptism. Conversion and baptism mark our gracious incorporation into the body of Christ

39. Hauerwas and Pinches, *Christians among the Virtues*, 63.
40. Charles, "2 Peter, Jude," 267, observes (contra Käsemann and others) that "what plagues the community hearing this epistle are ethical lapse and apostasy, and not the doctrinal emphasis (on the delay of the parousia) presupposed by 'early Catholic' proponents."

(being joined to Christ in his death and resurrection) and our deliverance from
the power of sin (being freed for obedience and faithfulness toward God), as
Paul so clearly lays out: "What then are we to say? Should we continue in sin in
order that grace may abound? By no means! How can we who died to sin go on
living in it? Do you not know that all of us who have been baptized into Christ
Jesus were baptized into his death? Therefore we have been buried with him by
baptism into death, so that, just as Christ was raised from the dead by the glory
of the Father, so we too might walk in newness of life" (Rom. 6:1–4). With Paul,
Peter believes that baptism creates a clear break with the past and the power of
sin and death over us and creates the time and space for a new life in the body of
Christ, which Peter spells out in terms of the virtues. We remember our baptism
not simply passively, in the manner of a mere recollection, but actively, by striving
for the "newness of life" inaugurated in our baptism. Remembering our baptism is
a matter of wholehearted striving and concrete bodily practice, as we work toward
forming a life of personal and ecclesial righteousness.

This is what Peter means when he urges us to be eager to "confirm [*bebaian . . .
poieisthai*] your call and election [*klēsin kai eklogēn*]" (2 Pet. 1:10). He has already
made it clear in 1:3 that Christ "calls" us by his own glory and excellence, and, as
we have seen, he presents the virtues as our living out of and being conformed to
this calling. The virtuous life is the way we remember our baptism. Peter surely
does not have later Reformation-style controversies over the doctrine of election
in mind when he writes these words (controversies reflected in both Calvin 1963:
333–35 and Luther 1967: 158–59). But just as clearly he does not understand our
striving after virtue as that which creates the occasion of our calling and election.
Exactly the reverse.[41] At the same time it is necessary that our calling and election
take on the flesh and blood of our daily dispositions and practices. Our calling
and election are not theological abstractions; they are the gospel soil, water, and
sunlight that grow our Christian life: they elicit and incite our own eager participation and effort toward growth in the gospel.[42] Our failure to enter fully and

41. Consider the description of the logic of faith in Paul by J. Louis Martyn, *Galatians: A
New Translation with Introduction and Commentary*, Anchor Bible 33A (New York: Doubleday,
1997), 276: "When Paul speaks about placing one's trust in Christ, he is pointing to a deed that
reflects not the freedom of the will, but rather God's freeing of the will." The logic of the virtues
in Peter is like that.

42. Compare again Martyn, *Galatians*, 277, on faith: "The gospel is itself an invasive event,
not merely the offering of a new option. It is in the gospel-event that Christ's faith elicits our faith."
Our faith is "incited by the preached message." I cannot agree with Bauckham 1990: 59 that for
Peter "the ethical fruits of faith are *objectively* necessary for the attainment of final salvation. The
divine initiative in our calling to be Christians will not reach its goal—our entry into Christ's
kingdom—unless it is ratified by our response in moral effort" (emphasis original). First, Peter
nowhere speaks about "attainment" of salvation, only about its being "richly provided" (1:11), as
the final outcome of Christ's divine power, calling, and promises (1:3–4). Second, as Bauckham
1983: 190 notes, the phrase *bebaian . . . poieisthai* likely does not have a strictly legal or contractual
meaning in this context. To speak of moral effort "ratifying" or "guaranteeing" salvation seems to
run against the grain of Peter's emphasis on personal moral *participation* in Christ's prior reality

personally into that growth may in time render the gospel inert and fruitless in us, even to the point that we might again become "entangled" and "overpowered" by the very "defilements of the world" from which our calling and election freed us (2:20). Conversely, when we fully and personally participate in our calling and election by living a virtuous faith, we "will never stumble" (1:10).

Peter states in 1:4 that the goal of Christ's power, provision, and promise is that we might become sharers in the divine nature. In 1:11 he renders the same goal with different language, speaking of our "entry into the eternal kingdom of our Lord and Savior Jesus Christ." In 3:13 he writes of our life in the "new heavens and a new earth, where righteousness is at home." Peter does not speak of the faithful "going to heaven."[43] When he depicts the final destiny of believers, and indeed of the whole creation, he envisages a radical and qualitative change in the very character of existence ("the elements will melt with fire"; 3:12) rather than a move to another space, so to speak. Our entry into the eternal kingdom of Christ will be God's gracious, rich provision of a qualitatively new life, in a qualitatively new creation (heavens and earth), in which Christ's own divinity, power, and righteousness sustain, pervade, and direct all things. That is the sum of Christian hope. "What we need to enter God's kingdom is a willingness to share the mode of existence practiced there, which is eternal love, self-offering, self-renunciation and sacrifice. In order to be filled with divine life, we have to give away all life of our own to God and to all the created beings united with him."[44] In this light, we must regard our living the virtues not as a means to an end (in the sense that we must do this to get to heaven), but as a kind of early acclimatization to the full virtue of existence in the new and eternal kingdom of Christ, and therefore also as that kingdom already invading the old world order that is in bondage to corruption. Then we must also say that we are not simply waiting for the new creation. In living the virtues we are also "hastening . . . the day of God" (3:12). The new creation itself is already on its way—and it is not slow in coming—among the people who take up its way of life, the life of virtuous faith. Paradoxically, the hastening parousia creates an even more piquant experience of its delay among the faithful (Rom. 8:18–25). The parousia is experienced as *merely* delayed only by those who refuse its radical alteration of *present* existence—and we must then understand the delay as God's *patience* for the sake of their salvation, that is, a delay of the day of judgment (2 Pet. 3:9).

Peter's Imminent Death (2 Peter 1:12–15)

Peter now for the first time directly states his purpose in writing the letter. It is a "farewell testament" that he leaves for his readers shortly before his imminent

and work. "Confirm" seems right—living the virtues is our wholehearted yes to Christ, "incited" by the grace of Christ.

43. Contra, e.g., Kraftchick 2002: 101: "a heavenly realm to be entered."
44. Harrison, "Theosis as Salvation," 442.

death (the removing of his earthly "tent" [*skēnōma*]; 1:13; cf. 2 Cor. 5:1–4). In like manner Jacob pronounced his final words to his sons (Gen. 49), Moses instructed Joshua and the people before his death (Deut. 31–32), and Jesus left the disciples with a summary of his teaching (Luke 22:24–38) and the promise of his continuing presence with them after his death and resurrection (John 13–17; see Harrington 2003: 253). Peter's letter thus takes on all the gravity that such a testament should have. These are the carefully considered words of one who must leave us with the most important thing that he has to give us from his life: the truth of the gospel, which he has just summed up in 2 Pet. 1:3–11. It is not as if we have not heard these things from the apostle before. He says that we "know them already and are established in the truth that has come" to us (1:12). But the point is that it is exactly that truth that will come under attack from false teachers (2:1–4); so Peter, in a final and solemn written testimony, "make[s] every effort" not only to remind us of that truth, but also to warn us of the dangers that will come from those who distort and malign the truth. The truth requires vigilance and ongoing defense against its enemies. That Peter's final testimony is now being put down in writing will enable us "at any time to recall these things" (1:15) in our own effort to withstand the attack of falsehood. We see then that his final testament is not merely intended for the present occasion of threat, but in fact for all posterity, reaching even to us who read his letter nearly two thousand years after his death and must bear our own faithful witness to the truth.

Peter mentions that the Lord Jesus Christ "also" (*kathōs kai*; 1:14) made it clear to him that his death was imminent.[45] In John 21:18–19 we hear these prophetic words from Jesus to Peter: "'Very truly, I tell you, when you were younger, you used to fasten your own belt and to go wherever you wished. But when you grow old, you will stretch out your hands, and someone else will fasten a belt around you and take you where you do not wish to go.' (He said this to indicate the kind of death by which he would glorify God.) After this he said to him, 'Follow me.'" By recalling these words of Jesus we are reminded that Peter's death was not "natural" but in fact a specific form of his discipleship, his own taking up of the cross and sharing in the sufferings of Christ. The final words of Peter in this letter (as in 1 Peter) thus bear all the weight and authority of one whose own life and death was an imitation of Jesus Christ, whom the apostle confessed as Messiah, God, and Savior. With this letter, therefore, Peter also fulfils the Lord's command to him in John 21: "Feed my lambs" and "Feed my sheep" (Harrington 2003: 254). We are fed by the faithful words of the apostle.

45. In other words, Peter's knowledge of his impending death is a result both of his own discernment and of what he was shown by Jesus (following Bauckham 1983: 199). Bauckham provides a thorough discussion of the event Peter might have been referring to by this phrase (200–201), concluding that John 21:18 is most likely.

Transfiguration: Jesus Christ Revealed in Glory (2 Peter 1:16–18)

What is the ground of confidence and authority for Peter's proclamation of the divine sovereignty and powerful coming of Jesus Christ? Are such claims merely "cleverly devised myths" (*sesophismenois mythois*; 1:16), fanciful fables fabricated by the apostle to support what he construes as an appropriate cosmic and moral order? Is not the story about a divine sovereign who will "come to judge the living and the dead" simply the means of creating fear of judgment in order to circumscribe and control the freedom of others' opinions and conduct—and to coerce them toward a life of virtue? We find out in 2 Pet. 2 that those are the kinds of challenges posed by false teachers who would undo the work of the apostles. Peter now sets out to respond to them by recounting the transfiguration.[46]

The apostolic claim about Christ's cosmic majesty and coming in power, far from being a fabricated tale, is instead firmly based on the experience of eyewitnesses—Peter himself being one of them. "Let us remember that from the beginning the Gospel was not made up of vague rumours, but that the apostles were the authentic heralds of those things which they had seen" (Calvin 1963: 338). The apostles were there on the "holy mountain" (Mount Tabor, according to tradition) and heard the divine voice when God the Father (who is himself the "Majestic Glory," *megaloprepous doxēs*) made the decisive declaration to Jesus: "This is my Son, my Beloved, with whom I am well pleased" (1:17).[47] Calling upon the scene depicted in Ps. 2, this declaration to Jesus in the hearing of the apostles is in fact a revelation of his *eschatological enthronement* and ultimate divine sovereignty and authority over all things, including the authority to destroy God's enemies and to inherit all the nations of the earth:

> "I have set my king on Zion, my holy hill."
> I will tell of the decree of the LORD:
> He said to me, "You are my son;
>   today I have begotten you.
> Ask of me, and I will make the nations your heritage,
>   and the ends of the earth your possession.
> You shall break them with a rod of iron,
>   and dash them in pieces like a potter's vessel." (Ps. 2:6–9)

46. An indispensable volume on the transfiguration is McGuckin 1986, which contains a study of the transfiguration in Mark and in patristic theology, as well as extensive texts and commentaries on the transfiguration (in English translation) by over thirty Greek and Latin fathers from Irenaeus to Gregory Palamas. Especially instructive are the oration of John of Damascus (pp. 205–25), Homily 34 of Gregory Palamas (pp. 225–34), Homily 28 of Augustine (pp. 274–77), and Homily 51 of Pope Leo I (pp. 281–85). Dorothy Lee's *Transfiguration* (New York: Continuum, 2004) is an excellent biblical and theological study of each of the New Testament transfiguration texts.

47. The declaration by God in 2 Pet. 1:17 (which is nearly identical to Matt. 17:5) "is a pastiche of OT phrases: Ps. 2:7 ('You are my Son'—about the king/messiah); Gen. 22:2 ('your only son'—about Isaac); and Isa. 42:1 ('my chosen, in whom my soul delights'—about the Servant of God)" (Harrington 2003: 256).

The transfiguration of Jesus is therefore an *apocalypse*, a heavenly revelation ("we ourselves heard this voice come from heaven"; 2 Pet. 1:18) granted to the apostles of the coming "eternal kingdom of our Lord and Savior Jesus Christ" (1:11), a glorious revelation of the day when "the kingdom of the world [shall] become the kingdom of our Lord and of his Messiah, and he will reign forever and ever" (Rev. 11:15). "Peter and the Sons of Thunder saw his beauty on the mountain more radiant than the very radiance of the sun, and they were found worthy to see with their eyes the preliminaries of his glorious advent" (Basil of Caesarea, *Homily on Psalms* 44.5, in McGuckin 1986: 169). "And he flashed like lightning on the mountain and became brighter than the sun, intimating mysteries of the age to come" (Gregory of Nazianzus, *Oratio* 29.19, in McGuckin 1986: 171).[48] The transfiguration is an apocalypse like that granted to John when he was taken up into heaven and allowed to stand before the throne of God and of the Lamb (Rev. 4–5) and to see the triune God being worshiped by all the creatures and peoples of the earth, as if the final goal of all creation had already arrived. It is like the apocalypse of Jesus Christ that suddenly came upon Saul when he was struck down by the blinding light from heaven as he traveled on the road to Damascus (Acts 9:1–9).

In the Gospel of Matthew Jesus announces that he will "come with his angels in the glory of his Father, and then he will repay everyone for what has been done" (Matt. 16:27). This is the same "powerful coming" (*dynamis kai parousia*) of which Peter writes in 2 Pet. 1:16 and 2 Pet. 3. But Jesus goes on to say, strangely: "Truly I tell you, there are some standing here who will not taste death before they see the Son of Man coming in his kingdom" (Matt. 16:28; cf. Mark 9:1: "until they see that the kingdom of God has come with power [*dynamis*]"). What can he mean, since all of the apostles do in fact die before Jesus's powerful parousia? As Cyril and many of the church fathers recognize, the question is answered in the very next scene of the gospel (Matt. 17:1–8):

> Surely [Jesus] did not mean that such a span of life would be drawn out for them that they would survive even into those times of the consummation of the ages, when he would descend from the heavens and restore to the saints the kingdom that had been prepared for them? . . . But the Kingdom he spoke of was the vision of his glory in which he will be seen in that time when he will shine out upon all men on earth. . . . So how did he make them see this wonder, those who had received his promise? Going up the mountain he took three chosen ones from among them and then he was transfigured into a certain extraordinary and godlike radiance", so that even his garments seemed to shine at the touch of this light. (Cyril of Alexandria, *Homiliae Diversae* 9, in McGuckin 1986: 177)

---

48. Many patristic commentators on the transfiguration texts (usually in the gospel accounts) understand the transfiguration as a proleptic revelation of Christ's glory in the age to come.

The revelation of the Son of Man in his glory to "some standing here" (Peter, James, and John) is in fact the transfiguration itself: *that* is the moment when *they see* the "Son of Man coming in his kingdom"; they are granted an advance glimpse of the day of his coming in power to judge the whole world in righteousness. "The disciples truly saw him coming into his kingdom when they saw him shining in glory on the mountain. This is that glory in which he shall be seen by all the saints in his kingdom, once the judgement is over" (Bede, *Homily* 28, in McGuckin 1986: 291). The transfiguration is a prophetic apocalypse of the eschatological enthronement of Jesus Christ as Lord, "a prophecy of Jesus' parousia" (Harrington 2003: 258; see also Bauckham 1983: 219–21). Because the apostles (not only Peter, but also those with him; he speaks of "we" in 2 Pet. 1:16–19) at the transfiguration have, for a moment, *already seen and heard* Jesus Christ enthroned at the end of the ages in his divine majesty and glory, they are now also *already certain* ("we have the prophetic message more fully confirmed"; 1:19) that he will in fact come to judge the earth and its inhabitants and set up his eternal reign over all things and all peoples.

> Listen to what the blessed Peter says: "It is good for us to be here." So if he, seeing an obscure image of the things to come, immediately cast out everything from his soul, for the sake of the delightfulness of what he saw being placed in his soul, then what can be said when the very truth of these things comes about; when the kingly halls are thrown open and the King himself can be seen no longer in riddles or through a mirror, but face to face; not by faith any longer but before our very eyes? (John Chrysostom, *Ad Theodorum Lapsum* 1.11, in McGuckin 1986: 173)

The transfiguration grants us a partial and temporal glimpse of the eternal divine reality and glorious beauty of the kingdom of Christ and calls us to enter into that kingdom and begin to experience its glory.

Now we understand why Peter recalls the transfiguration (rather than, say, the resurrection) as the ground of his confidence and authority in writing this letter of promise and warning and, in fact, as the criterion for everything he writes.[49] The transfiguration is the revelation to the apostles, and in them to the whole church and all of humanity, of the final truth and reality of all things. The knowledge of the truth of all things—of the world and all human existence—is given only in the knowledge of the divine majesty and the powerful coming of Jesus Christ our Lord, because he is the one exalted and enthroned by the creator of the universe as the king and judge of the world. He is the uncreated light of the world. The light that shines on the apostles on the mountain of transfiguration is the light that shines in the darkness when God creates the world, the light that

---

49. Edith M. Humphrey, in conversations early on in this commentary project, suggested to me that 2 Peter is in reality an extended meditation on the transfiguration. My original doubts about that suggestion have dissipated. See her meditation on the transfiguration in her *Ecstasy and Intimacy: When the Holy Spirit Meets the Human Spirit* (Grand Rapids: Eerdmans, 2006), 79–101.

enlightens all of creation, which the darkness cannot overcome, the light that will shine from the new Jerusalem. It is the divine Logos of God. "And the Word became flesh and lived among us, and we have seen his glory, the glory as of the Father's only Son, full of grace and truth" (John 1:14 NRSV margin).[50] Not to know Jesus Christ in the truth of this brilliant revelation of his divine glory, not to have a share in him, in the personal, participatory way of knowledge to which Peter has called us, is to be left in a world of darkness, ignorance, irrationality, and immorality—as Peter makes abundantly clear in 2 Pet. 2. But on the day of the Lord's coming "the earth and everything that is done on it will be disclosed" (3:10): on that day the light of the transfiguration revealed only momentarily to Peter, James, and John on the holy mountain will overcome the darkness and be revealed to everyone.

The transfiguration figures large in the iconographical tradition and the liturgical calendar of Eastern Orthodoxy.[51] The all-encompassing scope of Christian truth is in some sense revealed in this extraordinary event of Christ's life, as David Bentley Hart writes:

> In the icon of the Christ's transfiguration upon Mount Tabor—as in the feast of light to which it is liturgically attached—the entire "logic" of Eastern Christian theology, devotion, worship, and mysticism is uniquely concentrated. . . . As an object of contemplation, the Transfiguration image comprises within itself the whole story of creation, incarnation, and salvation in a particular way, with a fixed harmony of elements, and with a singular intensity. It allows us, in one fixed instant of visionary clarity, to see and to reflect upon the entire mystery of the God-man and of the divinization of our humanity in Him. . . .
>
> The icon also, however, offers us a glimpse of the eschatological horizon of salvation; for the same light that the three disciples were permitted to see break forth from the body of Christ will, in the fullness of time, enter into and transform all of creation, with that glory that the Son had with the Father before the world began (John 17:5), and that the whole of creation awaits with groans of longing and travail (Rom. 8:19–23). Then, to use an image favored by a host of Orthodox spiritual writers, the entire universe will be like the burning bush seen by Moses: radiant with the fire of God's holiness, but not consumed. And the Christian who prayerfully turns his gaze to the Transfiguration icon, and holds it there, should see himself taken up into the incarnate God, and refashioned after the ancient beauty of the divine image.[52]

50. Lee, *Transfiguration*, 103–5, draws out important common themes (as well as some differences) between John 1:14 and the Synoptic accounts of the transfiguration.

51. It may be, however, that this emphasis on the transfiguration is waning in the Eastern churches: "In the East, despite the rich theological thought that surrounds it—especially within the tradition of hesychasm—its liturgical importance has been dwarfed by its proximity to the feast of the Dormition of the Mother of God"; Andreas Andreopoulos, *Metamorphosis: The Transfiguration in Byzantine Theology and Iconography* (Crestwood, NY: St. Vladimir's Seminary Press, 2005), 15.

52. David Bentley Hart in Solrunn Nes, *The Uncreated Light: An Iconographical Study of the Transfiguration in the Eastern Church* (Grand Rapids: Eerdmans, 2007), xiii–xiv.

By recalling the glorious apocalyptic event of the transfiguration of our Lord, Peter directs a strong word against the theological rationalisms, reductionisms, and relativisms of his age and ours. While he offers a vigorous apologia for the truth of the gospel, he does not appeal to a foundation in universal rational first principles, available to everyone everywhere, or to an a priori universal religious sense, variously modified by historical and cultural experience—the standard post-Enlightenment modes of apologia for religious truth. Instead, Peter goes directly to his and the other apostles being *eyewitnesses of an apocalypse* of the truth of Jesus Christ. That apocalypse of the truth of all things is itself the origin and criterion of all claims about God and the beginning and end of all things.[53] "If Jesus' action and passion are genuinely for the life of *the world*, then their power and significance extends to all creation. And the difference Jesus makes to the rest of reality is not superficial or transitory, but utterly basic; it is the difference between death and life, between non-being and being, for every particular thing."[54] The glorious reality of Jesus Christ revealed in the transfiguration itself constitutes, defines, and illuminates the world in which we live. The transfiguring judgment and new creation that Peter envisages in 2 Pet. 3 amount to nothing less than God's act of dissolving all other rational or ordering principles (the *stoicheia*; 3:10, 12) of the world and recreating the world in conformity with the truth of Jesus Christ. When we deny or diminish the significance of the apocalyptic enthronement of Jesus Christ, and of his coming in power, we are attempting to live in some other world, a world that does not exist by the word and judgment and action of the one creator God (3:5–7, 13)—and therefore does not exist in any true sense. Such a world is in fact a mere fantasy, spun by those whose imaginations are like "waterless springs and mists driven by a storm" (2:17). Such a fantastic world is the very *tohu wabohu*, the "formless void" of Gen. 1:2, in all of its sterility, ugliness, and insubstantiality, from which the creator delivers us by his powerful, gracious, and beautiful word spoken in Jesus Christ.[55]

The Authority of Prophecy and Scripture (2 Peter 1:19–21)

"You will do well to be attentive to this"—that is, this apocalyptic revelation of the glorious majesty and authority of Jesus Christ, the beloved Son of the Father—"as to a lamp shining in a dark place, until the day dawns and the morning star rises in your hearts" (1:19). When the day dawns (an everlasting day; Rev. 21:25; 22:5), the light of Christ, "the bright morning star" (22:16), will rise not only in our

53. This conviction is the root and branches of Karl Barth's entire theological work.
54. Bruce D. Marshall, *Trinity and Truth* (Cambridge: Cambridge University Press, 2000), 109 (emphasis original).
55. Hart, *Beauty of the Infinite*, 35–125, provides a trenchant critique of such fantastic worlds (which hover insubstantially over the void: the "empty sublime") imagined by many postmodern philosophies.

hearts; it will illuminate the whole of creation with the truth and beauty of God. "And the city has no need of sun or moon to shine on it, for the glory of God is its light, and its lamp is the Lamb. The nations will walk by its light, and the kings of the earth will bring their glory into it" (21:23–24).

The transfiguration, the revelation to the apostolic eyewitnesses of the enthronement of Jesus Christ as the eschatological divine king and judge by God the Father, is *itself* the "prophetic word" (*prophētikos logos*) announcing the coming day of the Lord. What was revealed to the apostles on the mountain anticipates and proclaims the final revelation of Christ in glory. That is Peter's point in the first part of 2 Pet. 1:19.[56] The apostles themselves saw and heard this powerful, reality-constituting word of promise and hope. In 1:20 Peter says that the transfiguration is also a *fulfillment* of the prophecies of scripture, of Ps. 2 in particular, but also of others. He is reflecting the gospel accounts of the transfiguration, in which Moses (the law) and Elijah (the prophets) appear with Jesus in his glorification. The truth that the Old Testament prophecies are caught up by and given new life in the revelation of the coming glory and sovereignty of Jesus Christ is not a matter, Peter says, of "one's own interpretation," but a matter of confidence in two things. First, there is the fact of the transfiguration itself. Far from being a conclusion about Jesus that the apostles drew from their own reflection on their experiences of him, and in turn their own ascription of wonderful titles and status to him, the prophecies were interpreted by the divine voice itself in relation to Jesus (Kraftchick 2002: 118). *The transfiguration is God's own exegesis of the prophetic word of Ps. 2*, as God himself declares Jesus to be the one about whom the words of the psalms and the prophets are written. Thus the transfiguration may be taken as testimony against the endless sterile claims of modern and postmodern theologies since Kant that "the divine," if it can be spoken of at all, is an inert, silent, and finally empty transcendence, merely subject to the multitude of diverse attempts by individual or collective human subjects to image or name God, or identify the transcendent significance of Jesus, through an exegesis of one human experience or another. Therein biblically speaking lies idolatry. By contrast, the transfiguration, since it is the declaration of the divine sonship of Jesus Christ by God the Father, amounts to a reiteration of the first commandment, "You shall have no other gods before me," seen and overheard by the apostolic eyewitnesses. Jesus is identified by the words of the Father in such a manner that God cannot be thought as other than the Father whose beloved Son Jesus Christ is. Conversely, Jesus Christ cannot be thought as other than the beloved Son of the Father.

> When the Father said, "This is my beloved son in whom I am well pleased," they heard quite plainly: This is my Son who is from me and with me and who is eternally. The Begetter is not prior to the Begotten, nor the Begotten subsequent to the Begetter. This is my Beloved Son whom Godhead does not separate from me,

56. I am here following some of the suggestions by Harrington 2003: 256–57, 259–60.

power does not divide and eternity does not distinguish. This is my Beloved Son, not an adopted son but a true son. He is not created by another, but begotten from me; not made like me from a different nature, but from my own essence born equal to me. This is my Son through whom all things were made and without whom nothing was made. All that I do, he does equally, and in whatever way I am active he too is active with me without separation and without difference. The Son is in the Father and the Father in the Son, and our unity is never divided. (Pope Leo I, *Homily* 51, in McGuckin 1986: 284)

To know Jesus Christ as the Father's own exegesis of Ps. 2 is to know him with the Father as, in truth, the one God. This is the core affirmation of the whole of the New Testament, apart from which there is no authentic Christian faith. Those who propose doctrines of Jesus Christ that reduce or deny his divine identity as revealed in the transfiguration are not only in contradiction of the witness of the New Testament; they must be regarded as "false teachers" (*pseudodidaskaloi*; 2 Pet. 2:1) whose opinions are fundamentally destructive of the life of the church.

Second, the prophecies of the Old Testament are themselves not merely human words. They are the words of God, spoken as men and women "moved by the Holy Spirit spoke from God" (1:21). In other words, neither prophecy nor its interpretation come "through human will"; they are from beginning to end, from origin to destination, the work of the triune God. The transfiguration reveals to us the proper understanding of the origin and interpretation of holy scripture. God the Holy Spirit—who is the cloud that descends on the holy mountain— utters the prophecies through the law (Moses) and the prophets (Elijah). God the Father exegetes the prophecies by speaking in his own voice. God the Son in his very own person is the exegesis, the meaning and truth, of the prophecies. The apostles on the mountain, and with them the whole church, are caught up into prophetic revelation, interpretation, and fulfillment as recipient hearers and witnesses. They "suffer divine things."[57] The church's faithful interpretation of scripture in preaching, theology, and doctrine comes about from beginning to end through its ongoing witness to and participation in the speech of the triune God. The unity of the scriptures, that is, their coherence in speaking of the one God and his Son Jesus Christ, is not something first *constituted by* a theological idea, worldview, doctrine, practice, or method of interpretation. The unity of scripture is constituted by God the Holy Spirit who speaks prophetically in the Old Testament, also being God the Father who draws Old Testament prophecy toward its goal as witness to Jesus Christ, who as the Son of God is himself the content of Old Testament prophecy. The unity of the Old and New Testaments is given in God's own triune action with respect to the text of scripture, an action

57. Reinhard Hütter, *Suffering Divine Things: Theology as Church Practice*, trans. Doug Stott (Grand Rapids: Eerdmans, 2000); idem, "The Church: The Knowledge of the Triune God: Practices, Doctrine, Theology," in *Knowing the Triune God: The Work of the Spirit in the Practices of the Church*, ed. James J. Buckley and David S. Yeago (Grand Rapids: Eerdmans, 2001), 23–47.

in which the church by the Holy Spirit is granted participation *through* its preaching, doctrines, and practices.[58]

Ascending the Holy Mountain: Coda on 2 Peter 1

We have ascended with Peter on a short, steep, and demanding climb to the top of the holy mountain of transfiguration. Here a vista of the gospel opens before us; but it is not the gospel as some *thing*—a story, an idea, a doctrine—that we in turn "believe in." Rather, the gospel revealed on the mountain is the beautiful and glorious divine reality in which we live and move and have our being, the triune God. We hear the voice of the Majestic Glory as he speaks to and about his beloved Son. We see the majesty and glory of Jesus Christ in his divine sovereignty over all things. We know the meaning of the prophetic word spoken by the Holy Spirit and exegeted by the Father through the incarnation of the Son. What is this but our participation, already, by grace and in some measure, in the divine nature—knowing and living the life of the triune God from the inside so to speak?

We do not ascend the mountain without our own determined effort. Peter calls us to "make every effort" toward a life of virtue, and each of the virtues that he names is a handhold or foothold on the rugged path of ascent. But we discover as we climb with him that every step of our way to this high holy place is made possible, indeed is *given* to us, through the power and rich provision of Jesus Christ himself. We ascend the mountain with Christ and in Christ. It is not that our effort is "worth it in the end." Rather, in striving to live each of the virtues we already share in the powerful divine life of Jesus Christ, who himself is the *aretē*, the excellence and strength of our own striving in the ascent from faith, through steadfastness and the other virtues, to self-giving love, and finally to the vision of Christ's glorious reign with the Father over all things. "Our citizenship is in heaven, and it is from there that we are expecting a Savior, the Lord Jesus Christ. He will transform the body of our humiliation, that it may be conformed to the body of his glory, by the power that also enables him to make all things subject to himself" (Phil. 3:20–21). We find ourselves drawn onto the way of truth and righteousness because we are promised a vision of God's own triune glory.

"Why does [Christ] lead his disciples onto a high mountain? Because divine scripture figuratively calls the virtues 'mountains.' And set as the pinnacle and citadel of all the virtues is love" (Gregory Palamas, *Oratio, De Transfiguratione*, in McGuckin 1986: 215). As we ascend and stand on the mountain of Christ's transfiguration with Peter and the apostles, we find that our own lives are already being transfigured through assimilation to the life of Christ. "And all of us, with

58. David S. Yeago, "The Bible: The Spirit, the Church, and the Scriptures: Biblical Inspiration and Interpretation Revisited," in *Knowing the Triune God: The Work of the Spirit in the Practices of the Church*, ed. James J. Buckley and David S. Yeago (Grand Rapids: Eerdmans, 2001), 49–93.

unveiled faces, seeing the glory of the Lord as though reflected in a mirror, are being transformed into the same image from one degree of glory to another; for this comes from the Lord, the Spirit" (2 Cor. 3:18).[59] The "coming of the day of God" is therefore not only a future hope for those on the holy mountain. "The Lord is not slow about his promise, as some think of slowness" (2 Pet. 3:9). Those who live "lives of holiness and godliness" do not merely wait for the day; they already experience it in part and hasten its final arrival. To ascend with Peter and the apostles to the top of the mountain is to know in some measure, here and now, the reality of that coming day, of Christ's eternal kingdom, of our sharing in the divine nature.

59. Lee, *Transfiguration*, 112–13, suggests that there are transfiguration themes in Phil. 3:20 and 2 Cor. 3:18.

2 PETER 2

Destructive Opinions (2 Peter 2:1–3)

Only by standing with Peter on the holy mountain are we given an accurate perspective on the dangerous and distorting opinions of the false teachers. In the bright light of the glorious truth revealed on the mountain of transfiguration, their teachings are exposed as paltry, miserable, dark and destructive, and therefore worthy of vigorous condemnation. Having separated themselves from the life of the triune God through their denials, falsehoods, and manner of living, the false teachers already have their own share in the reality of God's coming day—the day of his wrath.

"False prophets" are not a new phenomenon. Peter reminds us in 2:1 that they were also there in the history of Israel, vying with God's own prophets for the people's attention and loyalty. And Peter warns that they will threaten the church as well. Despite "teachers of falsehood" (*pseudodidaskaloi*) almost invariably presenting their message as good news, "gospel" (as Paul also knows; Gal. 1:6–9), their words are in fact "destructive opinions" (*haireseis apōleias*), teachings that erode, diminish, and distort the truth of God (2 Pet. 2:1). The most serious challenges to the truth of Christian faith rarely come directly from those outside the Christian church; they usually come from those who were once loyal servants of "the Master who bought them," but who now in one way or another deny their master (cf. Acts 20:29–30). The undoing of the faith is usually an "inside job," done by (post-)Christian teachers who assert the authority of their own supposed enlightened and liberated opinions over against the prophetic and apostolic word of scripture.[1] As Luther clearly saw, those trained for the teaching ministry of the church, the *doctores* (for Peter, the *didaskaloi*), are often particularly culpable:

---

1. See, for example, the many books of this nature by John Shelby Spong, listed on his website, www.BishipSpong.com.

Peter "hits the schools of higher learning, where such people [*falsi doctores*] are turned out. . . . For the whole world thinks these schools should be the springs from which those who are to teach the people should flow" (1967: 169). Luther is certainly not against schools of higher learning, but he wants to disabuse us of the notion that the best seminary training, conducted at the highest scholarly level and under the banner of Christian teaching, is going to build up the church of God. It is not necessarily so, as Luther himself learned from the schools of the "Papists." Teaching destructive *haireseis* is usually done by theologians and bishops in the church, from Marcion and Valentinus in the second century, to Arius in the fourth, and to Matthew Fox, John Shelby Spong, and the Jesus Seminar in the twenty-first, who manage to win over many within the church as well as beyond it. "It is no small stumbling-block to those who are weak to see false teachings received by the common approbation of the world, and a huge number of men led astray, so that only a few remain in the pure obedience of Christ" (Calvin 1963: 346).

Peter notes that false teachers will "bring in" their destructive opinions surreptitiously (2:1; see Bauckham 1983: 239 on *pareisagō*, "to bring in [secretly]"). It is not that the false teachers themselves come from outside—as Calvin colorfully suggests, "infiltrating by flanking attacks and by underground tunnellings" (1963: 346). It is rather that some of those *already on the inside* have become persuaded that the world beyond the church tells a bigger and better story than the gospel of the sovereignty and powerful coming of Jesus Christ. For these teachers there is some other account of cosmic and human reality that the wider (philosophical, scientific, political) culture tells that seems more plausible, more scientific, more useful for human "flourishing." The Christian gospel (so it seems to them) will therefore need to justify itself in relation to this larger, culturally established story.[2] The false teachers do not usually present that story in direct opposition to the truth of Jesus Christ. In fact Jesus Christ is invariably given a role to play in the "gospel" of Christian heresies—and so these "gospels" often sound a good deal like the real thing. The destructive heresies are thus introduced surreptitiously. Christ is made a character (perhaps even the highest, most representative one: the "symbol") in a larger cosmic, political, social, or personal story; he is a redeemer or liberator or social reformer or spiritual guide or example. Where is the heresy in that, since in some respect Christ is indeed all of these things? The heresy is that the constitution, definition, parameters, and conditions of the larger story or world in which Jesus Christ is given his role, or of which he is the symbol, are already in place before he arrives on the scene; as such they set the terms, conditions, and limits for understanding who he is and what he does or is able to do in

2. John Howard Yoder provides an insightful description and critique of this kind of apologetic effort in "'But We Do See Jesus': The Particularity of Incarnation and the Universality of Truth," in his *The Priestly Kingdom: Social Ethics as Gospel* (Notre Dame, IN: University of Notre Dame Press, 1984), 46–62; and "On Not Being Ashamed of the Gospel: Particularity, Pluralism, and Validation," *Faith and Philosophy* 9 (1992): 285–300.

relation to that story or world. Christ may function as the highest manifestation, symbol, or expression of some truth or principle already known and operating in that world; but far from being our "God and Savior" (1:1), coequal with the Father and the Holy Spirit in his being and acts, he is constrained by the present world order and realistically can act only within its limits and according to its determining rules.

Most major heresies in the history of the church amount to this: they in some manner deny the transcendent divine glory of Jesus Christ and his divine sovereignty over all worldly limits, structures, and powers—his sovereignty revealed to the apostles on the holy mountain.[3] But, against the heresies, Peter and all of the New Testament declares that Christ does not have a "part" in another story. Christ himself is the one and only *author* of the story of all things, the one by whom and through whom and for whom all things exist, the one in whom everything coheres, the one through whom God judges the world in righteousness and graciously reconciles all things to himself, the one who is the head of his body, the church, the one who will come again in power (cf. Col. 1:15–20). If this is the truth of reality, the truth that heresies deny, then it is the heresies themselves that are "plastic words" (*plastois logois*; 2 Pet. 2:3 DH), *"feigned words* that are artfully designed to deceive" (Calvin 1963: 347). Heresies are, in fact, "cleverly devised myths" (1:16), not the truth of Christ's powerful parousia. Therefore, the false teachers' "destruction" of the truth of "the Master who bought them" can only lead to their own destruction, because they do not merely distort *a* truth but "the way of truth" (*hē hodos tēs alētheias*; 2:2). They fail to grasp the very ontological and moral character of reality itself, the reality in which they in fact exist. Denying that reality, false teachers and heretics proclaim and promote a world that does not exist and a way of life that runs against the "grain of the universe."[4] Exactly for this reason, Peter says in 2:3, their destruction is neither uncertain nor far off (it is not "dozing"; see Harrington 2003: 262 on *nystazō*): it is *already* in some measure upon them, for, by dwelling spiritually, intellectually, and morally in their denials and distortions of the way things are, false teachers in the church already willingly participate in their own devolution and destruction, their own nonbeing (2:12–13)—the very same end to which they will be given over on the day of judgment (3:7).

The kingdom [of God] wears the aspect of damnation, as well as of redemption, and the language of hell enters Christian discourse alongside the language of peace; this is the shadow side of the gospel that promises the rescue of the world by way of a history in which God tells correctly the story that a sinful humanity tells awry,

3. See Ben Quash and Michael Ward, *Heresies and How to Avoid Them: Why It Matters What Christians Believe* (Peabody, MA: Hendrickson, 2007).
4. The phrase, originally from John Howard Yoder, is borrowed by Stanley Hauerwas as the title of his 2001 Gifford Lectures: *With the Grain of the Universe: The Church's Witness and Natural Theology* (Grand Rapids: Brazos, 2001).

and so saves not by unifying the many strands of human history in a great synthesis but by electing one story as the truth of the world.[5]

Heresy in the church is the failure to tell that one story truthfully; it is a question of the truthfulness of Christian *teaching*. No doubt many of those whom the church judges heretical in their teaching nevertheless live apparently saintly lives. Still, Peter makes us aware that crucial and destructive shifts away from truthful Christian teaching often occur along with, and perhaps as justifications for, unfaithfulness in Christian living. Those against whom he warns not only teach false doctrines; they also live in "licentious ways" (*aselgeiais*) and in their "greed" (for wealth? for fame?) deceive their followers to do the same. This is the reverse image of what Peter presents in 2 Pet. 1, where the knowledge of Jesus Christ is not merely followed up by a virtuous life, but where a life of virtue and the knowledge of Jesus Christ are inseparable and mutually sustaining features of the Christian life. So, conversely, a diminished doctrine of Christ's divine sovereignty and coming judgment often exists in a mutually symbiotic relationship with the justification of vice, of "dissolute practices"—all too often the immoral sexual practices of the wider unbelieving society (see Bauckham 1983: 241 and Harrington 2003: 262, on the meaning of *aselgeia*). Because of that, people in the wider world not only fail to see the truth of God; they also "malign" (*blasphēmeō*) the truth because all they see is its distortion. "The way of truth will be blasphemed by the heretics not only in those people whom they manage to win over to their errors but also in those who reject Christianity by the wicked things which they see these heretics doing, and because they know no better, imagine that all Christians must be caught up in the same depravity" (Bede, *On 2 Peter*, in Bray 2000: 145–46).

God Destroys and Rescues: Three Stories of Warning and Hope (2 Peter 2:4–10a)

God will not ignore false teachers, nor will he forget those who stand fast against them. In a long conditional sentence that extends nearly the entire length of these verses, Peter reminds us that God brings judgment on the ungodly and rescues the righteous. Peter draws our attention to several well-known biblical stories that make that fact abundantly clear.

The teachers of destructive opinions and ungodly ways of life, and those who follow them, are already actively bringing about their own destruction; but God will not simply leave them alone to destroy themselves. God will also not "spare" them from his own direct act of judgment. How could we think God would spare unrighteous human teachers if he "did not spare [even] the angels when they

5. David Bentley Hart, *The Beauty of the Infinite: The Aesthetics of Christian Truth* (Grand Rapids: Eerdmans, 2003), 399.

sinned" (2 Pet. 2:4; cf. Gen. 6:1–4)? And if he "did not spare the [entire] ancient world" in the time of Noah (2 Pet. 2:5; cf. Gen. 6–8)? And if he "condemned . . . to extinction" the entire cities of Sodom and Gomorrah in the days of Lot (2 Pet. 2:6; cf. Gen. 19:1–29)? In these scriptural stories (and many others), God's judgment is always decidedly active and apocalyptically destructive. God lays hold of the rebellious angels and "cast[s] them into hell and commit[s] them to chains of deepest darkness" (2 Pet. 2:4). God comes in wrath upon the ancient world of the ungodly and "[brings] a flood on" the entire world (2:5). God sees the wickedness of the cities of Sodom and Gomorrah and "turn[s] . . . them to ashes" (2:6).

These dramatic, drastic Old Testament stories of God's severe judgment on the "ungodly" (*asebēs*; 2:5–6) stand as a warning not only to false teachers, but also to those who are tempted to follow their often plausible and attractive accounts of the way things are—accounts that in fact deny God's coming final judgment on all powers and peoples that is prefigured precisely in these Old Testament stories. But the stories also speak a word of promise about how God delivers those who stay the course, abiding in the truth of Christ amid the powerful spiritual and cultural forces that oppose God's word and way.

The stories that Peter recalls follow the narrative order of the biblical text. But we discern a theological logic to this order as well. The first story occurs in the *heavenly realm*, where some of the cosmic suprahuman powers (angels) rebel against the authority of God and their rightful role in the cosmic order.[6] Rather than serving God and God's purposes for his creatures, as they were created to do, these angels turn to serve themselves and to bend the minds, wills, and bodies of human beings to their own unrighteous ends. They become "the rulers, . . . the authorities, . . . the cosmic powers of this present darkness, . . . the spiritual forces of evil in the heavenly places" (Eph. 6:12) opposed to God and his reign. They are the malignant "rulers of this age, who are doomed to perish," the very same powers that "crucified the Lord of glory" (1 Cor. 2:6–8). They are the great uncontrollable cosmic and historical forces (appearing in the form of powerful ideals, religions, isms, worldviews, causes, movements) that lay hold of epochs, empires, peoples, nations, societies, institutions, and persons, enslave them, and make them serve systems of enmity, exploitation, destruction, warfare, and violence—the systems of sin and death. They are the "diverse manifestations of a seamless web of reality hostile to God" (→1 Pet. 3:18–22).[7]

God conquered those powers through the cross of Christ, who "disarmed the rulers and authorities and made a public example of them, triumphing over them in [the cross]" (Col. 2:15; cf. 1 Pet. 3:22). The rebellious powers, Peter says, God

6. For what follows on "principalities and powers," see especially John Howard Yoder, *The Politics of Jesus: Vicit Agnus Noster*, 2nd ed. (Grand Rapids: Eerdmans, 1994), 134–61; and Marva J. Dawn, *Powers, Weakness, and the Tabernacling of God* (Grand Rapids: Eerdmans, 2001). For an excellent discussion of the powers in relation to the "natural order," see David Bentley Hart, *The Doors of the Sea: Where Was God in the Tsunami?* (Grand Rapids: Eerdmans, 2005).

7. Thomas R. Yoder Neufeld in Dawn, *Powers, Weakness, and the Tabernacling of God*, 19.

has cast into "Tartarus" (2 Pet. 2:4)—in Hellenistic thought, the place of divine punishment—and holds them there in "chains of deepest darkness." There they await their final destruction.

Still, the rebellious powers, defeated, imprisoned, and condemned though they are through the cross of Christ, maintain a hold on nations and individuals, insofar as we continue to put our trust in the powerful worldviews and religions represented by them for our salvation, rather than in the cross of Christ that is the power of God. We see the effects of that idolatry among nations and peoples, in homes and in hearts, every time we read the news or critically examine life in our nations, cities, and families. Scripture instructs us to arm ourselves with the power of the gospel to stand against their attacks (Eph. 6:10–17). Peter tells of their imminent destruction as a way of warning the church not to come again under their power through false teaching and finally be destroyed along with them.

The second story that Peter recalls, of Noah and the flood, occurs in the *earthly realm* made for good creaturely existence, but a realm now filled up and corrupted with human evil. "The LORD saw that the wickedness of humankind was great in the earth, and that every inclination of the thoughts of their hearts was only evil continually. . . . Now the earth was corrupt in God's sight, and the earth was filled with violence . . . for all flesh had corrupted its ways upon the earth" (Gen. 6:5, 11–12). Here the emphasis is on human evil and culpability. This is, as Peter says, the "world of the ungodly" (*kosmō asebōn*; 2 Pet. 2:5) that presses in upon Noah from all sides and ridicules the seeming irrationality of his faith in God's coming judgment and new creation as he builds a huge seaworthy boat in a dry land. "By faith Noah, warned by God about events as yet unseen, respected the warning and built an ark to save his household; by this he condemned the world and became an heir to the righteousness that is in accordance with faith" (Heb. 11:7). Noah was indeed a righteous man in his world, but *he could not deliver himself* from it. He stood firm and trusted God to rescue him from that corrupt world through the flood. But the flood did not wipe out the sinful inclination of the human heart itself, as God himself acknowledges (Gen. 8:21). The world of humankind, the very progeny of righteous Noah, remains the world of the ungodly and the weak, the world of sinners and enemies of God. Unless God simply destroys all sinners and enemies (a plan that he does not countenance), the violent and destructive evil inclination must be met with an even more radical act of God to deal with it: it requires the atoning and reconciling death of Jesus Christ (Rom. 5:6–11), "the righteousness of our God and Savior Jesus Christ" (2 Pet. 1:1) who delivers us "from the corruption that is in the world because of lust" (1:4). Peter warns the church to stand firm in that deliverance, in the powerful coming of Jesus Christ and the new creation, against the denials and corruption of the false teachers. If we do not, we will share in their destruction.

As the third lesson, Peter brings forward the story of Lot in Sodom and Gomorrah. This story takes place in *the city*, the *polis*, that sphere in which worship, history, culture, politics, economics, and social order might come together for the sake of the common good and human flourishing.[8] But in Sodom and Gomorrah these things do not appear in their rightful function of serving the peace and well-being of the city; they are thoroughly distorted and corrupted by rebellious powers and the evil inclination of human hearts. For the *polis* (or the *ethnos* or the *imperium*) is that place where these two forces so often come together in deeply destructive ways. Like Noah in his world, Lot is (according to Peter) a righteous man in the midst of the wicked city, "tormented" by the sight and sound of their unlawful doings (2 Pet. 2:8; Bauckham 1983: 253). But Lot, righteous though he is, is *not able to save himself.* According to the Genesis story, he is a man also deeply indebted to the city and attracted by it—no doubt by its great power and beauty, its rich cultural and social life, and its economic wealth. So in the end he is unable to leave the city of his own will, even though it faces imminent destruction: "When morning dawned, the angels urged Lot, saying, 'Get up, [go]. . . . But he lingered; so the men seized him and his wife and his two daughters by the hand, the LORD being merciful to him, and they brought him out and left him outside the city" (Gen. 19:15–16).

Even the sturdiest of the faithful find themselves surrounded on all sides by the strong powers of unrighteousness—destructive cosmic powers, rampant human evil (which is not merely out there, but always also the inclination of the human heart), and the often distorted, damaging, and deadly forms of the cultural, social, and political life in which we all participate. Noah and Lot are figures of the people of God, the church, and individual Christians, none of which are able by their own righteousness and power to extricate themselves from the destructive grip of these ungodly powers. Indeed, like Lot, we often do not *wish* to be delivered from those "cities" that seem to give and promise so much freedom and life, but that, because of their ungodliness, are as much places of injustice, destruction, and death. Our churches, like those of Philippi and Corinth in Paul's time, find it difficult to relinquish the power, associations, goods, privileges, and practices that come with full citizenship and sociocultural establishment in the earthly city, for fear of ending up with a life in Zoar—the small town on the edge of the Plain (Gen. 19:20–23)—or, worse still, a life of homelessness, in a cave in the hills (19:30). Life on the margins of the *polis* holds little attraction. So the church and its members linger and hesitate and ask whether some realistic compromise might not be possible, by which to ease the stark opposition between true worship and idolatry, between the truth and the lie, between righteousness and unrighteousness to secure our long-term future in the ungodly city.[9] That is the moment in which the false teacher is born. That is the moment of our temptation to follow

---

8. For an instructive theology of the city, see Bernd Wannenwetsch, "Representing the Absent in the City: Prolegomena to a Negative Political Theology according to Revelation 21," in *God, Truth, and Witness: Engaging Stanley Hauerwas*, ed. L. Gregory Jones, Reinhard Hütter, and C. Rosalee Velloso Ewell (Grand Rapids: Brazos, 2005), 167–92.

9. R. R. Reno, *In the Ruins of the Church: Sustaining Faith in an Age of Diminished Christianity* (Grand Rapids: Brazos, 2002), 97–126, offers an incisive analysis of the (Episcopal) church's (or

them. That is the time of trial, from which we pray to be delivered. Will the righteous live?

"The Lord knows how to rescue the godly from trial" (2 Pet. 2:9). The Lord will come with power to deliver the faithful from the powers of unrighteousness and their promoters and to establish righteousness in the earth. That is the apocalyptic hope of the church (3:13), established in the *apokalypsis* of the *dikaiosynē theou* ("the righteousness of God") in the cross and resurrection of Jesus Christ (Rom. 1:16–17). For Peter this apocalyptic hope is the ground of confidence upon which he instructs the church to stand against the tide of false teaching, and it assures the church that, despite its weakness, hesitation, and temptation to compromise, it will be delivered on the day of judgment. The righteous one will live because God "himself is just and . . . he justifies the one who has the faith of Jesus" (Rom. 3:26 DH):

> Therefore, since we are justified by faith, we have peace with God through our Lord Jesus Christ, through whom we have obtained access to this grace in which we stand; and we boast in our hope of sharing the glory of God. And not only that, but we also boast in our sufferings, knowing that suffering produces endurance, and endurance produces character, and character produces hope, and hope does not disappoint us, because God's love has been poured into our hearts through the Holy Spirit that has been given to us.
>
> For while we were still weak, at the right time Christ died for the ungodly. . . . God proves his love for us in that while we still were sinners Christ died for us. Much more surely then, now that we have been justified by his blood, will we be saved through him from the wrath of God. For if while we were enemies, we were reconciled to God through the death of his Son, much more surely, having been reconciled, will we be saved by his life. (Rom. 5:1–10)

In Jesus Christ, God has already delivered us from the rebellious powers and the evil inclination, reconciled us to himself, and made us sharers of the divine life. That is the church's "mighty fortress" of confidence in an ungodly world that is perishing. It is our fortress against false teachers in the church. Peter utters a powerful warning not to be taken in by their denials and lies, lest the church perish with them. Beyond Peter's warning, forged in the heat of a life-and-death controversy with the false teachers, we might ask whether false teachers and heretics—ungodly ones, sinners, enemies of God and the gospel (which we also once were)—might *also* finally be rescued from the rebellious powers, from the sin of the human heart, and from the ungodly city—indeed, from themselves— and be reconciled to God through the death of Christ, saved by his life. That is indeed Peter's hope: "The Lord . . . is patient . . . , not wanting any to perish, but all to come to repentance" (2 Pet. 3:9). Such a hope should lead the orthodox in

---

rather, the church's leaders') "lingering" and compromise with the world to avoid marginalization in the wider society.

---

the church to correct, contend with, pray for, serve, and love even the heretics in its midst; for if God's powerful grace is not also for the heretics, then neither is it for the orthodox.

Ad hominem (2 Peter 2:10b–18)

Without a doubt Peter perceives a grave threat to the faith, to the church, and to individual believers, from the false teachers. They surely appear to have the persuasive power to lead Peter's flock into apostasy (2:14, 18), as they themselves have already apostatized (2:20–21). It is a situation of crisis, which calls for a strong and decisive intervention, with Peter employing all of the rhetorical strategies at his disposal. After all, he is dealing with "bold and arrogant" characters (2:10; following Harrington 2003: 268) who do not fear to scorn the demonic cosmic powers, indeed, denying that they have any power, even though God's angels themselves "do not bring against them [the rebellious powers] a slanderous judgment from the Lord" (2:11; see Bauckham 1983: 261–63 for discussion of this difficult verse). In an effort to convince us not to follow false teachers, Peter exposes the many spiritual, intellectual, and moral faults of the teachers: they are irrational, living instinctually like animals (2:12); they revel in broad daylight and at the communal table and are insatiable adulterers (2:13–14); they exploit the weak and are greedy and morally stubborn and stupid. Acting like animals, their end—destruction—will be like that of animals. Like stubborn Balaam, they deserve to be rebuked by a dumb ass:

> It was a dreadful judgment of God that the angel revealed himself to the ass before the prophet, and that the ass seeing that God was displeased did not dare to go further but rather retraced its steps, while the prophet under the blind impulse of his own avarice pressed on in the face of the clear prohibition of God. . . . As a final, crowning indignity the mouth of the ass was opened, so that he who had refused to submit to the rule of God had to accept the orders of the ass. (Calvin 1963: 354)

Should Christians today avoid or reject such ad hominem arguments as Peter engages in here? Through the centuries theologians have often not hesitated to imitate Peter in this—think of Athanasius or Luther or Calvin—as they preached against the heretics of their days. But, with Peter, they believed that the life or death of the church was at stake in the question of heresy—*and so it is*. The church will not stand if it believes that Jesus Christ is less than the Lord and God of all things or that he will not come again, in the same glory by which he was transfigured, to render God's rectifying judgment on all things. Failure to stand firm in these critical matters spells the corruption and death of the church.

The church will not stand, for example, by faith in the insubstantial figure often presented to us by the Jesus Seminar, which denies his divinity and lordship and his coming again. Should we not mock the irrational and fundamentalist seriousness of this group, which markets itself as the very paradigm of scientific rationality in search of the pure facts about the historical Jesus, by which they might save gullible and hapless Christians from the church and the creeds?[10] But "they are waterless fountains and a fog driven by the storm" (2 Pet. 2:17 DH): their supposed rigorous rationality—in a mode discredited by most contemporary philosophy—is dry and spiritually fruitless, yielding a nonapocalyptic Jesus who is theologically insubstantial and boring as hell. Should we not expose the seminar's media publicity, public acceptance, and publication royalties for what they are—the benefits that come from finding so many eager consumers in the church as well as the world, ready to pay well for its cheap and diminished Jesus who was neither rescued from the powers of unrighteousness himself nor has the power to rescue anyone?[11] "They entice unsteady souls. They have hearts trained in greed" (2:14). Should we not mention that where such a diminished Jesus is bought and sold in the churches, those very same churches also often display and promote a moral life, particularly in matters of human sexuality, that is no different from that found in the wider society? Should we not ask about the relationship between theological heresy and immorality, between the act of "despis[ing the] authority [*kyriotētos*]" of Jesus Christ and "indulg[ing the] flesh in depraved lust" (2:10)? "For with fatuous and vacuous teaching and through lust and sexual immorality [the false teachers] lure back those who are only just escaping from their life in paganism" (2:18 DH).

Back into Slavery (2 Peter 2:19–22)

False teachers promise a gospel of "freedom" (2:19)—freedom from the divine authority of Jesus Christ (who, they say, has no such authority; 2:10); freedom from the coming judgment (which, they say, will never come; 3:4); freedom to shape life on one's own terms and to walk a path toward one's own chosen future. But Peter makes it clear that we are never "our own." If we are not mastered by the authority of Jesus Christ, who lays hold of us and takes us through virtue into his own divine power and glory, then we will surely be overcome by something else. "For a person is enslaved to whatever overcomes one" (2:19 DH). What overcomes us, Peter says, is "corruption" (*phthora*). Every human being is, because of sin, *already* held in bondage to decay and under the regime of death. Apart from Christ this is the only human condition there is (Rom. 8:20–21). While the enlightened, libertine false teachers pretend to place before us the choice between what they construe as constricting servitude to the church's historic doctrine and practice

10. See, for example, the introduction in Robert W. Funk and Robert W. Hoover, *The Five Gospels: The Search for the Authentic Words of Jesus* (New York: Macmillan, 1993).

11. See, for example, the account of the death and resurrection of Jesus by John Dominic Crossan, *Jesus: A Revolutionary Biography* (San Francisco: Harper, 1994), 123–201.

on the one hand and a life of uninhibited, creative, individual self-expression on the other, Peter places before us life and death. The only possible deliverance from the enslaving moral and physical corruption that ends in death and disintegration is to be made a sharer of the incorruptible divine life and virtue that is given "through the knowledge of our Lord and Savior Jesus Christ" (2 Pet. 2:20). True human freedom is the freedom of this knowledge and virtue and participation, for it is the freedom that already bears within itself the incorruptible seed of God's own life and freedom.

Libertine heretics invariably fail to see that the original relation between the life and freedom of the triune God and the life and freedom of the human creature is not a competition in an economy of scarce sovereignty. Denying or forgetting that freedom is a *gift* of participation in the life of God, they believe that humans, in order to be free, must assert themselves over against or apart from God and his sovereignty. Or perhaps they have come to see freedom as that bit of sovereignty they have been able to eke out for themselves in their struggle with an implacable cosmos and its evolutionary process (which perhaps they falsely equate with God's sovereignty) or with an authoritarian tradition and its sacerdotal system. But Peter, as we have seen, draws our attention to another vision, to our participation in the inexhaustibly rich livingness and freedom of the Father, Son, and Holy Spirit in their eternal divine unity. Submission to the authority of the living *kyrios* Jesus Christ is our act of acknowledgement, against our pride, rebellion, and war against God, that this participation is the only true life and freedom there is.

There was a time when the false teachers knew that life and freedom through personal faith, the practice of virtue, and the apostolic tradition: they once lived in "the knowledge of our Lord and Savior Jesus Christ" (2:20), they once knew "the way of righteousness" and had once received "the holy commandment that was passed on to them" (2:21). By these things they had once escaped the corruption of the world through the hope of sharing in the divine nature. How could they now turn against the truth of the gospel? But the impossible possibility happens. Having since become, as they imagine, enlightened and free, they leave behind the saving knowledge of Jesus Christ, they turn from the path of virtue to which they were called, they reject the truth and teaching that they had received from the Lord and the apostles. But their condition is now far from enlightened and free—it is in fact a more desperate descent into darkness and a more thorough enslavement in corruption than they knew before their baptism; for, having reckoned the light and freedom of the gospel to be blindness and bondage, they are no longer able to see their own darkness and bondage exposed for what it is by the glorious light of the gospel. In this state, their future is dim indeed: "For it is impossible to restore again to repentance those who have once been enlightened, and have tasted the heavenly gift, and have shared in the Holy Spirit, and have tasted the goodness of the word of God and the powers of the age to come, and then have fallen away, since on their own they are crucifying again the Son of God and are holding him up to contempt" (Heb. 6:4–6).

The church announces the gospel to the *world* and, in the light of the gospel, it is made clear that wrongdoers will not inherit the kingdom of God: "Fornicators, idolaters, adulterers, male prostitutes, sodomites, thieves, the greedy, drunkards, revilers, robbers—none of these will inherit the kingdom of God" (1 Cor. 6:9–10). When those who are *in the world* hear that, they often actually believe it. They might say, "Get lost! I want nothing to do with such a kingdom of God." Or they might say, "What must I do to be saved?" But either way they become aware that sinful deeds are incompatible with life in the gospel-created kingdom. It seems so often to be those *in the church* who are able, by all manner of means (perhaps precisely as a declaration of "freedom in Christ"), to master the art of reconciling such deeds with life in the kingdom.[12] Just in this way, the church enters more deeply and dangerously into the deadly slavery from which it was delivered, and the world is left without a witness to its need for rescue and the only possibility of its liberation. As Hauerwas often says, the world needs the church to be the church so that the world might know that it is the world. Instead, the church often becomes a chaplain to the world, including, blessing, baptizing—in the name of a vague nonjudgmental deity—attitudes, practices, and deeds (e.g., greed, war, sexual immorality) that the world itself, when it hears the truth of the gospel, knows to be enslaving, destructive, and deadly.

Will Peter's sharp concluding proverbs about the disgusting habits of dogs and pigs (2:22) be heard by our churches? Or will it be that these words will "make the mind of this people dull, and stop their ears, and shut their eyes, so that they may not look with their eyes, and listen with their ears, and comprehend with their minds, and turn and be healed" (Isa. 6:10)?

Descending into the Abyss: Coda on 2 Peter 2

In 2 Pet. 1, Peter leads us up with him onto the holy mountain of the transfiguration of Jesus Christ, where we are given a glimpse of the transcendent glory and power in which Christ will come to judge the world in righteousness. In 2 Pet. 2, by contrast, Peter shows us in graphic images and with severe warnings the reality and the consequences of false teaching and apostasy in the church: false teachers, by their distortions and denials of the truth of Jesus Christ and his coming and by their dissolute practices, lead themselves and their followers into the dark abyss of self-destruction and God's judgment. Will the church and its members stand fast in faithfulness and justice, as did Noah and Lot, and be delivered by God's power; or will they succumb to false teaching and apostasy and be delivered over to sin and the cosmic powers of destruction, which themselves will finally be destroyed? Peter leaves us with this question as he turns to "the end."

12. Reno, *In the Ruins of the Church*, 113–17.

2 PETER 3

What Parousia? (2 Peter 3:1–7)

Peter writes this "second letter" as a reminder and an encouragement to stand fast against the scornful scoffing of skeptical teachers (3:1, 3).[1] He does so by urging us to remember the reliable words spoken by the prophets and apostles, whose testimony and authority can be fully trusted because, as Peter has already declared, they spoke "from God" as they were "moved by the Holy Spirit" (→1:19–21). The words that the prophets speak and "the commandment of the Lord and Savior" (3:2) that the apostles announce bring about a whole new way of being and thinking (*eilikrinēs dianoia*; 3:1) through Jesus Christ. Translators and commentators provide a variety of possibilities for rendering the phrase *eilikrinēs dianoia*: "sincere intention" (NRSV), "wholesome thinking" (NIV; Peter Davids),[2] "sincere understanding" (Bauckham 1983: 287), "pure mind" (Harrington 2003: 281). The idea is that the moral and intellectual are bound together, an idea very inadequately captured by NRSV. As we have seen, Peter consistently binds together the moral and intellectual aspects of participation in Christ (as also of heresy; 2 Pet. 2). The person as moral and intellectual unity is laid hold of by Jesus Christ and as such apprehends and participates in the "knowledge of God and of Jesus our Lord" (1:2). *Eilikrinēs dianoia* is about being known by the one who is the source and goal of all reality, and knowing reality through moral and intellectual participation in him.

Nonetheless, the mocking of the scoffers puts that altered way of thinking into question. Doubts creep in. Once again old habits of thought begin to appear

1. For a thorough discussion of what might be the first letter that Peter refers to, see Bauckham 1983: 285–86. Bauckham and most other commentators take it to be 1 Peter.

2. Peter H. Davids, *The Letters of 2 Peter and Jude*, Pillar New Testament Commentaries (Grand Rapids: Eerdmans, 2006), 259–60.

persuasive. The skeptics' truths seem self-evidently undeniable: all things are fated to decay and death; nothing changes for the better; human strife, sickness and disease, and natural disasters continue as they always have; the gods are powerless; there is clearly no coming finality that is fundamentally different from the depressing past and present—if it were, why would we not have caught at least a glimpse of it by now? "Realism" speaks its ever powerful word against the promise of a new order. And so Peter must, by way of reminder, arouse again that *eilikrinēs dianoia*, that revolutionary moral and intellectual knowledge of things as they are, which the gospel generates, that whole pattern of being and thinking that challenges and overturns the old mode of being in the world, time, and history.

The "scoffers will come," Peter says, "in the last days" (*ep' eschatōn tōn hēmerōn*; 3:3). These scoffers will taunt the faithful with the question, "Where is the promise of his coming [*hē epangelia tēs parousias*]?" Ironically, though, Peter says that the scoffers are asking their question "in the last days," those same last days before the coming of Christ that they are denying; their scoffing is itself a negative eschatological sign of the imminent parousia. Yet, how can this be, since such scoffing is already on the scene when Peter writes and has continued on, inside the church and out, throughout the subsequent two thousand years of history? It is with us today, while we, like Peter's first readers, still await the parousia. Isn't that exactly the force of the scoffers' taunt when they say, "For ever since our ancestors died, all things continue as they were from the beginning of creation [*ap' archēs ktiseōs*]"? Skeptics and scoffers seem to have a very strong case against the holy prophets, the apostles, and Peter himself, whose collective claim about the powerful coming of Christ appears to be empty. That such a claim was more fully confirmed by Christ's transfiguration on the holy mountain, and the presence with him of at least two "ancestors" (*hoi pateras*), Elijah and Moses, who were not asleep or dead, is unconvincing to the scoffers. All of nature and history is an argument against it.

Nevertheless, Peter declares, the skeptics and scoffers are fools, for they do not understand the ways of God; indeed, they do not even grasp the meaning of the very words they are using—words like *parousia* ("coming") and *ktisis* ("creation"), which mean something only in relation to the God who comes and creates. Not only do they fail morally, "indulging their own lusts" (3:3); they fail theologically as well, through a *culpable* lack of godly vision and understanding of the strange new world that Christ revealed in his transfiguration and is about to reveal in his coming. "For by their own choice they keep things hidden from themselves" (3:5 DH). The scoffers were once believers, indeed sharers, in God's coming new order (2:20–21). But now, deliberately choosing to ignore the revelation of the truth in Jesus Christ—their failure of knowledge is both spiritual and intellectual—they see only what they want to see: they see the physical world and human history marching along, causally, monotonously, necessarily, as "one damn thing after another," showing no progress or development (as they might hope) toward something better. And, given only what they are able to see when they hide from themselves what God has revealed according to the testimony of faithful eyewitnesses, how can they *not* be skeptical and pessimistic about the long-time-coming of Christ's parousia? "This hour [of Christ's parousia] will not enter into the series of historical events, such as the fall of Rome, the Crusades, the Great War. It is not in history, because it lies *beyond* history. Therefore, the end is essentially an object of faith *par excellence*, and thus it is so easy and natural not to believe in it, to remain self-sufficient in the life of this world."[3] Failing in faith, the skeptics and scoffers see only nature and history in its bondage to the rebellious spiritual powers, to death and decay, and to the sinful inclinations of the human heart, and they take this visible normal as normative. They see only "time's surface." "History, as a strictly causal sequence, has no salvific power, reflects no universal or providential order, has no metaphysical yield."[4] Looked at from this angle—and this is the only angle that ancient Epicureanism or modern secular scientism or postmodern nihilism (and the Christian heresies shaped by them) offer us—is there any choice but to join the skeptics in asking, "Where is the promise of his coming?" There are no signs of another world, or of the end of this one, or of the reign of God. Even the natural and historical catastrophes that might suggest some kind of an end, that might perhaps expose the abyss beneath time's surface, that might reveal the inherent *incapacity* of nature and history to sustain or direct themselves to any final good, can be read otherwise, assimilated into the scheme of the normal. "One can find physical and historical signs to explain these catastrophes ('rumours of wars . . . famines, and pestilences, and earthquakes, in divers places' [Matt. 24:6, 7]), but this is only 'the beginning of sorrows' (v. 8), not yet the end (v. 6). On the contrary, all this is situated on *this* side of cosmic being. In effect, it is still possible to believe that this world is stable."[5] It is still possible to proclaim an earthly "peace and security" (1 Thess. 5:3) and believe in it, with no thought of an apocalyptic interruption, a "day of the Lord" (2 Pet. 3:10), that would expose it as a false description of things as they are. The world seen from this point of view is the only world that ever was, is, or will be. It suffers no beginning, no end, no interruption, no alteration. It suffers the simulacra of endless change, but no final purifying judgment. It is a dead end. It is the "real" world, the world as we know it.

But which world is that? It is not the world that Peter knows. He knows a world that not only has a divine beginning (*ktisis*) and a divine end (*parousia*), but also one that has already been invaded, and in every moment is about to be invaded, purified, redeemed, and transfigured by the sovereign saving power of God and our Lord Jesus Christ. The real world, as those in Christ know it, is therefore never merely the world of time's surface—though it is always also that

3. Sergius Bulgakov, *The Bride of the Lamb*, trans. Boris Jakim (Grand Rapids: Eerdmans, 2002), 385 (emphasis original).

4. David Bentley Hart, *The Beauty of the Infinite: The Aesthetics of Christian Truth* (Grand Rapids: Eerdmans, 2003), 396, 397.

5. Bulgakov, *Bride of the Lamb*, 418 (emphasis original).

in an ephemeral sense not to be despised: see the book of Ecclesiastes. It is also the world of "eternity's light,"[6] that world in which God's apocalyptic reign is ever imminent, always ready suddenly to break in:

> The kingdom of God, the Gospels assert, is adventitious to history: it comes sud-denly, like a thief in the night, and so fulfills no immanent process, consummates none of our grand projects, reaps no harvest from history's "dialectic." Only thus does it complete all things. And in the light of an eschaton that has already, in the resurrection [and transfiguration] of Christ, been made visible within history, the eschatological interruption of time . . . is seen to press upon each moment within time, an ironic syncopation that unsettles the stern and steady beat of history, a word of judgment falling across all of our immanent "Truths," whether of power, privilege, or destiny.[7]

Peter proclaims the reality of this *apocalypsed* world, the world revealed as cre-ated, formed, preserved, judged, destroyed, and made new by the powerful word of God: "By the word of God heavens existed long ago and an earth was formed out of water and by means of water, through which [word] the world of that time was deluged with water and perished. But by the same word the present heavens and earth have been reserved for fire, being kept until the day of judgment and destruction of the godless" (3:5–7). With these words Peter proclaims not only the power of the Word, but also of the Holy Spirit. Throughout the scriptures, water and fire are the manifest signs and instruments of the Spirit's purifying arrival. Creation is brought into being by the power of the Word and Spirit of God. Creation is again and again judged and renewed by the Word and Spirit of God. *This the real world.* If creation is finally to be fully liberated and made new by the Word and the Spirit, the divine parousia must consume everything that now holds creation and history in bondage to unrighteousness, death, and decay. The coming fiery purification and glorious transfiguration of creation are not two events in a sequence; they are the double effect of the final divine parousia of the Spirit and Word of God. It is for this that "the present heavens and earth have been reserved" (3:7).

The Day of the Lord (2 Peter 3:8–13)

The world apocalyptically revealed in the transfiguration of Jesus Christ is a world in which the past is never simply bygone and the future is never simply beyond. It is not a world made and remade by the steady forward unfolding in time of dispensationalist sequences or progressivist millennial kingdoms or inevitable evolutionary processes. It is, rather, a world constituted by this: "With the Lord

6. Hart, *Beauty of the Infinite*, 396.
7. Ibid., 396–97.

one day is like a thousand years, and a thousand years are like one day" (3:8). "The net of time is torn, and a supertime suddenly shines through it."[8] In the world revealed in the transfiguration of Jesus Christ, the "long dead" prophets Moses and Elijah stand alive on the holy mountain in the living presence of Jesus Christ and the apostles, and Jesus Christ is already present with the prophets and apostles in the eschatological glory that will be his when he comes with power to judge the earth. Here time's surface—past, present, and future—is wondrously interrupted, invaded, and gloriously illuminated by eternity's light and opens up to what is infinitely more than what merely appears in ordinary time. Reality thus transfigured by apocalypse cannot be contained in memorial shrines (cf. Matt. 17:4) or scientific formulas, as if the transfiguration were simply one more happening in the ordinary causal sequence of things rather than *the* apocalyptic revelation of the way, the truth, and the life of all reality created through, in, and for the Lord of glory. The transfiguration inaugurates a fundamentally new pattern of thought (*eilikrinēs dianoia*; 2 Pet. 3:1) that discerns all of reality as in truth a participation in the transcendent, coming, glorious power of Jesus Christ and the Holy Spirit. "If anyone is in Christ, there is a new creation" (2 Cor. 5:17). Under the impact of this new pattern of thought, a Christian account of things cannot be historicist, in the mode of the scoffers who cannot conceive of an apocalypse interrupting the unbroken causal continuity of all things. Walter Benjamin writes:

> Historicism contents itself with establishing a causal connection between various moments in history. But no fact that is a cause is for that very reason historical. It became historical posthumously, as it were, through events that may be separated by thousands of years. A historian who takes this as his point of departure stops telling the sequence of events like the beads of a rosary. Instead, he grasps the constellation which his own era has formed with a definite earlier one. Thus he establishes a conception of the present as the "time of the now" which is shot through with chips of Messianic time.[9]

The one who, like Peter, knows the reality of Christ transfigured, is now able to "[grasp] the constellation which his own era has formed" with other, earlier eras, such as those of Noah, Lot, and Balaam. Those ancient eras become historical "posthumously" in the messianic present of Peter's time, though he is separated from them by thousands of years. In the illuminating truth of the transfiguration-apocalypse of Christ's powerful coming, Peter is able to draw our attention to those other apocalypses (which is to say, to the singular messianic apocalypse, refracted in other times and places): the heavens were created by the word of God; the earth was created out of water; the rebellious angels were cast into hell; the great cities on the plain were burned to ashes

---

8. Bulgakov, *Bride of the Lamb*, 384–85.
9. Walter Benjamin, "Theses on the Philosophy of History," in *Illuminations*, ed. Hannah Arendt, trans. Harry Zohn (New York: Schocken, 1968), 263.

by fire; the rebellious powers, the false teachers, and the whole ungodly world are being reserved for judgment by fire. "People were talking this way [that is, saying, Where is the promise of his coming?] as if the flood had never occurred and as if fire had never come down from heaven in the past" (Hilary of Arles, *Introductory Commentary on 2 Peter*, in Bray 2000: 156). There has been no shortage of God's powerful messianic comings.[10] And surely there is more to come. Our world is not one that has been "waiting for Godot" who never shows up. To the taunt "where is the promise of his coming?" the apostle responds: God's reign has broken out in the heavens and upon the earth again and again in the past! God's reign is upon us now! Christ was transfigured before our eyes! God's kingdom is ready to break in soon! "The Lord is not slow about his promise, as some [those self-blinded to God's apocalyptic ways] think of slowness. . . . The day of the Lord will come like a thief" (3:9–10).

For those who share Peter's godly vision of an apocalyptically charged world, the present time is never simply dead time or metered time, as a historicist would have it: it is time pregnant with the *patience* of God: He "is patient with you, not wanting any to perish, but all to come to repentance" (3:9). We live not in a time of empty waiting. We live in the fullness of time of God's gracious patience—a time given to us in which to repent. This is the time for the church and the heretics and the whole world to wake up to the reality of the bondage of all things to corruption and perishability through desire; to wake up to the reality of the destruction that we bring upon ourselves, even seek out, through our sin and submission to the rebellious powers; to wake up to the reality of the purifying trial to which God will put us on the day of judgment.

> Alas for you who desire the day of the LORD!
>   Why do you want the day of the LORD?
> It is darkness, not light;
>   as if someone fled from a lion,
>   and was met by a bear;
> or went into the house and rested a hand against the wall,
>   and was bitten by a snake.
> Is not the day of the LORD darkness, not light,
>   and gloom with no brightness in it? (Amos 5:18–20)

Not only should the church not be impatient that the Lord is slow in coming; perhaps it should also *pray* that the Lord will indeed be slow, that the day of the Lord will *not* come upon us "like a thief," so that the church might have the time necessary to repent of the many and various ways it corrupts faith and life: seeking "peace and security" for itself by compromising with the powers of this

10. "On time and divine glory: imagine a cloth folded and pierced by a single pin. If it is unfolded (time), then the hole made by the pin will recur again and again, even though it is the same hole made by the single pin" (R. R. Reno correspondence).

age; gaining worldly power by joining cause with the latest and most influential political agenda; growing numerically and economically by using the latest marketing and communications techniques; achieving intellectual, social, or cultural respectability by aligning itself with the latest philosophy, social movement, or interest group. In the time of God's patience the compromised church is called to repent. For "when they say, 'There is peace and security,' then sudden destruction will come upon them, as labor pains come upon a pregnant woman, and there will be no escape" (1 Thess. 5:3). But for those whose lives have been purified, whose eyes are awake, and whose minds are constantly alert to the approaching parousia of the Lord, the glorious day of the Lord is already dawning: "But you, beloved, are not in darkness, for that day to surprise you like a thief; for you are all children of light and children of the day; we are not of the night or of the darkness. . . . But since we belong to the day, let us be sober, and put on the breastplate of faith and love, and for a helmet the hope of salvation" (5:4–5, 8). For the faithful people of God, the day of the Lord is not "a thousand years" away; it is even now coming upon us, for "with the Lord one day is like a thousand years, and a thousand years are like one day" (2 Pet. 3:8). Christ is already transfigured; the day of the Lord's apocalypse is on the way.

And a radical and catastrophic apocalypse it is! "Then the heavens will pass away with a loud noise [*rhoizēdon*, 'roar'], and the elements [*stoicheia*] will be dissolved [*lythēsetai*] with fire, and the earth and everything that is done on it [*ta en autē erga*] will be disclosed [*heurethēsetai*] . . . [on] the coming of the day of God [*parousian tēs tou theou hēmeras*], because of which [*di' hēn*] the heavens will be set ablaze [*pyroumenoi*] and dissolved [*lythēsontai*], and the elements [*stoicheia*] will melt [*tēketai*] with fire" (3:10, 12). It is an astonishing, even frightening, vision of the coming "day of God." But long before Peter, the prophets of Israel had already spoken of that day in similar terms. One Greek version of Isaiah says, "And all the powers of the heavens shall melt [*takēsontai*], and the heaven shall be rolled up like a scroll" (Isa. 34:4). And Malachi declares, "For, behold, a day comes burning as an oven, and it shall consume them" (Mal. 4:1 LXX).[11] Jesus said, "For as the lightning comes from the east and flashes as far as the west, so will be the coming of the Son of Man" (Matt. 24:27). When the Holy Spirit came in the rushing wind and tongues of fire at Pentecost, Peter himself recalled the words of the prophet Joel: "In the last days it will be, God declares, that I will pour out my Spirit upon all flesh. . . . And I will show portents in the heaven above and signs on the earth below, blood, and fire, and smoky mist. The sun shall be turned to darkness and the moon to blood, before the coming of the Lord's great and glorious day" (Acts 2:17, 19–20, quoting Joel 2:28–32 LXX). What are we to make of all of this?

11. Bauckham 1983: 304–6, 316 provides a helpful discussion of the connections between 2 Pet. 3:10, 12 and Isa. 34:4; Mal. 4:1.

Russian Orthodox theologian Sergius Bulgakov reflects at length and with great profundity on 2 Pet. 3 and other New Testament apocalyptic texts:[12]

The Lord's eschatological discourse [Matt. 24:29–30] establishes a direct relationship ("immediately . . . then") between the cosmic catastrophe and the parousia, which relationship signifies the inner unity of this event—the end of the aeon. Clearly, the symbolic language of the images that describe this event cannot be interpreted literally. In general, it conforms to the language of the apocalypses of this period. It expresses the fundamental idea that the world will undergo a catastrophic *transcensus*: on the one hand, it will perish in a cosmic fire; on the other hand, it will be transformed inwardly. The world becomes new, a "new heaven and a new earth." . . .

In conformity with the depth of the cosmic catastrophe, the end will arrive not only in the physical plane. It will not be limited to *changes* of cosmic being within the framework of cosmic evolution. The end transcends these limits. It presupposes a meta-empirical change of cosmic being. . . .

The end of the world must first be understood *in connection with* the parousia and even in a certain sense *as* the parousia in its cosmic aspect. The earth and the world are not only the physical or geographic (cosmic) place of the parousia in a purely external sense, but also its metaphysical receptacle. This place must conform to its purpose: It must be worthy of meeting the Lord in glory. For, in its present state, the world cannot encompass the parousia. The world catches fire from the approach of the parousia, melts in its fire. In this sense the *present* world *will not see* the coming Lord; His coming in consuming glory will not occur on this earth. The parousia must first occur *inside* the world itself. The world will be illuminated by the lightning of the parousia, which will blaze out from the east to the west. The world will not remain in a state indifferent to the approach of the coming Lord; all of creation trembles at His coming. And this trembling of creation will be its burning.[13]

Bulgakov helps us to account for Peter saying that the elements are dissolved and the heavens set ablaze "because of" (*di' hēn*) "the coming of the day of God." It is the divine advent itself that effects the fundamental transformation. Bulgakov further explicates the character of the parousia in terms of Pentecost:

In Scripture, the parousia is accompanied by the fire of the world, the destruction of the world, followed by its transfiguration, but this does not signify a succession or coincidence in time of two parallel events. It is one and the same event: the coming of Christ in glory and the revelation of glory to the world correspond to the action of the Holy Spirit. This fire—in which the present heavens and earth will be consumed on the day of judgment . . .—signifies the passage of the world through the Pentecost. The Pentecost's fiery tongues become the flame of the world

12. Indeed, I can no longer imagine how to comment on 2 Pet. 3 apart from Bulgakov, *Bride of the Lamb*, 379–526.
13. Ibid., 417–18 (emphasis original).

fire, not consuming but transmuting the world. This figure represents a hieroglyph of the cosmic Pentecost.[14]

The "cosmic Pentecost" of creation brings about a radical and fundamental alteration in the very being of things, in which their nature is both preserved and glorified—that is, all things are transfigured. Bulgakov continues:

> The end of the world is not physical but metaphysical. In reality, the world does not end but is transfigured into a new being, into a new heaven and a new earth. The changes that will take place in it will not be limited to a new combination of the same cosmic elements and the action of the previously existing cosmic forces. Rather, a new supercosmic force will enter the being of the world and transform it. The introduction of this force will affect the entire physical structure of the world, but it will be preserved in its natural being. However, the latter will open up to receive a new element of being: "glory." And this appearance of glory, the glorification of the world, will inwardly change all the elements of its being, will impart a new quality to them.[15]

Bulgakov's reflections enable us to grasp some important things about Peter's words in 3:10, 12. First, he rightly steers us away from literalizing interpretations of this and all other apocalyptic texts, interpretations that are often a troubling aspect of popular thinking about the end-times. The consuming fire of the apocalypse is the approach of the thrice-holy God himself in the persons of the transfigured Christ and the Holy Spirit. The image of the Holy Spirit as fire is already given to us in the event of Pentecost. Fire is a purifying and transforming force. God comes in purifying and transforming power. And yet, the transformation required to make creation into the new heavens and the new earth is so radical and qualitative—a death and resurrection of the universe—that we can no more know *how* it will happen than we can know *when* it will happen. We know *that* it will happen because Christ was crucified and was raised from the dead and was glorified and because the Holy Spirit has been shed abroad in our hearts and given to the church.

Second, Bulgakov helps us to see that in Peter's apocalypse the parousia effects an alteration in the very being of creation as well as in the moral quality of human existence within it. Creation itself must be made ontologically fit for those who by grace have become sharers of the divine nature—indeed, made fit for the eternal dwelling of God among mortals, as the vision of the new Jerusalem in Rev. 21 has it.

Third, Bulgakov assists us to see that the parousia of the Son and the Holy Spirit effects a fundamental transfiguration of what is *already given in creation*. The consuming fire of the divine advent is finally not about destroying all things,

14. Ibid., 400.
15. Ibid., 401.

but about liberating, purifying, healing, renewing, and exalting all things. Peter's own language is more precise about this point than Bulgakov's. Peter writes in both 3:10 and 3:12 that "the elements [*stoicheia*] will be dissolved" and that "the heavens" will "pass away" or "be set ablaze."[16] If the *stoicheia* (cf. *ta stoicheia tou kosmou*, "cosmic principles," in Gal. 4:3, 8–9 and Col. 2:20) and "the heavens" (cf. *pasai hai dynameis tōn ouranōn*, "all the powers of the heavens," in one Greek version of Isa. 34:4) refer to the spiritual principles and powers under which the creation currently exists, indeed, as the immanent principles and forces that make it all too easy to see creation as merely fated nature, then it is precisely these— sin and death in Pauline terms; physical, social, and psychological causality in ours—that hold creation in bondage to decay, robbing creaturely being of its original goodness and freedom, and blinding us to it. The liberation of creaturely being into "the glorious freedom of the children of God" (Rom. 8:21 NIV) will absolutely require the destruction of these. They must be "dissolved," "melted," "set ablaze," in order that creation might be reestablished absolutely in a wholly other spiritual principle and power, the reality of the Word and Spirit.[17] Further, Peter writes that "the earth and everything that is done on it [*ta en autē erga*] will be disclosed [*heurethēsetai*]" (2 Pet. 3:10).[18] We may take "the earth" to refer to creaturely being in its original created goodness, after all enslaving powers have been dissolved in the divine approach; and we may take "everything that is done on it" as all of the works of human beings done in response to the original divine commands to be fruitful and multiply and fill the earth, to have dominion over the many other creatures, and to till and keep the garden, after all of the corrup- tion and moral disorder has been melted in the divine parousia, and the goodness, truth, and beauty of creaturely being and human work are finally revealed. The point is this: while the transformation of all creaturely being in the parousia of God will be radical beyond imagining, it will nonetheless be a transfiguration *of creaturely being*, including human beings and the many works that they have done

16. Bauckham 1983: 315–16 discusses various understandings of "the elements" and "the heavens." My reading here is not identical to his, but is consistent with it.

17. Douglas J. Moo, "Nature in the New Creation: New Testament Eschatology and the Envi- ronment," *Journal of the Evangelical Theological Society* 49 (2006): 468, notes that *lyō* (the root of *lythēsetai* and *lythēsontai* = "dissolve" in these verses) "does not necessarily mean total physical anni- hilation, but a dissolution or radical change in nature." That would support Bulgakov's reading.

18. A number of ancient manuscripts have variant readings instead of *heurethēsetai* ("will be disclosed"). The variant *katakaēsetai* ("will be burned up"), which has influenced a number of En- glish translations (King James Version, Revised Version, Revised Standard Version, Jerusalem Bible), is now judged to be very unlikely. Bauckham 1983: 316–20 provides a lengthy discussion of the variants and a definitive argument (accepted by nearly all recent commentators) for *heurethēsetai*. It is interesting that Bulgakov works with the reading *katakaēsetai*, but against that reading he writes: "However, this should not be understood to mean the earth's destruction, for immediately after this it is said: 'we . . . look for a new heavens and a new earth' (3:13)" (*Bride of the Lamb*, 400n14). Bulgakov's instincts are thus in fact supported by the better textual evidence for *heurethēsetai*.

and will do on the face of the earth. The transfigured new heavens and the new earth are made to be the "home" of "righteousness" (3:13).

Some worry that 3:10, 12 (especially under the impact of the now discredited textual variant *katakaēsetai* ["will be burned up"] in 3:10), with its vision of such a radical dissolution or transformation of all creaturely being, undercuts all motivation for Christians to care for creation and the environment.[19] If all things are to be transformed in this way anyway, so the argument might go, what is the point of worrying about what sorry state the creation is in on the day of the Lord's parousia? But to that argument Peter himself provides us with some important lines of response. First, the day of the Lord comes "like a thief" and no one knows the time of its arrival. Just because humans may at some future time scorch the earth and render it uninhabitable because of their rapacious desire, that does not mean that the day of the Lord is the next event on the horizon. Who knows what temporal suffering may still lie ahead? Second, for Peter the time of "waiting" for the day is simultaneously the time of "hastening" its arrival (3:12) through "leading lives of holiness and godliness" (3:11). That is hardly compatible with leading lives of lust, greed, undisciplined consumption, and gluttony that will result, inevitably it now seems, in environmental destruction. Third (and moving now beyond Peter), Christians have always taught that appropriate care of our physical bodies, as temples of the Holy Spirit, is one essential aspect of the Christian life—and this in spite of (or because of) our physical bodies inevitably eventually dying and dissolving, before they are raised from the dead and filled with glorious divine life. Why should it be otherwise with the body of the earth?

"What sort of persons ought you to be in leading lives of holiness and godliness, waiting for and hastening the coming day of God?" (3:11–12). The life of the church in the time before the Lord's coming is to be characterized not only by turning from its own compromised and corrupted ways, but also, positively, by turning toward holiness and godliness, those very virtues that are undermined and despised by false teachers and their followers. The church and its members are called to reflect the very character of God, the "Holy One of Israel." We do so through knowing "our God and Savior Jesus Christ"—that is, through right worship ("godliness" as orthodoxy) and through living the virtues ("holiness" as orthopraxis). In living in godliness and holiness we both enact and display, even now, our participation in God's life, our ongoing assimilation to the glorious reality of Christ's transfigured body, and our rescue from the corruption of the world.

That is why Peter urges us both to wait and to hasten the coming of our God through orthodoxy and orthopraxis. We wait (in the gracious patience of God), because "about that day or hour no one knows, neither the angels in heaven, nor the Son, but only the Father" (Mark 13:32). No right worship or right practice, no careful liturgy or revolutionary movement, can bring in or build up the kingdom

---

19. Moo's "Nature in the New Creation" makes a persuasive effort to address these concerns on the basis of a thorough examination of many New Testament texts, including 2 Pet. 3:10, 12.

of God, for the coming of the kingdom is a matter of God's sovereign decision and action, his lordship over time and space, as the transfiguration of the Son shows. And so we wait for him to come. At the very same time we hasten his coming, because we participate even now in the glorious coming of Jesus Christ, in his veritable reign over all things, through worshiping our God and Savior and living the virtues as our present mode of "sharing in the divine nature" (2 Pet. 1:4). In that sense we already have in some measure what we wait for, what will come in its fullness on the day of the Lord. We have hastened his coming. And just so (that is, because we have already been made sharers in Christ's glory), we need not be afraid of the day of God's coming, which for us will be the transfiguration of our waiting and hastening alike.

Final Words (2 Peter 3:14–18)

Peter's letter is full of wonderful teaching about "our God and Savior Jesus Christ" (2 Pet. 1), terrible warnings about the words and ways of the heretics (2 Pet. 2), and strong exhortation to steadfast hope for transfiguration on the day of the Lord's coming (2 Pet. 3). All of this is for the sake of those whom Peter calls his "beloved" (3:14), now for the third time in this chapter (3:1, 8, 14 and again in 3:17). Peter's love for God's people takes the shape of such teaching, warning, exhortation, encouragement, and the declaration of bonds of affection. This is a strange and difficult love letter from Peter to the church, in order that the church might "grow in the grace and knowledge of our Lord and Savior Jesus Christ" (3:18). In our own time of "waiting" (3:14) we must receive it as such. For when Christ comes in power, we will "be found" (*heurethēnai*) by him when all things are disclosed (*heurethēsetai*; 3:10). And how shall he find us? Peter urges us to be found in holiness ("without spot or blemish"; 3:14), and "in peace." With these words he reiterates his encouragement to both hasten and wait for "the coming of the day of God" (3:12), for waiting and hastening is our mode of being and acting in this time of "the patience [*makrothymian*, 'longsuffering'] of our Lord" (3:15). The time that remains is anything but empty time, for Jesus Christ's patience is anything but passive inaction. It is the time of his active self-restraint in the face of all that is done on the earth, the time of his continuing to suffer the ongoing injustice of humankind, and therefore the time that he gives to human beings in which to repent, entrust their lives to him, and live for him. Christ's patience is itself our "salvation" insofar as we are taken up into his own time of waiting and hastening the day of his coming, and graciously given time to live "without spot or blemish" and "in peace." "This peace is the quietness of a soul at ease which rests on the Word of God" (Calvin 1963: 366). But not the quietness of only "a soul." Also the confident quietness of the community of Christ whose members have learned to be at peace with one another because their life together is founded on the hope of the imminent transfiguration of all things in the Word and Spirit, rather than on their own efforts to make all things right by their own power.

Peter now joins the purpose of his own letter with that of the apostle to the Gentiles, whose letters, Peter assumes, the recipients of his own letter have read. The difficulty is that Paul's letters are "hard to understand" (3:16), since "the wisdom given him" (*dotheisan autō sophian*; 3:15) is hardly what accords with ordinary common sense, as even Paul himself acknowledges in several places (e.g., 1 Cor. 1:18–2:16; Rom. 11:33–36). It is, after all, divine wisdom: "The participle *dotheisan* ('given') . . . is a 'divine' passive: God has supplied the wisdom Paul has received. . . . In this regard Paul's letters (and Paul) are functionally equivalent to 'the prophecy of scripture' and its interpreter ([2 Pet.] 1:20–21), all conveying truth supplied by God. . . . Paul was not relaying his opinions when he wrote about how Christians should live as they await the second coming; his writing was the result of divine revelation" (Kraftchick 2002: 171). What is important in this text is the unity of the testimony of the apostles among themselves, as each is commissioned by the same Lord and endowed with the same Holy Spirit of apostolic revelation, *and* the unity of the apostles with the prophets and scriptures of the Old Testament that are given by the same Holy Spirit and confirmed by the same Lord (1:19–21).

One of the tactics of heretics is to divide and conquer the unified witness of scripture—for example, to set the "new and liberating" witness of the apostles against the legalistic and outdated prophets, or to set the ethical Jesus against the doctrinal Paul, or to pit one apostle (e.g., Paul) against others (e.g., James, Peter, Jude), or even to set some "authentic" (Protestant) letters of Paul against other "spurious" (Catholic) letters claiming to be by him. Peter will not have it. He does not suggest, however, that the unity of the witness of scripture, or the unity of Paul's testimony with his own, is always straightforward and simple to discern. He openly admits the difficulties in interpretation that might lead some to "twist [scripture, including Paul's letters] to their own destruction" (3:16). That the scriptures are a unity is not in the first place a *theory* about their coherence (e.g., a scriptural worldview or a biblical narrative), but a *confession* that in all their variety they are given by one God the Father through the inspiration of the Holy Spirit and confirmed in the history of the Son. The difficulties are not resolved in that confession. Indeed the confession is not itself a guarantee that they will all be resolved by their human interpreters. But to confess the unity of scripture becomes the occasion and invitation and challenge to *work at discerning how all of scripture does indeed testify together* to the one truth in the light of the "rule of faith" (i.e., minimally, the Nicene-Constantinopolitan Creed). In other words, the unity of scripture is also a *practice*. We cannot say specifically what Peter has in mind when he refers to the difficulties of understanding Paul, or which aspects of Paul's writings Peter means when he writes that some who are "ignorant and unstable twist [Paul's writings] to their own destruction, as they do the other scriptures [*loipas graphas*]." It may well be those sections of Paul's letters in which he too speaks of the parousia of Jesus Christ (1 Thess. 4:13–5:11; 2 Thess. 1:5–2:12), but we cannot be certain. In any case, Peter declares that his testimony in this letter is finally at one with that of Paul, and that to reject that unity is to court self-destruction.

Peter concludes therefore with a warning: do not be "carried away with the error of the lawless and lose your own stability" (2 Pet. 3:17). He has already provided a strongly worded description of the "lawless" ones and warned against the destabilizing deceitfulness of their errors. We need only look back to 2 Pet. 2 to be reminded of them. The antidote to their errors, however, is not to become familiar with the ways and works of the heretics, in order perhaps to refute them. Rather, Peter turns us finally to the one whose transfiguration he himself witnessed, to the one whose coming in transfiguring power we now await with eager anticipation, to the one in whom we will be made sharers of the divine nature, to the one to whom all glory belongs "both now and to the day of eternity" (3:18): "Grow in the grace and knowledge of our Lord and Savior Jesus Christ.... Amen."

BIBLIOGRAPHY

Frequently cited works are listed here. Other works are documented in the footnotes.

Achtemeier, Paul J. 1996. *1 Peter: A Commentary on First Peter*. Edited by Eldon Jay Epp. Hermeneia. Minneapolis: Fortress.

Bauckham, Richard. 1983. *Jude, 2 Peter*. Word Biblical Commentary 50. Waco: Word.

———. 1990. *Word Biblical Themes: Jude, 2 Peter*. Waco: Word.

Boring, M. Eugene. 1999. *1 Peter*. Abingdon New Testament Commentaries. Nashville: Abingdon.

Bray, Gerald, ed. 2000. *James, 1–2 Peter, 1–3 John, Jude*. Ancient Christian Commentary on Scripture: New Testament 11. Downers Grove, IL: InterVarsity.

Calvin, John. 1963. *The Epistle of Paul the Apostle to the Hebrews and the First and Second Epistles of St Peter*. Translated by William B. Johnston. Calvin's Commentaries 12. Grand Rapids: Eerdmans.

Elliott, John H. 2000. *1 Peter: A New Translation with Introduction and Commentary*. Anchor Bible 37B. New York: Doubleday.

Green, Joel B. 2007. *1 Peter*. Two Horizons New Testament Commentary. Grand Rapids: Eerdmans.

Harrington, Daniel J. 2003. "Jude and 2 Peter." Pp. 159–299 in Sacra pagina 15. Collegeville, MN: Liturgical Press.

Jobes, Karen H. 2005. *1 Peter*. Baker Exegetical Commentary on the New Testament. Grand Rapids: Baker Academic.

Kraftchick, Steven J. 2002. *Jude, 2 Peter*. Abingdon New Testament Commentaries. Nashville: Abingdon.

Luther, Martin. 1967. *The Catholic Epistles*. Translated by Martin H. Bertram and Walter A. Hansen. Luther's Works 30. St. Louis: Concordia.

McGuckin, John Anthony. 1986. *The Transfiguration of Christ in Scripture and Tradition*. Lewiston, NY: Mellen.

Senior, Donald P. 2003. "1 Peter." Pp. 1–158 in Sacra pagina 15. Collegeville, MN: Liturgical Press.

SUBJECT INDEX

abortion, 107
Abraham, 29, 31, 39, 50, 136–37
abuse, 91–92
abyss, 174
Achtemeier, Paul J., 21, 27, 53n44, 61n52, 68n6, 76n15, 76n17, 80n24, 86n1, 91n8, 99n15, 108, 113n11, 125n7
ad hominem arguments, 171–72
adoption, 144
alienation, 35
aliens and exiles, 74, 80
American empire, 136
Amish, 36
Anabaptists, 141n16
"angels, authorities, and powers," 54, 101–3, 167
animals, 171
anxiety, 126–27
apocalypticism, 22
apologetics, 95
apologia, 94–96
apostasy, 150n40, 171, 174
apostles, as eyewitnesses, 144, 158
Apostles' Creed, 99n16
apostolic calling, 27–28
apostolic letters, 133
apostolic message, 133, 134, 187
Arius, 164
ark, 100–101, 103
ascent, 161–62
Athanasius, 141, 171
atonement, 42, 84–85
Augustine, 74, 90, 141n16, 146–47, 154n46
authenticity, of faith, 49

author, of epistles of Peter, 23
authorities. *See* powers
authority, 77, 93
  of messianic leadership, 124
  of rulers of this age, 104

Babel, 30n5
Babylon, 28, 33, 35, 71
  Rome as, 130
Balaam, 171
baptism, 41, 44, 101, 103, 125, 150–51
Baptists, 69n8, 97n12
Barmen Declaration, 136n6
Barth, Karl, 21, 43n27, 47n31, 75, 76, 79, 101–2, 144n29, 158n53
Basil of Caesarea, 155
Bauckham, Richard, 22, 145n30, 153n45, 181n11
beauty of the infinite, 138
begotten anew, 62–63
beloved, 186
benediction, 42
Benjamin, Walter, 21, 52, 179
bishops, 120, 121n1
blessing, 92
blessing God, 42–43
blindness, 150
Bockmuehl, Markus, 147n36
body of Christ, 68–69, 89, 103, 144
Bonhoeffer, Dietrich, 78–79
Boring, M. Eugene, 21, 47, 53, 59n51, 62n55, 66
Boyarin, Jonathan and Daniel, 36n13, 38n16
brotherly love, 91, 149
brothers and sisters, 91

SCRIPTURE INDEX